Organisation, Interaction and Practice

T0300485

Ethnomethodology and conversation analysis have an elusive relationship with organisation studies (OS). They are often used to motivate and inform developments in the field, including for example the 'linguistic turn' and the growing interest in 'practice'. However, empirical contributions informed by ethnomethodology and conversation analysis remain rare within OS. This book provides a significant reference point for scholars interested in this work by showing how research based on ethnomethodology and conversation analysis can contribute to key issues and debates in OS. Drawing on audio/video recordings from a diverse range of work settings, a team of leading scholars present a series of empirical studies that illustrate the importance of the real-time achievement of organisational processes and practices. These studies demonstrate how apparently unremarkable aspects of our daily working lives turn out to be critical in understanding how people accomplish, experience and constitute work and organisation.

NICK LLEWELLYN is Associate Professor (Reader) in Organisation Studies in the Industrial Relations and Organisational Behaviour Group at Warwick Business School, University of Warwick.

JON HINDMARSH is Reader in Work Practice and Technology in the Department of Management, King's College London.

Organisation, Interaction and Practice

Studies in ethnomethodology and
conversation analysis

Edited by

NICK LLEWELLYN

AND

JON HINDMARSH

CAMBRIDGE
UNIVERSITY PRESS

CAMBRIDGE UNIVERSITY PRESS
Cambridge, New York, Melbourne, Madrid, Cape Town,
Singapore, São Paulo, Delhi, Tokyo, Mexico City

Cambridge University Press
The Edinburgh Building, Cambridge CB2 8RU, UK

Published in the United States of America by Cambridge University Press, New York

www.cambridge.org
Information on this title: www.cambridge.org/9780521300285

© Cambridge University Press 2010

First published 2010
First paperback edition 2011

A catalogue record for this publication is available from the British Library

ISBN 978-0-521-88136-4 Hardback
ISBN 978-0-521-30028-5 Paperback

Contents

List of contributors   *page* vii

Preface   xi

Part I   Orientations   1

1 Work and organisation in real time: an introduction
NICK LLEWELLYN AND JON HINDMARSH   3

2 Finding organisation in detail: methodological orientations
JON HINDMARSH AND NICK LLEWELLYN   24

Part II   Studies   47

3 A kind of governance: rules, time and psychology in
organisations
JONATHAN POTTER AND ALEXA HEPBURN   49

4 On the reflexivity between setting and practice: the
'recruitment interview'
NICK LLEWELLYN   74

5 The situated production of stories
DAVID GREATBATCH AND TIMOTHY CLARK   96

6 Orders of bidding: organising participation in auctions of fine
art and antiques
CHRISTIAN HEATH AND PAUL LUFF   119

7 Some major organisational consequences of some 'minor',
organised conduct: evidence from a video analysis of pre-
verbal service encounters in a showroom retail store
COLIN CLARK AND TREVOR PINCH   140

8 The work of the work order: document practice in
   face-to-face service encounters
   ROBERT J. MOORE, JACK WHALEN AND E. CABELL
   HANKINSON GATHMAN   172

9 The interactional accomplishment of a strategic plan
   DALVIR SAMRA-FREDERICKS   198

10 Peripherality, participation and communities of practice:
   examining the patient in dental training
   JON HINDMARSH   218

List of references   241
Index   263

Contributors

Editors

Jon Hindmarsh is Reader in Work Practice and Technology in the Department of Management at King's College London. He is involved in a range of studies concerned with the interactional organisation of work in settings such as operating theatres, research labs and student dental clinics. He co-edited *Workplace Studies* (Cambridge University Press, 2000) and is currently co-authoring a text on *Video in Qualitative Research* and co-editing a volume on *Communication in Healthcare Settings*.

Nick Llewellyn is Associate Professor (Reader) in Organisation Studies at Warwick Business School (IROB Group). His research focuses on work and interaction in workplaces and public settings. He has published work in journals such as *British Journal of Sociology*, *Sociology*, *Organization Studies*, *Human Relations* and *Discourse Studies*.

Contributors

Colin Clark is Professor of Marketing at Fundação dom Cabral, Belo Horizonte, Brazil. He has held positions at institutions in the United Kingdom, France and Brazil. His research considers real-life marketing and business communication, in particular, the analysis of video recordings of selling, marketing, negotiation and consumer behaviour. He has published articles in leading journals such as *Sociology*, *Discourse and Society* and *Discourse Studies*. He co-authored *The Hard Sell* (1995) with Trevor Pinch.

Timothy Clark is Professor of Organisational Behaviour at Durham Business School, University of Durham. He has conducted a series of research projects into different aspects of consultancy work and more recently has focused on speaker–audience interaction in management guru lectures. The findings from these projects have been published in a number of journal articles and books. His most recent books are *Management Speak: Why We Listen to What the Management Gurus Tell Us* (2005, with D. Greatbatch) and *Management Consultancy: Boundaries and Knowledge in Action* (forthcoming, with A. Sturdy, K. Handley and R. Fincham).

E. Cabell Hankinson Gathman is a Ph.D candidate in sociology at the University of Wisconsin–Madison. Her dissertation research is an ethnomethodologically informed ethnographic study of self-presentation and relationship maintenance on the social networking website Facebook, where user profiles and the self-presentation that they facilitate are largely shaped by forms.

David Greatbatch is a visiting professor at Durham Business School, University of Durham, and Special Professor in the School of Education at the University of Nottingham. His research focuses on public speaking and interpersonal communication in organisational settings. He has published widely in journals such as *American Journal of Sociology*, *American Sociological Review*, *Human Relations*, *Language in Society*, *Law and Society Review* and *Sociology of Health and Illness*. He recently co-authored *Management Speak* (2005) with Timothy Clark.

Christian Heath is Professor of Work and Organisation and leads the Work, Interaction and Technology Research Centre at King's College London. He specialises in video-based studies of social interaction, drawing on ethnomethodology and conversation analysis, with a particular interest in the interplay of talk, bodily conduct and the use of tools and technologies. He is currently undertaking projects on auctions and markets, medical consultations and operating theatres, and museums and galleries. He has published five books and more than a hundred academic articles in journals and books and is co-editor of the book series 'Learning in Doing' (Cambridge University Press). He has held positions at the Universities of Manchester, Surrey and Nottingham and visiting positions at various universities and industrial research laboratories in the UK and abroad.

Alexa Hepburn is Senior Lecturer in Social Psychology in the Social Sciences Department at Loughborough University. She has studied school bullying, issues of gender, and violence against children, as well as interaction on child protection helplines. She has also written about the relations of the philosophy of Jacques Derrida to the theory and practice of social psychology. Currently she is applying conversation analysis to core topics in interaction. She has two recent books – *An Introduction to Critical Social Psychology* (2003) and, as co-editor, *Discursive Research in Practice* (2007) – and has co-edited a special issue of *Discourse and Society* on developments in discursive psychology (2005).

Paul Luff is Professor of Organisations and Technology at the Department of Management, King's College London. His research involves the detailed analysis of work and interaction and draws upon video recordings of everyday human conduct. With his colleagues in the Work, Interaction and Technology Research Centre, he has undertaken studies in a diverse variety of settings including control rooms, news and broadcasting, health care, museums, galleries and science centres, and within design, architecture and construction. This research and related studies have been reported in numerous articles in the fields of computer-supported co-operative work, human–computer interaction, requirements engineering, studies of work practices and ubiquitous and mobile systems. He is co-author with Christian Heath of *Technology in Action* (Cambridge University Press).

Robert J. Moore is a sociologist and virtual-world designer. While at the Xerox Palo Alto Research Center (PARC), he conducted ethnographic and conversation analytic studies in a variety of workplaces including copy shops, automobile assembly plants, offices and mobile repair services. In addition, he founded the PARC PlayOn project, the first large-scale sociological study of virtual worlds. PlayOn examined player sociability from the micro to the macro levels of analysis. He also worked as a video game designer at the Multiverse Network, where he designed virtual worlds optimised for social interaction, both synchronous and asynchronous.

Trevor Pinch is Professor of Science and Technology Studies and Sociology at Cornell University, Ithaca, NY. His research interests focus on the sociology of scientific knowledge, the sociology of markets, the sociology of technology and the sociology of music. He has published thirteen books including *The Hard Sell* (1995, with Colin Clark), *The Golem: What Everyone Should Know About Science* (Cambridge University Press, 1993, with Harry Collins), and *Analog Days: The Invention and Impact of the Moog Synthesizer* (2002, with Frank Trocco). He has also published numerous scholarly articles in journals such as *Sociology*, *Discourse and Society* and *Journal of Management Inquiry*.

Jonathan Potter is Professor of Discourse Analysis at Loughborough University. He has studied racism, argumentation, fact construction and topics in social science theory and method. His most recent books include *Representing Reality* (1996), which attempted to provide a systematic overview, integration and critique of constructionist research in social psychology, postmodernism, rhetoric and ethnomethodology, and *Conversation and Cognition* (2005, with Hedwig te Molder) in which a range of different researchers consider the implication of studies of interaction for understanding cognition. He is one of the founders of discursive psychology.

Dalvir Samra-Fredericks is Reader in Organisational Behaviour at Nottingham Business School, University of Nottingham. She previously worked at Aston Business School (Aston University) and University of Derby. Earlier, in a different 'life', she worked in private and public sector companies (in sales and marketing, and training and development functions). Her research interests pivot upon a talk-based ethnographic approach – extended to include audio/video recordings – of managerial elites/strategists doing their everyday work over time and space. This research has been published in a number of journals; current writing projects include papers on magic and on process-theorising and a book on *Researching Practice as It Happens* (with F. Bargiela-Chiappini).

Jack Whalen is Principal Scientist in the Computing Science Laboratory at Palo Alto Research Center (PARC). He received a Ph.D in sociology from the University of California, Santa Barbara. Before joining PARC, Whalen was Associate Professor of Sociology and Department Head at the University of Oregon, and served as a research scientist at the Institute for Research on Learning in Menlo Park, California. His current research interests are (1) the design of systems to support knowledge sharing in work communities; (2) the design and use of artificial intelligence applications in the workplace; and (3) the role of documents in co-ordinating organisational activities. Whalen is currently leading a study of software engineering work practice in Xerox and recently led a three-year study in Japan on system engineering work. Prior to that, he led a project with a US auto manufacturer to develop an information system for manufacturing engineers.

Preface

> Soon after our studies began it was evident from the availability of empirical specifics that there exists a locally produced order of work's things; that they make up a massive domain of organisational phenomena; that classic studies of work, without remedy or alternate, depend upon the existence of these phenomena, make use of the domain, and ignore it.
>
> (Garfinkel 1986: vii)

When the term 'organisation' is used in common parlance, it is typically to label this or that place of work. People can say that an 'organisation' has acted in a certain way, that they have joined an 'organisation' or even that an 'organisation' has certain values. The term is clearly short-hand, a neat lexical gloss for something fairly complex and abstract. The minute we try to push the term analytically, things get quite complex. Does the term refer to an entity or a set of processes? Is it possible to say where an 'organisation' begins and ends? Is this a legal question or a matter of economic function? Is it a matter of where particular social and cultural boundaries lie?

These questions, concerning where organisations begin and end and with what material consequences, may seem purely theoretical in character, but they have practical counterparts. In different ways and towards different ends, everyone (at least tacitly) addresses these questions many times each day in the course of engaging with organisational members and settings. This is such a taken-for-granted feature of living in society that we often do not even notice.

For example, when we enter a high street shop we are suddenly in an 'organisation'. We have crossed a boundary. The world has shifted a little – for us anyway. We recognise new constraints and possibilities. We can expect things of shop assistants that we cannot expect of other shoppers or of people passing along the street. Let us say we have to find an assistant and get their attention. They are dealing with someone else, so we wait. As they become available, we ask whether they have an item in a particular size and colour. They check and return with the item in question. We are happy and so we locate and join the queue to pay. We purchase the goods and catch the assistant's eye on the way out to thank them.

Theorising this boundary – or these boundaries – raises difficult issues for the analyst, and yet members find no trouble 'resolving' them towards practical ends. That is to say, in and through ordinary conduct, people recognise the organisational location of their actions many times over, not abstractly but concretely. We establish how to shape our conduct to being in a shop, how to recognise a staff member as opposed to a fellow customer and how to order the exchange of goods for money. Moreover, these solutions to the many small 'problems' faced by the organisational locations of our actions *work*. With respect to the example at hand, it is not just that we bought the right item, but that we competently played our part in the social and moral order of the shop.

The point we are making is that in the first instance 'organisation' is a members' phenomenon and not just a phenomenon for the social scientist. Indeed, 'organisation' is not *primarily* a phenomenon for the social scientist. If the social sciences did not exist people would not forget how to shop or how to act during meetings or job interviews. People do not need social scientists to pick their way through the organisational world. They already have methodic ways of doing this. As such, one thing social science might do is recover these methodic practices. We know people can already *do* 'organisation'; one job of the social scientist should be to find out how. This is the project that the authors pursue in this volume.

We first discussed the idea for this book at a conference on ethnomethodology and conversation analysis in Boston. At that conference we heard plenty of work that, we thought, had something to say to organisation studies (OS). We wondered why this work so rarely featured in OS conferences and journals, despite the fact that it appears in many disciplines throughout the social sciences. Of course, there were some connections between these fields. The linguistic turn engages Deirdre Boden's work and is increasingly looking to 'live' recordings. The practice turn engages Lucy Suchman's work and debates the studies of Julian Orr. Various established areas of research, such as the sensemaking perspective associated with Karl Weick, clearly owe quite a debt to Harold Garfinkel's early writings and so on. There are numerous other points of connection, but few OS researchers actually do ethnomethodological research.

The primary aim of the book is thus to *introduce* a particular way of studying work and organisations. We devote the first two chapters to framing connections between OS and ethnomethodology/conversation analysis, and we highlight key methodological issues and orientations. The volume then presents eight empirical chapters exploring issues, settings and concerns that bear upon contemporary debate in organisation studies. Each chapter shows how resources from ethnomethodology and conversation analysis can be applied to the study of work and organisations, sometimes in subtly different ways. Some chapters direct attention to embodied and material aspects of interaction, whereas others focus more on the organisation of talk. Differences are also apparent in the ways that data are presented, ranging from subtle variations in the notation used in transcripts to the ways that authors represent moving pictures on the printed page.

The first two empirical chapters explore how key features of organisational settings are worked into being through episodes of social interaction. Jonathan Potter and Alexa Hepburn consider the orientation to, use of and engagement with 'rules' during organisational meetings. Nick Llewellyn analyses how interviewers and interviewees constitute the distinctive character of the recruitment interview.

The following three chapters explore not only the talk of organisational members, but also the embodied resources that members bring to bear in their work by focusing on aspects of persuasion and sales. David Greatbatch and Timothy Clark pursue their interests in organisational storytelling by demonstrating the ways in which management gurus 'sell' their ideas to different audiences through the radically situated delivery of stories. Christian Heath and Paul Luff reveal the ways in which auctioneers order and organise the participation of multiple potential customers through the deployment of a specific turn-taking organisation. They especially highlight the embodied conduct of the auctioneer in accomplishing this work and in making the process 'visible, transparent, witnessed and witnessable'. Colin Clark and Trevor Pinch then explore the very foundations of the notion of the 'customer' by considering the ways in which shoppers order and organise their bodily conduct with regard to the presence or preoccupations of retail sales staff. They are found to engage in quite delicate forms of conduct in the course of initiating or avoiding verbal encounters with staff – and it would also seem that salespeople are highly attentive to these variable forms of conduct.

Chapter 8 also considers retail encounters, but the focus comes moments after the previous chapter's analysis finishes. Whereas Clark and Pinch focus on the pre-verbal aspects of sales encounters, Robert Moore, Jack Whalen and Cabell Gathman analyse the sales conversations between copy shop staff and customers. In particular they explore how staff translate customers' vernacular and embodied descriptions of an order to fit within and/or work around the 'standardising' tendencies of the order form.

In Chapter 9, Dalvir Samra-Fredericks also explores the production of documents in organisational conduct, but in her case she considers how two strategists collaborate in producing a strategy document. In doing so she demonstrates the ways in which the 'professional vision' (C. Goodwin 1994) of the strategist is revealed in and through the joint production of the strategic plan. Chapter 10 similarly pursues interests in 'professional vision' but this time in the context of the clinical training undertaken by student dentists. However, rather than focus exclusively on expert and novice, Jon Hindmarsh explores the ways in which the patient engages in a peripheral and yet central role during training conversations.

As this very brief synopsis reveals, there are many cross-cutting themes in this volume relating to issues of rules, exchange, practices, identities, formalisms and knowledge, but at their core all are fundamentally preoccupied with how 'organisation' becomes manifest in real-time social interaction.

For a volume such as this to work it needs to attract leading scholars in the field, and we are extremely grateful to all those who agreed to participate in this project. The book includes chapters by some of the most significant scholars engaged in ethnomethodological studies of work today, and all have been generous and enthusiastic about the project. We take this opportunity to thank them. We would also like to thank Paula Parish at Cambridge University Press, who has shown significant patience and support throughout the process and Karen Anderson Howes for her thorough, considered and thought-provoking work in copy-editing the draft typescript.

PART I

Orientations

1 | Work and organisation in real time: an introduction

NICK LLEWELLYN AND JON HINDMARSH

No social institution can be treated as a self-subsistent entity which exists independently of the accounting practices of its participants. The reproduction of institutional settings and the accounting practices through which they are constituted is an elementary and fundamental fact of institutional life. And to demand that institutions function in independence from these reproductive processes is, to adapt an earlier observation of Garfinkel's, ... 'very much like complaining that if the walls of a building were only gotten out of the way one could see better what was keeping the roof up'.

(Heritage 1984: 229)

Introduction

The studies in this volume are rather distinctive. For one, they all utilise audio and/or video materials. This alone is rare. With few exceptions, organisation studies has tended to rely on empirical materials that are removed from the flow of 'real-time' or 'live' conduct within organisations. Even where researchers have studied work activities up close (see Roy 1960; Burawoy 1979; Casey 1995), they have rarely established permanent records of work activity that can be viewed repeatedly and sustain detailed analysis (but see Gephart 1978; Gronn 1983; Boden 1994).

A second point flows from this. Historically, the discipline of organisation studies has been surprisingly uninterested in 'work itself'. This is not the first time this point has been made. Anselm Strauss (1985), Harold Garfinkel (1986), Lucy Suchman (1987) and Julian Orr (1996) have made this argument with respect to the sociology of work; John van Maanen and Stephen Barley (1984), Barley and Gideon Kunda (2001), Jon Hindmarsh and Christian Heath (2007), Anne Rawls (2008) and Nick Llewellyn (2008) with respect to organisation studies. This argument is explored below, but at this stage it is enough to present the bare bones. Research in organisation studies has rarely treated 'what ordinary work consists of' and 'how ordinary work is practically accomplished' as *analytic problems*. Overwhelmingly, ordinary work has been treated descriptively, rather than analytically (Strauss 1985). In research papers, what some domain of work practically entails is normally covered in a section *before* the analysis begins.

The third and final introductory point concerns the subject matter of ethnomethodologically informed studies. The opening quote by John Heritage (1984: 229) is helpful in this regard. In this quote the term accounting practices is used to refer to practical ways in which people display or orient their conduct to matters including the nature of the activity at hand and who they and others are. Consider a basic example. In what practical ways might an actor display that they have joined a queue to purchase some goods and that they are working on the presumption that another party, who is perhaps in front of them, is part of the same queue? The accounting practices through which actors publicly display, recognise and handle such matters are 'elementary facts' of organisational life (Heritage 1984: 229), in the sense they are going on all the time and no organisational scene could be sustained without them. As a basic form of social organisation, the queue is only witnessable, and thus joinable, because people are able to recognise, and orient their conduct to, 'what queues look like' and 'what queuing practically involves'. When we see a queue that we might join, we trade on the products of these continual methodic labours (Garfinkel 1967).

For ethnomethodologically informed studies this point applies grossly. It is only possible to witness, as seemingly objective and concrete phenomena, a business presentation, a recruitment interview or an auction because they are continually being built and reproduced that way by members. Were these interactional practices somehow paused, these apparently concrete settings would stall. In these terms, ethnomethodologically informed studies are interested in how people practically sustain a shared social world consisting of familiar persons, commonplace happenings and definite contexts.

It should be noted that there have been a number of attempts within ethnomethodology and conversation analysis (EM/CA) to develop a distinctive approach to the study of work. There is a long tradition of ethnomethodological studies that consider the ways in which rules and procedures are deployed in organisational and institutional practice (e.g. Bittner 1967; Zimmerman 1971a; Wieder 1974b; Sacks 1972), the production of everyday organisational action in and through talk in interaction (e.g. Drew and Heritage 1992b; Arminen 2005) and the ways in which tools and technologies feature in and are constituted by work practice (e.g. Button 1993; Heath and Luff 2000; Luff, Hindmarsh and Heath 2000). However, as we shall argue, these developments have failed to fully draw in scholars within management and organisation studies. At various points, EM/CA scholars including Deirdre Boden (1994), David Silverman (1997b) and Richard Harper, Dave Randall and Mark Rouncefield (2000) have sought to engage the discipline more explicitly, but only very recently has organisation studies incorporated an emerging body of ethnomethodologically informed studies. These are mostly those studies that analyse recordings of real-time organisational conduct (see Greatbatch and Clark 2002, 2005; Samra-Fredericks 2003b, 2004b; Alby and Zucchermaglio 2006; Hindmarsh and Pilnick 2007; Llewellyn 2004, 2008; Llewellyn and Burrow 2007; Suchman 2005). These are some of the most noticeable efforts not simply to review or evaluate EM/CA, but to practically undertake research *within* the field of organisation studies.

The present volume builds on these developments by bringing together some of the most significant scholars driving the study of real-time organisational conduct. Drawing on audio/video recordings from a diverse range of work domains, these authors both explicate the local organising properties inherent to organisational conduct and consider the relevance of these properties for (re-)understanding core concepts in organisational literatures. Rather than 'chasing important events' (Czarniawski 2004: 776) and imagining 'organisation' always to be elsewhere, ethnomethodological studies allow analysts to access thousands of 'small ways' in which people locally recognise and reproduce the organisational location of their actions (Sacks 1984).

Locating the collection: ethnomethodology and conversation analysis

The studies presented in this volume draw heavily on the work of Harold Garfinkel and Harvey Sacks, the central figures in the development of ethnomethodology and conversation analysis respectively. Each chapter explores methods through which 'members produce and manage settings of organised everyday affairs' (Garfinkel 1967: 1), including strategy meetings, auctions and interviews. Each does this by examining how people assemble work activities in real time. At the same time, the chapters illustrate only one way of doing ethnomethodology: namely through the sequential analysis of recordings of real-time naturally occurring organisational conduct. There are other ways of doing ethnomethodology, whether through ethnography (see, for example, Button and Sharrock 2002; Garfinkel 1986; Harper, Randall and Rouncefield 2000) or through more theoretical work concerned to 're-specify' conventional categories of social science (see Coulter 1989; Button 1991).

This particular approach to analysing recorded materials is now widespread across the social sciences. Much of this work has been done in organisational settings and yet tends not to feature within organisation studies. It has been influential in psychology (Potter and Weatherell 1987; Edwards and Potter 1992; te Molder and Potter 2005) and sociology (Boden and Zimmerman 1991b; Drew and Heritage 1992b). Furthermore it has contributed to debates in health studies (Heath 1986; Silverman 1997a; Heritage and Maynard 2006; Pilnick, Hindmarsh and Gill 2009) and education (Mehan 1979; McHoul 1978; MacBeth 2000; Hester and Francis 2000; Rendle-Short 2006). It has greatly shaped the development of interdisciplinary fields such as human–computer interaction (HCI) and computer-supported cooperative work (CSCW) (Suchman 1987; Heath and Luff 2000). In more specific ways this type of research has considered work in media and news settings (Greatbatch 1988; Clayman and Reisner 1998; Clayman and Heritage 2002), courtrooms (J. M. Atkinson and Drew 1979), meetings (Boden 1994; Samra-Fredericks 2003b; Llewellyn 2005; Mirivel and Tracy 2005), negotiations (Walker 1995; Greatbatch and Dingwall 1997), call centres (J. Whalen, Zimmerman and Whalen 1988; J. Whalen, Whalen and Henderson 2002; Potter and Hepburn 2003; Greatbatch *et al.* 2005), control centres (Suchman 1997; C. Goodwin and Goodwin 1996; Heath and Luff 2000), sales work (C. Clark and Pinch 1995a; C. Clark, Drew and Pinch 2003; B. Brown 2004; Heath *et al.* 1995; Heath and Luff 2007b) and so on.

Much of this research has addressed topics that are very much central to organisation studies, which makes the separation between these fields all the more surprising. Consider some examples. Christian Heath, Paul Luff and Marcus Sanchez Svensson (2002: 181) examined how '[London Underground] personnel constitute the sense and significance of CCTV images'. Despite considerable interest in *surveillance* within organisation studies, few studies have analysed how people practically accomplish overview of some domain, the real-time doing of surveillance. Similarly, emergency situations have become topics of research within organisation studies, mainly as a result of Karl Weick's (1993) work. But Weick only ever analyses post hoc materials. In contrast Jack Whalen, Don Zimmerman and Marilyn Whalen (1988) studied an emergency call that went badly wrong and had direct access to participants' sensemaking as it happened. They did not need to imaginatively reconstruct events; they were densely and concretely apparent in the empirical materials.

As we shall suggest, this kind of argument can be applied to many topics within organisation studies, whether *time* (Clayman 1989), *authority* (Maynard 1991), the *body* (Hindmarsh and Pilnick 2007), *exchange* (Heath and Luff 2007b), or whatever. In each case ethnomethodologically informed studies of real-time conduct bring something distinctive to the table. The present volume is interested in demonstrating the nature and value of this distinctive focus.

Ethnomethodology's place within organisation studies

As we have already suggested, there are relatively few people doing ethnomethodological research within the organisation studies community. But at the same time Garfinkel and ethnomethodology do continue to be widely cited; Sacks and conversation analysis less so. These citations are interesting because they are so diverse. Ethnomethodology is invoked by authors working in varied traditions whose problematics differ from one another and from those of ethnomethodology. Scholars have typically interpreted ethnomethodology in the context of their own distinctive intellectual projects – rarely have scholars committed to the project of ethnomethodology as an approach in its own right, which provides a distinctive analytic agenda and methodological orientation (for this see also Burrell and Morgan 1979; Hassard 1993; T. Watson 1995). Consider some of the ways in which ethnomethodology features in management and organisation studies.

First there are some positive 'passing references' to ethnomethodology. In a discussion about the theorisation of 'discourse', Rick Iedema (2007: 936) welcomes Garfinkel's focus on *in situ* interaction and 'performativity'. By engaging with real-time interaction, Iedema argues, analysts might establish a 'unique position' from which to engage with practice. Ola Bergström and David Knights (2006: 372) draw on Garfinkel in an argument about the position of agency in some Foucauldian studies. Bergström and Knights suggest that in some of these studies social actors are reduced to nothing more than 'cultural dopes' (see Garfinkel 1967: 68). In the context of a practice-based approach, Davide Nicolini (2007: 894) references ethnomethodology in a discussion about the normative character of ordinary work practice. To be involved in a practice, Nicolini argues, is to know how to contribute appropriately to unfolding courses of action.

On the flip side, there are numerous passing 'swipes' at ethnomethodology in the course of wider debates, most often in theoretical considerations of the ontology of organisation, or structure–agency. For Paul Adler and Bryan Borys (1993: 664), ethnomethodology is firmly idealist, an approach that 'reduce[s] society to a cognitive order'. Steve Fleetwood (2005: 209) suggests that ethnomethodology 'confuses' retrospective accounts of events and events *as they really happened.* He suggests that Garfinkel's insights into the work of jurors were 'mistaken'. Ethnomethodology might be a good deal more sympathetic to Fleetwood's position than he seems to realise. It does not understand itself as constructivist, interpretivist or post-modern. Meanwhile, Hugh Willmott takes ethnomethodology to task for lacking 'politico-emancipatory intent' (Willmott 2005: 749), something that we will return to later.

Whether positive or negative, for the most part Garfinkel and ethnomethodology are cited 'in passing'. Scholars draw on the odd concept here and there but typically leave the overall project of ethnomethodology unexplored. That said, there are three key areas of recent research in organisation studies that draw more heavily on Garfinkel. These are the new institutionalism associated with Paul DiMaggio and Walter Powell (1991), the sensemaking approach associated with Weick (1995), and the organisational discourse project (Grant *et al.* 2004). These are deserving of greater attention but, as we shall suggest, they also fall short in embracing ethnomethodology in its own terms, as a distinctive intellectual project.

In writing on the new institutionalism, ethnomethodology is invoked in the context of the enduring structure–agency debate:

most [practitioners of new institutionalism] move back and forth among ethnomethodology, phenomenology and conventional resource dependence arguments. Zucker is the most ethnomethodological, suggesting that many typifications are 'built up' from ground level by participants in interaction. (DiMaggio and Powell 1991: 25)

When DiMaggio and Powell state that Lynne Zucker is the 'most ethnomethodological', they do not mean that she does ethnomethodological research. In fact, Zucker undertakes historical studies, rather than studies of 'practical actions as contingent ongoing accomplishments' (Garfinkel 1967: 11). In this literature, Garfinkel is invoked in the construction of a grand theoretical framework that shifts attention from the very subject matter of ethnomethodology: members' *ethnomethods* for the accomplishment of ordinary actions (Garfinkel 1967). Indeed Silverman (1997b) argues that while the new institutionalism project is innovative it does not develop clear guidelines regarding the collection and analysis of data. The resulting problem is that the overarching aims of the project fail to resonate with the quite significant commitments of ethnomethodology and conversation analysis to understanding practices and practical reasoning.

Posing a quite different set of problematics, Weick (1995: 24) notes the 'continuing influence of ethnomethodology on the study of organisational sensemaking' (also see Gephart 1978). More specifically, Garfinkel's study of jurors is invoked to support the notion of 'retrospective sensemaking' (see Garfinkel 1967: 41), the idea that clarity and rationality often work in 'reverse'. Weick (1993, 1995) also draws on other terms associated with ethnomethodology, not only 'retrospective sensemaking', but also 'accountability', sensemaking as an 'ongoing accomplishment' (Weick 1993: 635) realised 'in and through interaction' (Weick 1995). Whilst Weick draws on such terminology, quite legitimately he does not *do* ethnomethodologically informed work. Indeed it rather seems that ethnomethodological categories and terms are pulled out of their original context and given new work to do. Despite the frequency with which sensemaking is rhetorically framed as social activity accomplished 'in and through interaction with others' (Maitlis 2005: 21; Balogun and Johnson 2005: 1576), studies in this literature have conspicuously *not* analysed sensemaking in real time.

The burgeoning and wide-ranging field of organisational discourse is where the greatest concern with conversation analysis (as opposed to ethnomethodology) arises, most notably through citation to Boden's (1994) text *The Business of Talk*. The linguistic turn in organisation studies is most clearly associated with, even constituted by, the emergence of studies of organisational discourse as a field. Many of the programmatic texts that underpin these developments highlight the prevalence of talk in organisations, and how standard management practices are routinely and massively accomplished through talk; they also consider importance of talk *as*, rather than separate from, action (Grant *et al.* 2004). The foundations of the claims for the importance of organisational discourse rely, in no small measure, on the argument that discourse is, in the first instance, a medium for the accomplishment of social activity. However, when we consider the empirical studies in this literature, the focus shifts quite significantly away from real-time talk-in-interaction (but see Woodilla 1999; Forray and Woodilla 2002; Cooren and Fairhurst 2004). The overwhelming bulk of the studies are *about* talk rather than *of* talk. These studies will routinely abstract from the concrete situations in which language resides to consider the *form* of stories or narratives, metaphors, analogies, rhetoric, dialogues and the like. The concern becomes language use widely conceived, and these studies are often deployed to consider the discourses that are implicit in language. Once more, ethnomethodology and conversation analysis are invoked, rather than actively pursued as a distinctive intellectual project.

Ethnomethodology and the 'practice turn'

Tony Watson (1995: 62) is right to note the contrast between widespread reference to ethnomethodology and the 'limited number of people ... who wholeheartedly [adopt] it'. Ethnomethodology is not 'at home' in the production of historical studies or research that aims to imaginatively reconstruct sensemaking from *post hoc* sources (Weick 1993, 1995). It will not serve those who hope to 'document the systematic "distortions" of communication, and the routinized "reproduction" of historically structured relational asymmetries' (Lynch 1993: 31). Ethnomethodology is at home in the context of studies that give 'to the most commonplace activities of daily life the attention usually accorded extraordinary events', that treat ordinary work activities as 'phenomena in their own right' (Garfinkel 1967: 1). In the context of organisational studies, to pursue ethnomethodological research, as an approach in its own right, is to analyse ordinary work practice.

Of all the intersections between ethnomethodology and organisation studies the most relevant is the recent 'turn to practice'. This is because practice-based studies seem to share with ethnomethodology an interest in the fine details and normative character of ordinary work; these studies begin with work (see Gherardi 2001: 134; Gherardi and Nicolini 2002b; Nicolini 2007). In this literature, analysts have long since been attentive to easily missed details, competencies and practices of ordinary work. Such noticings include the ability to *feel* 'the tension of the sling' (Gherardi and Nicolini 2002b) or 'the roof through your feet' (Strati 2003: 60). Practice-based studies have sought to connect notions such as community, knowledge, learning and identity with the practical 'doings' of ordinary work (Gherardi 2001: 136), something that chimes nicely with ethnomethodological commitments to a 'practice-based theory of knowledge and action' (see C. Goodwin 1994: 606).

Of course, the practice literature is theoretically and methodologically pluralistic. When authors say they are analysing 'practices-in-use' (Jarzabkowski 2004) or how 'practices are actually used' (Whittington 2006: 624), they often steer clear of analysing live conduct. But some *have* done this by adopting approaches informed quite clearly by ethnomethodology and conversation analysis (e.g. Samra-Fredericks 2003b, 2004b; Alby and ZuccI hermaglio 2006). As practice-based studies are centrally concerned with the detail of 'ordinary activities' there is no need to bend or twist ethnomethodological terms and categories to the ends of some alternative project. It can be confronted and applied as an approach in its own right. Thus ethnomethodology and conversation analysis have rightly been presented as a distinctive approach to engage the burgeoning interest in 'practice' in organisation studies. This raises questions about the nature of ethnomethodological studies.

Organisation in the details

An initial point is that, broadly in common with many scholars in the field of organisation studies, ethnomethodologically informed studies hold to the idea that organisational settings and various components of organisation (hierarchy, procedure, rules, authority, expertise, decision-making and the rest) are best understood as ongoing accomplishments rather than predetermined social facts. This chimes with authors such as Robert Chia, who speaks of 'primary organizing micro-practices which generate stabilized effects such as truth, know-ledge, individual and organisation' (cited in Samra-Fredericks and Bargiela-Chiappini 2008: 668). At this broad level, such commitments are widespread within organisation studies, but we would suggest that the discipline is still struggling to find a way of *showing* these accomplishments in the everyday conduct of organisational members, how 'organisation' permeates the moment-by-moment accomplishment of work.

This point is also made by François Cooren and Gail Fairhurst (2004: 793–4) who argue that 'it still remains to be shown how the process of organizing can be identified through the details of naturally occurring interactions'. This might not be surprising given that few studies of 'naturally occurring interaction' have ever been published in the discipline's key journals (but see Gephart 1978; Gronn 1983; Boje 1991). There appears to be a general tension between theoretical framings, bound to images of fluidity and motion, and studies themselves, which are overwhelmingly disconnected from the flow and flux of ordinary work activities.

We are not the first to make these points. Some twenty-five years ago, van Maanen and Barley (1984: 350) argued that 'organisation studies has very little to say about the things people actually do at work'. This point was similarly made by Strauss (1985), Garfinkel (1986) and Orr (1996) in relation to the sociology of work. More recently Barley and Kunda (2001) have described organisation studies' lack of interest in ordinary workplace activity. Rawls (2008: 723) has argued that 'there never has been much known about work in details … because conventional methods reduce the details of practices to generalities'.

This can seem like a very strange argument because, in one way or another, virtually all research in organisation studies seems to be about work. What these authors are pointing to is the absence of a particular kind of engagement with ordinary work, one in which analysts treat the practical moment-by-moment accomplishment of work as an *analytic* problematic. In organisation studies it is rare indeed to see research papers or monographs that treat, as a matter of analysis, what work practically consists of and how that work gets done. Rather, the work itself tends to be reduced to something that is amenable to casual observation and description. In research papers, the 'work itself' is often described in a section *before* the analysis begins. What work entails, it is presumed, can be grasped descriptively and straightforwardly.

For ethnomethodology this is problematic on a number of grounds. First, it disconnects analysis from the material stuff of work and encourages a premature move to theorise organisational processes that have yet to be described in much detail. What ethnomethodologically informed studies show is that apparently 'ordinary work' consists of things that might not be easily imaginable ahead of time. But there is also a broader problem. If we assume that ordinary work practice is one of the main materials out of which the social facts of organisation are produced and sustained – that is, if we assume that work settings have to be continually accomplished in and through ordinary activity – then the absence of a tradition of scholarship that aims to show 'process of organising [in] the details of naturally occurring interactions' (Cooren and Fairhurst 2004: 793–4) becomes more of a worry. If one of the core problematics of the discipline is to show and analyse, rather than theoretically stipulate or presume, the reproduction of organisational settings, at some point the discipline will have to analyse how organisation is apparent in, and sustained through, ordinary work practice.

What ethnomethodology and conversation analysis provide is *one way* of accessing how organisation might be shown in the moment-by-moment flow of ordinary work. Such studies bring into focus 'seen but unnoticed' (Garfinkel 1967) ways in which people recognise and reproduce the organisational location of their actions, in and through each successive action (Sacks 1984). For more than thirty years, scholars aside from organisation studies have used resources from EM/CA in the name of such a project, and this volume is committed to exploring the ways in which the discipline of organisation studies might be enriched by attending more explicitly to its concerns.

Guiding assumptions and study policies

At its core ethnomethodology is engaged in a fundamental 're-specification' of the classical sociological concern with the nature of social order (see Garfinkel 1967, 1991). Garfinkel was keen to demonstrate the 'artful practices' through which participants produce and maintain orderly, mutually intelligible social encounters, how parties produce and maintain the very social facts and structures taken as given within classical sociology. Thus, order is not assumed; it is achieved by members and systematically described by analysts. In this sense, ethnomethodological studies do seem to begin with Émile Durkheim's suggestion that sociology's fundamental principle is the objective reality of social facts. But *contra* Durkheim they treat as their prevailing topic the 'endless, ongoing, contingent accomplishment' (Garfinkel 1967: 1) of such 'objective reality'; the very practices in and through which reality is (re-)produced; the taken-for-granted and tacit features of everyday activities.

For example, Max Atkinson (1978) re-considered the assumptions which formed the foundation of Durkheim's classic study *Suicide* (1952). Atkinson problematised or re-specified the concept of suicide by treating it as a matter of mundane practical significance for various kinds of work. For example, he described the coroner's practical reasoning in working up a verdict of 'suicide', as opposed to, say, accidental death. In this way, Atkinson demonstrated how a seemingly objective social fact, which forms the cornerstone of Durkheim's thesis, is recoverable through practices and procedures of work. As this example strongly suggests, ethnomethodologically informed studies see themselves not in competition with other approaches, but as exploring a distinctive subject matter, allied to a distinctive solution to the problem of social order. EM/CA authors routinely contrast their studies with 'more conventional' approaches (Silverman 1997b), not to denigrate them for their conventionality, but to demonstrate the unexplored features of standard accounts – the 'missing what' (Garfinkel 1986).

So, the first study policy is to recover the local practices and procedures that produce local occasions of order. Common scenes of work already possess their own local or endogenous organisation. Before analysts begin their work, the things they study have already been socially produced *as those things* and not as other things (Garfinkel 1967). Consider something as apparently straightforward as the description of a 'customer waiting to be served' (see Clark and Pinch, this volume). For someone to be seen as a 'customer waiting to be served' takes work. The witnessability of people and projects does not just happen. People have to *do* things for such an account of their bodily conduct to be witnessable and accountable that way.

The first analysis of the customers' conduct will be performed by shop assistants, and it is their analysis (rather than that of the researchers) that will be *reflexively implicated in the socio-interactional constitution of the scene itself* (Schegloff 1997). In the way people practically orient to unfolding courses of action, common scenes of work acquire their concrete and witnessable properties. It is on the back of these continual labours that professional researchers are able to see organisational phenomena and describe what is *obviously* happening. From this point of view, then, there *is* an opportunity to evidence this or that description of some scene, by showing how people themselves orient to those matters which the analyst brings to attention. For EM/CA, description is not casual; it involves analysis.

In a characteristically thought-provoking essay, Sacks (1984) sketched two further important study policies, which clearly reflected Sacks' engagement with Garfinkel and with ethnomethodological thinking. He suggested that social science tends to be governed by an overriding interest 'in what are in the first instance know to be the "big issues" of the day' (Sacks 1984: 22). This is a considerable generalisation, of course, but within organisation studies a great many scholars do come to topics such as power, teamwork, bureaucracy and customer service either because of a guiding interest in sources of oppression and subjugation or to learn more about the basis of firm efficiency and durability. Given such *a priori* interests, particular episodes of work may not seem interesting in and of themselves. They become interesting to the extent they can be read against some broader set of social, economic or political issues.

EM/CA studies take a difference stance. They take what appear to be mundane or routine activities – which are not obviously bound up with pressing social, cultural or economic issues – *seriously* (Garfinkel 1967: 1). This reflects a particular way of understanding the problem of order and, more particularly, where we might find solutions to that problem. Sacks' famous dictum was 'order at all points' (Sacks 1984). On the one hand, this means that, wherever the tape is stopped, we will find the activities of the auction, lecture or interview being built in ways that embody the rational properties of that setting. At all points, but in different ways and with different consequences, interview conduct will embody the interview-ness of the occasion. On the other hand, 'order at all points' brings into question the contemporary privileging of some empirical settings and processes, simply because they capture the spirit of the age. What are overlooked as a result are phenomena of order that, whilst less 'sexy', are nevertheless integral to the reproduction of organisations.

A related matter for Sacks (1984), and a third study policy, concerns the tendency to 'read' organisational activities against big analytic categories such as culture, hierarchy or discourse. In organisation studies, a great many sophisticated studies nevertheless adopt what EM/CA authors term an 'ironic' perspective towards organisational actors, in which the knowledge of the researcher is taken to be of primary significance for what is happening. For example, in a study of general practitioners Laurie Cohen and Gill Musson (2000) argue that, even though GPs may be unaware of the values and claims of enterprise, they inevitably reproduce it through their engagement in practices that are 'imbued with enterprise'. This is a familiar and powerful way of *reading* ordinary work practice, against a social formation whose 'relevance' (Schegloff 1991) is stipulated in advance by analysts on the basis of their knowledge of society. If actors themselves don't 'get it', that's irrelevant.

A key policy of ethnomethodologically informed studies is that 'the rational properties of practical activities' should not be read in this way, against rules or standards 'outside the actual settings within which such properties are recognized, used [and] produced' (Garfinkel 1967: 3–4). For EM/CA studies the key question is how 'parties embody, for one another, the relevancies of their conduct and this is understood to be an analytic problem, rather than one that can be resolved theoretically' (Schegloff 1991: 51).

This policy is often misread as the argument that social forces, broadly understood, somehow either do not exist or do not matter, as if people are free to do as they please. This is not the argument. A quite different point is being made, which concerns the possibility of analysing how 'social structure in the conventional sense enters into the production and interpretation of determinate facets of ... the actual conduct to which it must be finally referred' (Schegloff 1991: 51). Within such a project, the analytic problematic is 'how to examine the data so as to be able to show that the parties were, with and for one another, demonstrably oriented to those aspects of who they are, and those aspects of their context, which are respectively implicated in the social structures which we may wish to relate to their talk' or conduct (Schegloff 1991: 51–2).

Pursuing organisational concerns

Where might such study policies lead? What kinds of insights do they produce? There are many ways of addressing these questions, given

the scale and diversity of both organisation studies and EM/CA literatures. In three sections below, three overarching themes are discussed
that begin to show the relevance of ethnomethodologically informed
research for debates within organisation studies. These themes also
pervade the empirical chapters included in this volume and so, where
relevant, we elaborate these themes with examples drawn from the
empirical studies that follow.

Skill, knowledge and images of work

One problem often expressed about ethnomethodologically informed
studies is that they do not have any 'transparent political agenda'
(Lynch 1993: 31). They have been accused of being apolitical and
conservative. It is certainly true that EM/CA studies tend not to be
aligned with any specific political movement for social change, but the
question of their politics is more complex.

To explore this further, consider one quite visible theme arising
from EM/CA informed research. This challenges oppositions that
run to the heart of organisation studies, between mental and manual
labour and between knowledge-based and routine work. This distinc-
tion is historic and political, in the sense of being traceable back to
feudalism (Veblen, in Duguid 2006: 1797). Drawing on ethnomethodology and conversation analysis, Suchman (2000: 30) intervenes
directly in a contested ideological debate when she argues that images
of work have been

systematically biased to highlight judgmental, interpretative work amongst
the professions, while obscuring the work's mundane practical aspects.
Commensurately, mundane practical activity is foregrounded in so-called
routine forms of work, while reasoning is relegated.

Attempting to 'disrupt the received dualism of knowledge/routine'
(Suchman 2000: 30) EM/CA scholars have been engaged in two related
projects. One aims to reveal practical and embodied aspects of 'professional work' (see C. Goodwin 1994; Hindmarsh and Pilnick 2002,
2007). In the present volume, a number of chapters can be understood
in this light. Heath and Luff recover the embodied work of auctioneers;
David Greatbatch and Timothy Clark look at the live performances of
business gurus; Dalvir Samra-Fredericks considers the strategic work of
strategists; and so forth. These studies are diverse but they all point to

the fact that professional authority, legitimacy and expertise are not predetermined, but exercised 'through the competent deployment in a relevant setting of a complex of situated practices' (C. Goodwin 1994: 626). This does not suggest that the powers to 'legitimately see, constitute and articulate ... are homogenously distributed' across a society (see C. Goodwin 1994: 626); simply that professional power and 'vision' are *practised* in concrete, recoverable and thus analysable ways.

The related project involves recovering expertise and reasoning which feature as essential components of apparently routine work such as clerical tasks, servicing machines or selling goods over the phone or face to face (Suchman 2000; Orr 1996; J. Whalen, Whalen and Henderson 2002; Llewellyn and Burrow 2008). Such a project is possible once analysts have a permanent record of routine work, which captures the density of brief fragments of apparently mundane activity. In the present volume, Colin Clark and Trevor Pinch consider video recordings of 'shop work' and access how assistants recognised the projects of customers ('browsing', 'trying to initiate contact' or 'waiting to be served') from the way they manage their body conduct within the local ecology of the store. Clark and Pinch explicate the 'framework of socially organised communicative practices that, along with the interactional "rules", expectations, obligations and other situational factors ... inform these actions'. Their work clearly chimes with J. Whalen, Whalen and Henderson who considered the work of call centre staff:

> one aspect is the degree to which work that appears to be uncomplicatedly 'routine' or even scripted may in reality require considerable adroitness with an organisation that is conspicuously intricate. And, if this is the case, it suggests that the conventional (and recognisably vernacular) division in our discipline between 'routine' work and other, presumably more demanding and cognitively challenging kinds of work needs to be respecified. (J. Whalen, Whalen and Henderson 2002: 255)

This two-fold project challenges images of routine work that are apparent in self-consciously critical scholarship (see Willis 1978) and that seem, on occasion, to collude with managerial versions of low skill and thus support the status quo, in terms of pay and training. Authors such as Suchman, Orr and Whalen confront management and theorists with the 'surprisingly uncomfortable challenge of the knowledgeable worker' (Duguid 2006: 1795).

Of course, some consider such studies not political enough, because they say little about why employees, such as those studied by Orr (1996), were so willing to strive and innovate even when they have good reason not to trust the company. This is a good example of where EM/CA scholarship ends and other modes of research begin (Silverman 1997b).

Working with bureaucracy: rules, documents and formal orders

In a recent review Barley and Kunda (2001) argue for detailed studies of work in order to grasp the shift from an industrial to a post-industrial society. Whilst this is an important research agenda, it might also be fruitful to look in the opposite direction. This is because many familiar workplace institutions and practices, traceable back to the earliest characterisations of rational bureaucracy, are yet to be explicated in detail (Rawls 2008). These would include how people 'work with' standard forms and fill-in documents (Moore and Whalen, this volume), occasions where formal rules become relevant for the conduct of organisation members (see Potter and Hepburn, this volume), recruitment interviews practised in light of standard protocols (see Llewellyn, this volume). We are not arguing that such things have not been studied at all. We are pointing to an absence of studies that are attentive to the 'situated integration of tools, documents, action and interaction' (Barley and Kunda 2001: 89).

By pursuing such matters, chapters in the present volume contribute to rich lines of EM/CA work, which date back to early studies by Zimmerman (1971b) and Wieder (1974b). These studies examined how people 'work' organisational systems: how people apply formal rules and enliven standard protocols. Insights from such studies have direct relevance for core debates in organisation studies, going back to Max Weber's account of the 'ethos of office' (Weber 1978). This notion assumes an actor who is able to block out 'extra official conscience' (du Gay 2000: 75) and act only in accordance with formal rules and prescribed procedure. For EM/CA studies such an image of conduct, oriented *only* to formal procedures, protocols, plans and the like, is problematic (see Suchman 1987). EM/CA studies hold to an alternative picture of bureaucratic conduct, where the labour of officials is inescapably informed by bodies of knowledge, normative considerations and modes of reasoning that have their origins well beyond legal-rational organisational boundaries.

For example, Garfinkel (1967), and as we have seen Max Atkinson (1978), sought to recover practical and inferential work through which suicide cases were discovered in the details of 'sudden, unnatural death' (Garfinkel 1967: 11). In lucid terms, Garfinkel describes the activities of an SPC (suicide prevention centre)

> various ways of living in society that could have terminated with that death are searched out and read 'in the remains'; in the scraps of this and that like the body and its trappings, medicine, bottles, notes, bits of pieces of clothing, and other memorabilia ... Other 'remains' are collected too: rumors, passing remarks, and stories ... These whatsoever bits and pieces that a story or a rule or a proverb might make intelligible are used to formulate a recognizably coherent, standard, typical, cogent, uniform, planful, i.e., a professionally defensible, and thereby, for members, a recognizably rational account of how the society worked to produce those remains. (Garfinkel 1967: 17)

The Weberian formulation of ethicality would make relevant the conduct of the examiners in relation to the formal bureaucratic procedures governing the allocation of death certificates. But, in very concrete ways, no amount of formality can hope to capture what officers draw upon to do their work, the 'ways of living in society' through which they are able to determine the practical relevance of various 'remains'. The establishment of cases is always and inevitably an 'achieved organisation' (Sacks 1992), with conventions and precedents acting as resources through which cases are witnessed and reported in recognisably rational ways.

A second line of research, well illustrated by Jonathan Potter and Alexa Hepburn's chapter in the present volume, concerns the moral and inferential demands that bureaucratic processes place 'on both actors and situations' (Rawls 2008: 723). These authors examine how a chair of a school board meeting tried to constrain the contribution of speakers in light of a 'two-minute' rule. They describe local adaptations to formal rules that allow for the smooth running of the board. Rather than a clinical enforcement of exact procedure, rules are applied in light of moral-ethical considerations. Significantly, Potter and Hepburn also describe how officials imposed rules, apparently against the will of people who, momentarily, found themselves to be subjects of formal authority. Potter and Hepburn access the real-time production and negotiation of formal authority (Weber 1948): how the chair both invoked rules, upheld their legitimate character and dealt with resistance.

Finally, the chapter by Bob Moore, Jack Whalen and Cabell Gathman weaves together two lines of EM/CA research, on the work of writing-in documents (Garfinkel and Bittner 1967; J. Whalen, Whalen and Henderson 2002) and on the practical accomplishment of standardized procedures (Suchman 1987; Suchman and Whalen 1994). Based on their study of a copy shop, these authors show how standard forms and procedures do not, in and of themselves, provide for co-ordination or control across space and time. They are 'chronically insufficient' in the sense that they cannot handle all possible contingencies and specifications without expanding ludicrously in length. Moore, Whalen and Gathman describe informal literary practices – free-text notes, annotations and tagging – which overcome such deficiencies and enable single orders to be grasped across time and space. This echoes classic themes in organisation studies, where action animated exclusively by rational bureaucracy is shown to be counterproductive for the achievement of desired ends (see Blau 1956). EM/CA studies recover 'improvisations' (J. Whalen, Whalen and Henderson 2002) and 'artful interpretative work' which sustain and make durable complex organisational processes.

Subjects of work: delineations of identity, expertise and authority

A recurrent question for organisation studies has been how to locate, and differentiate between, subjects of work. The pages of research papers and monographs are, of course, full of references to subjects of work, including 'managers', 'entrepreneurs' (Cohen and Musson 2000), 'team members', 'scapegoats' (Casey 1995), 'old timers' (Burawoy 1979), 'younger sales managers' (du Gay 1996) and so forth. A quite separate set of (EM/CA) questions is how, when and why do organisational actors 'orient to' such categories in the midst of various kinds of work? This is the 'missing what' of the now considerable literature on identity within organisation studies (Trowler 2001; Meriläinen *et al.* 2004; A. D. Brown and Coupland 2005).

This is an alternative project, which considers identities that are 'relevant' and 'consequential' for the concerted activities of the workplace (Schegloff 1991). In the first instance, questions of identity are confronted and resolved by members and their solutions, rather than by analysts and theirs. As Llewellyn and Robin Burrow (2007, 2008) suggest, whether a *Big Issue* vendor is a 'salesperson' or a 'homeless person' is simply not resolvable from within a theoretical attitude. It is only resolvable by members *in situ*, and this raises questions about how such determinations are locally established or shown.

This is not just a matter of exploring individual identity. What is often quite apparent is that people find themselves subjects of a particular *ordering* of identity within a scene (see Sacks 1992: vol. I, 253–7). Hence, questions arise about how 'customers' stand in relation to 'sales staff' (Clark and Pinch, this volume); 'clinicians' to 'students' and 'patients' (Hindmarsh, this volume); senior managers in relation to each other (Samra-Fredericks, this volume); and so forth. By pursuing such interests, studies show how social relations and the division of labour between participants are oriented to and practically resolved moment by moment. Insights are produced which can then inform broader debates.

For example, despite the elevated status of customers in both critical (du Gay 1996) and managerialist literature (Osborne and Gaebler 1992), 'rarely, if ever, are they the focus of critical analysis – except as a disembodied object' (Bolton and Houlihan 2005: 686). In the present volume, Clark and Pinch situate the customer, and their study throws up some interesting matters, for example concerning a 'particular asymmetric ordering in the store' in the staff's favour.

The critical reader might ask how it is possible for EM/CA studies to invoke categories such as identity without an explicit theory of identity. This is a complex point. At a philosophical level, EM/CA authors are embarked upon a particular kind of project, to 'ground analytic work on human conduct in the logical grammar of our language, rather than in operational definitions and theoretical assertions' (Coulter 2005: 92). What Jeff Coulter describes is a kind of *knowing theoretical naivety* characteristic of EM/CA studies, which reflects the influence of Ludwig Wittgenstein, and to a lesser extent Edmund Husserl, who in different ways 'sought to construct methods which would inhibit the construction of further theories, and which would enable the recovery of pre-theoretical perceptions of phenomena' (Sharrock and Button 1991: 142). EM/CA studies try to do this by limiting their analysis to members' accounting practices (Heritage 1984), i.e. how people orient to various categories of personhood as they go about their business. For such a level of analysis there is no need to appeal to 'operational definitions and theoretical assertions' (Coulter 2005: 92).

Conclusion

Attempting to conclude on the distinctive feature of EM/CA studies is no easy feat. It is tempting to invoke some of Sacks' (1992: vol. II, 3) confidence in arguing

I'm proceeding this way for this kind of reason: basically what I have to sell is the sorts of work I can do. And I don't have to sell its theoretical under-pinnings, its hopes for the future, its methodological elegance, its theoretical scope, or anything else. I have to sell what I can do and the interestingness of my findings.

That is, it is tempting to argue what the collection has to sell are the phenomena of order described in each of the chapters, the interesting-ness of the findings. This is a nice attitude, for some, because it contrasts sharply with a mode of writing and research in which some piece of grand theorising is followed by a comparatively tame empirical analysis that neither requires nor particularly engages the theoretical materials. For Sacks, there had to be a clear pay-off. For him, this was the ability to bring new phenomena of order into view.

At the very least, it is no small thing to imagine what organisation studies would look like were analysts interested not in what people said about work, but in what they do as work. The consequences would be far-ranging, not least for subjects of academic research, who would be able to find themselves within the local organisational orders they help to sustain, reproduce or disrupt. Such a body of EM/CA knowledge would not compete with or try to 'trump' more conventional treatments, which gloss the local 'reproduction of insti-tutional settings' (Heritage 1984: 229) for their own good reasons, in the name of pursuing their own particular mode of analysis. But when such authors do gloss some category of person, scene or form of organisation, there will always be an opportunity for an ethnometho-dological re-specification that reveals ways in which members handle the practical and moral relevance of such delineations and, in doing so, find 'organisation' in the details of ordinary work.

2 | Finding organisation in detail: methodological orientations

JON HINDMARSH AND NICK LLEWELLYN

Introduction

Contributions to this volume direct attention to the real-time achievement of organisational processes and practices. This demands distinctive data and methodological resources, and the chapters that follow adopt one particular empirical approach to engage the ethnomethodological (EM) project, one that draws heavily from conversation analysis (CA). In all cases, the authors subject recordings of everyday work and organisational conduct to detailed sequential and interactional analysis.

The use of audio and/or video recordings offers intriguing opportunities for studies of work. The equipment to produce them is cheap and reliable, and they deliver real-time recordings of work in progress that can be subjected to repeated scrutiny and evaluation. As Harvey Sacks suggested, 'tape-recorded materials constitute a "good enough" record of what happened. Other things, to be sure, happened, but at least what was on the tape had happened' (Sacks 1984: 26). So, as with other data types they are limited in coverage, but unlike other data types they offer a density and permanence that can be very valuable (Grimshaw 1982). They exhibit density in that they are rich in the details of the recorded events; it is very common to notice new and subtle features of activity upon repeated re-viewing of recordings. They are also persistent and cumulative, providing researchers with the opportunity of preserving and comparing data across various projects. Furthermore, recordings allow researchers to show and share materials, so that others can judge for themselves the persuasiveness of insights and analyses.

The use of recorded data is by no means unusual in organisation studies. Most qualitative researchers use recordings of one form or another, for example to preserve the details of research interviews. However, the use of such recordings is more as an aide-mémoire. They are typically created to capture content rather than action; that is, they mainly are used to record answers to research questions rather than to explore the distinctive interactional organisation of the interview itself. In direct contrast, EM/CA studies generate recordings because they are interested in action and activity, as effectuated through language and the body. Recordings are not treated as a window to respondents' attitudes, opinions, beliefs and the like, but are instead seen as useful because they supply a robust and analysable record of one version of 'what happened'. From such a starting point, it is possible to build studies that are attentive to how organisational processes are practically sustained as recognisable and coherent phenomena.

Of course, recordings of organisational life become of vital importance only when work practice is transformed into a topic in its own right. Clearly there are a range of potential means for unpacking the details of work practice, but the authors of this volume seek to understand practical ways in which people craft contributions to unfolding activities *moment by moment*. In the argot of conversation analysis, each chapter is grounded at the level of *sequence organisation*, the relationships of each and every action to its immediate before and after. The idea that sense and coherence are interactionally achieved moment by moment underpins the analytic orientation brought to bear by the authors of this volume. The overriding aim of the present chapter is to explore these processes and unpack the notion of 'sequence' further before considering how these methodological resources can be applied to the study of work and organisation.

Understanding sequential organisation

Harold Garfinkel was keen to demonstrate the 'artful practices' through which participants produce and maintain orderly, mutually intelligible social encounters, how they produce and maintain the very social structures taken as given within classical sociology. So, instead of asking why in principle social order is as it is (or is claimed to be), he proposed examining how particular manifestations of social order are achieved and worked into being (Garfinkel 1967). In conversation analysis this concern with social order is pursued through a consideration of the organisation of interactional practices. For example the classic work on conversational turn-taking by Sacks, Emanuel Schegloff and Gail Jefferson (1974) considers the ways in which parties to a conversation orient to, and indeed reflexively constitute, order in conversation.

Along with his colleagues, Sacks pioneered conversation analysis (CA) and began to examine the nature of conversation's organisation:

This work is part of a program of work undertaken several years ago to explore the possibility of achieving a naturalistic observational discipline that could deal with the details of social action(s) rigorously, empirically and formally ... Our analysis has sought to explicate the ways in which the materials (records of natural conversations) are produced by members in orderly ways that exhibit their orderliness and have their orderliness appreciated and used, and have that appreciation displayed and treated as the basis for subsequent action. (Schegloff and Sacks 1973: 289–90)

Sacks and his colleagues initially worked on tape recordings of telephone calls. However, as CA developed, so the variety of data sources expanded to include audio and audio/video recordings of face-to-face encounters in both mundane and institutional settings.

The collection of recorded data poses numerous challenges, from using the appropriate equipment, to issues of informed consent, to deciding on where best to place the recording equipment and so on (see ten Have 1999; Heath, Hindmarsh and Luff forthcoming). However, in some ways the major challenges, and the distinctive features of this research approach, arise when the analyst begins to examine the data recorded. Often there are hours and hours of recordings and they provide rich and dense materials to work with; it is easy to get drowned in detail; and, as with many types of qualitative data, it can be an 'attractive nuisance' (Miles 1979). To exploit the density and permanence of the data record, the research progresses through the close and detailed analysis of small extracts or fragments. This helps to develop a disciplined understanding of these episodes. Furthermore the analytic lens adopted in interrogating the data is shaped by the recognition that interaction is *sequentially organised*. Understanding this notion is at the very heart of the analytic project for the authors of this volume.

Sequential organisation is often mistaken as simply being concerned with systems or patterns of conversational turn-taking. Its importance is, however, much more far-reaching. At a basic level, it refers to the idea that the sense of a turn at talk in conversation, or indeed any action in interaction, arises from its positioning with respect to an immediate before and after. Each turn at talk both displays an understanding of a prior and projects appropriate or relevant next actions. As Garfinkel (1967: 76–103) ingeniously demonstrated, even random (yes/no) answers will be heard this way, as recognisable and rational extensions of matters being discussed. There are no imaginable ways of escaping such constraints. Were someone to try to do this, perhaps by saying 'please disregard everything we have been talking about', their next turn would still inevitably be understood in relation to this prior comment. These constraints never stall; they are conditions within which talk is 'condemned to be meaningful' (Heritage 1984: 110).

The sequentially embedded nature of talk and action is not something that just analysts are able to see and report upon. More importantly, such matters are displayed, recognised and 'oriented to' by social actors themselves, as an essential feature of their participation in unfolding courses of action. Thus sequence organisation is a key practical resource through which people are able to find what some utterance is, or at least might be, trying to accomplish.

These points are perhaps most clearly illustrated in the case of paired actions or 'adjacency pairs' (Sacks 1992). Consider some very common social actions, such as greetings, questions, compliments or invitations. Each of these projects an appropriate next action – respectively, a return greeting, an answer, an acknowledgement, an acceptance/rejection. These are not just what might happen next: most likely they will be expected, and the absence of such a response may be 'noticeable and accountable' (Sacks, Schegloff and Jefferson 1974).

This latter point is worth expanding. Both Garfinkel (1967) and Sacks (1992) were centrally interested in what being a competent member of society involves, and part of this, perhaps a very substantial part, is knowing how to engage and respond appropriately to sequential constraints and opportunities. For example, it can be treated as deviant behaviour to withhold answers to questions unless an account for such an absence is forthcoming. The asking of questions projects, even demands, a next action. A major frustration in life can be when one's questions are routinely ignored. So at quite a general level there is a moral agenda to sequential phenomena.

A good example here is Mitchell Duneier's (1999) enlightening ethnographic study of a New York sidewalk, which considers how 'black street men' commit 'interactional vandalism' in their dealings with, typically, 'white middle-class women' (for these characterisations, see Duneier and Molotch 1999: 1263). He discusses how the men shout out questions, such as 'how you doin'?', 'where you goin'?' or 'how old's your dog?' These place the women in a very difficult, and often unsettling, position. If they answer they are entangled in the opening of a conversation. They could of course refuse to answer – but the moral obligations of paired actions are so strong the women feel that by not answering they are forced into being 'rude' (Duneier 1999). They are in a no-win situation. For them, as for us all, refusing to answer the question is morally problematic. So first pair parts, such as questions, greetings, compliments and summons, can place conflicting and powerful demands on their recipients.

Two points are worth emphasising. First, the focus on sequence represents a distinctive intellectual commitment, rather than a casual or incidental concern. From such a perspective metaphors, stories and other discursive phenomena have to be studied in relation to the sequential environment of their production. When such forms are abstracted from their sequential environment, the analyst has no way of evidencing how the utterance was treated by interlocutors. As this reflects what someone was doing (or was taken to be doing) through that talk, this is a very considerable constraint. Second, the chapters in the present volume address sequentially organised actions not just to learn more about sequence as an institution in its own right, but to grasp the interplay between interaction and apparently 'wider' social and organisational matters. As Duneier's (1999) study so nicely illustrates, 'wider' social issues and problems find their expression in, and are reproduced through, the sequential organisation of talk-in-interaction.

Sequence organisation forms the foundation of the ways in which conversation analysts attend to data. Moreover it leads to a distinctive approach to addressing two key concerns in any analytic endeavour: context and evidence.

Context

John Heritage refers to the 'standard approach' to the matter of context in the social sciences as the 'bucket' theory of context. That is to say, 'pre-existing institutional circumstances are seen as enclosing interaction' (Heritage 1997: 163). The argument is that these circumstances shape the nature of the organisation of the interactions that take place 'within' that context. But there are always endless and competing ways of glossing 'the context'. A participant can be 'female', a 'heterosexual', a 'manager', a 'mother', an 'entrepreneur', a political 'conservative', a 'wife', an 'owner', 'from Swansea' and so forth. The setting can be a 'small firm', a 'boutique agency', a 'competitor', 'in Wales', a 'success', a 'failure' and so on. This raises problems because each of these characterisations may in some senses be 'correct'. Also, such lists can extend indefinitely. We are reminded of how children sometimes address letters, e.g., 'the United Kingdom, Europe, the world, the universe ...'. Is everything to be included? If not, how does the analyst establish which features of 'the context' to prioritise? Who gets to have the last word (Schegloff 1997)?

The studies in the present volume are distinctive in that they seek an analytic-empirical warrant for how persons and apparently objective, or social structural, settings are characterised:

> It is one thing to register that there are many ways to characterize a person, a stretch of conduct, or a setting or context in which the person enacts that conduct. It is quite another to claim that they are all equally warranted, equally legitimate, entitled to identical uptake and weight. But how should one discriminate? On what grounds should some characterization of any of these aspects of a sociocultural event be preferred to another? (Schegloff 1997: 166)

For conversation analysts, then, the solution to the problem of 'relevance' (Schegloff 1991) comes by taking seriously the features of 'context' that participants themselves 'orient to'. The approach is radically local to accommodate how contextual relevancies shift, not simply over time, but within sequences of talk in interaction. For each and every moment of an encounter the 'context' has to be achieved, recognised and displayed.

In this way, the chapters in this volume approach any action or turn at talk as 'doubly contextual' (Heritage 1984: 242):

> 'context' is treated as both the project and product of the participants' own actions and therefore as inherently locally produced and transformable at any moment. (Drew and Heritage 1992a: 19)

It is clear that the same words on different occasions can constitute very different actions. For example if person X was standing at a bus stop and asked a stranger 'Do you know the time?', they might expect a reply of the form 'Yes, it's a quarter past ten.' However if a lecturer asked the same question during a 10 am lecture, when a student walked through the door fifteen minutes late, they might *not* expect the answer 'Yes, it's a quarter past ten.' Indeed if the student responded in this way it might be seen as rude (by the lecturer) and/or funny (by the other students). Asking 'Do you know the time?' on such an occasion might instead be expected to elicit an apology. The relevant context is achieved in practice; it is displayed in and through contributions to the conversation in hand. Furthermore it is amenable to transformation at each moment.

Evidence

An enduring concern of qualitative social science has been to prioritise the participants' perspective. An understanding of sequence delivers a specific means of engaging this concern, because within the unfolding course of sequences of interaction participants build an 'architecture of intersubjectivity' (Heritage 1984: 254) in which they display their ongoing and ever-updating orientations towards the business at hand and the emerging turns at talk. This furnishes the analyst with a unique resource for grounding or evidencing claims (Sacks, Schegloff and Jefferson 1974). As a consequence of participants displaying their understanding of a prior action to their co-participants, that understanding is simultaneously made available to the analyst. Therefore, the analyst is able to utilise participants' displayed understandings of prior actions, rather than imposing their own interpretations to make sense of those actions. Indeed, the analyst is obligated to demonstrate that members themselves are treating the action in the ways proposed.

A slightly different matter is how to 'evidence' the use of organisational characterisations of persons and settings. It is one thing to present evidence that someone is orienting to a 'question', perhaps quite another to suggest they are orienting to their identity as a 'customer' (see Clark and Pinch, this volume), 'chair' (see Potter and Hepburn, this volume) or 'auctioneer' (see Heath and Luff, this volume). At this level, presenting evidence of the relevance of this or that setting, such as 'school board meeting' or 'auction', is not simply a matter of justification. In a way, 'evidencing' forms the central part of the analytic process. What the analyst is doing, by evidencing their use of 'contextual categories', is showing how 'social structure in the traditional sense enters into the production and interpretation of determinate facets of conduct' (Schegloff 1991: 51).

For example, to evidence the use of the category 'candidate' is to recover how people practically 'do' being a 'candidate' (see Llewellyn, this volume), how they orient their conduct to the setting at hand. The question of what stands as evidence of such an orientation has to be found and argued for, but through such a process the analyst may begin to show how conduct is, in Michael Lynch's (1993: 259) terms, 'social structural all the way down' into the fine details. Of course, there is also a flip side to this. If it is not possible to demonstrate the relevance of this or that characterisation, then it is not clear that such characterisations should be mentioned. Analysts may rely on ethnographic understandings of the setting to do this, but still they are required to show how the participants themselves orient to these features in and through their conduct.

The approach then is evidential, but in a distinctively non-positivistic fashion. It does not attempt to draw on statistical defence of the claims of regularity:

Even if no quantitative evidence can be mustered for a linkage between that practice of talking and that resultant 'effect', the treatment of the linkage as relevant – by the parties on that occasion, on which it was manifested – remains ... And no number of other episodes that developed differently will undo the fact that in these cases it went the way it did, with that exhibited understanding. (Schegloff 1993: 101)

These arguments lead Schegloff (1993: 114) to suggest that 'quantification is no substitute for analysis'. The basis for evidential claims is shifted.

Furthermore ethnomethodological descriptions of everyday activities abstain 'from all judgements of their adequacy, value, importance, necessity, practicality, success, or consequentiality' (Garfinkel and Sacks 1970: 345). This position of 'ethnomethodological indifference' has become a basis for criticisms of ethnomethodology. In particular it is argued that ethnomethodology fails to recognise that activity and language are political (Willmott 2005: 768). However, this argument is rather spurious. Previous EM/CA studies have examined settings such as rape trials (Drew 1992), police murder interrogations (D. R. Watson 1990), union–management negotiation (Walker 1995), divorce mediation (Greatbatch and Dingwall 1997) and so on. These authors do not need to be told that interaction is political and contested at a great many levels. The question is clearly not *whether* social life is contested, equitable or asymmetrical, but rather how far the analyst allows their own *a priori* commitments to inform their work. As Lynch argues:

Ethnomethodologists are not oblivious to politics, and like others they are
capable of discussing and taking strong positions on contentious matters of
the day. For the most part, however, they do not try to use their investigations
as instruments for advancing one or another popular cause, remedial program, or normative policy. Nor do they endeavour to lend 'scientific' authority to their own political commitments. This has nothing to do with a personal
indifference to such matters. The desire for an authoritative critique of power
can be overwhelming and understandable, but all too often it encourages a
principled (and sometimes unprincipled) effort to pursue the unrealized
dreams of transcendental analysis. (Lynch 1993: 34)

It is suggested that when researchers assume *a priori* that a particular
injustice or asymmetry exists, and thereby ascribe priority in advance to
particular ways of defining people, processes and practices, then, no
matter how noble their intent, they may nevertheless find themselves
defining scenes, settings and social relations 'without regard for the
concerns of persons' (Weber 1948: 80).

Finding the organisation in interaction

Studying interaction in institutional and organisational settings brings
with it added complexity. The researcher is not simply unpacking the
organisation of interaction, but also the distinctive character and properties of the organisational setting at hand. This section considers in
more detail how this might be done.

A great deal of conversation analytic work that considers organisational interaction, an area known as the Institutional Talk Programme,
adopts a fundamentally *comparative method*. In looking at any stretch of
talk, such studies try to bring into view orderly deviations from 'ordinary
conversation', where such deviations might be taken to suggest some
distinctiveness to the setting at hand. This can be a useful starting place
for analysis, and Heritage (1997) provides very lucid guidance on where
to look for 'institutionality' in talk. He lays out six dimensions of interaction in which the institutional character of talk might be revealed.

(1) *Turn-taking organisation:* Are there distinctive procedures and
    practices for allocating turns at talk that differ from casual
    conversation?
(2) *Overall structural organisation of the interaction:* Are there routine
    stages or phases to an encounter that recur across occasions?

(3) *Sequential organisation:* Are there specific ways in which organisational members exploit an understanding of the sequential relationships between turns at talk?

(4) *Turn design:* Are there particular ways in which turns at talk (e.g. requests, invitations, questions, responses, rejections, etc.) are designed to accomplish organisational work?

(5) *Lexical choice:* Do references to people, objects or events reveal the institutional (as opposed to casual) nature of the activity at hand?

(6) *Interactional/institutional asymmetries:* Are there asymmetries in forms of participation, familiarity with organisational procedures or access to institutional know-how that reveal the different organisational roles that parties to the interaction are adopting?

Rather than review all of these (for which see Heritage 1997), it may be more useful to consider three in more depth – turn-taking organisation, sequential organisation and interactional/institutional asymmetries – that are especially relevant to the studies included in this volume.

Turn-taking organisation

Within casual conversation, exchanges between speakers are relatively flexible, though fundamentally ordered. Sacks, Schegloff and Jefferson (1974) discuss a variety of practices through which parties manage turn-taking so that they do not continually talk over one another and so that they avoid long pauses and moments of hesitation in conversation. These include practices that enable co-participants to assess when someone's turn is coming to completion and even how long a turn is likely to be. They also include practices for the selection of next speaker. These are all practices that seem to transcend sex, age, race and indeed topic of conversation. They have been shown to be orderly and describable at significant levels of detail (see Schegloff 2007).

Within organisational settings, turn-taking can be much more formalised or structured. Although on many occasions turn-taking is no different to ordinary conversation, some settings (at some times) systematically transform turn-taking practices. These transformations can reveal much of the business at hand. Take, for example, Deirdre Boden's (1994) study of the interactional organisation of business meetings. One practical problem for large meetings is to ensure that there is co-orientation to a single strand of conversation for a sustained period – consider as an alternative how social gatherings such as dinner parties quickly fragment into multiple groups of concurrent conversations. To avoid this, the organisational solution for many business meetings is to place someone in the role of the 'chair', who is oriented to by parties to the meeting as key to the allocation of turns at talk. The chair decides who speaks and often will dictate how long they speak for. They control the exchange of turns and they are also in a position to ensure that turns at talk remain 'on-topic'. This reveals an orientation to the problem of turn-taking in large meetings, and the larger the meeting the more likely it is that the group will appoint a chair to address this problem.

Taking another example, consider studies of the classroom (e.g. Mehan 1979; McHoul 1978). While there are a variety of forms of talk in school classrooms, there is a prevalent form that exists, that is, the instructional triad, variously termed initiation-response-feedback (I-R-F) or question-answer-comment (Q-A-C). Studies of classrooms reveal an orientation by members to parties engaging in particular 'types' of turn in particular orders – questions from a teacher, answers from students and then comments on those answers by the teacher. Furthermore the teacher routinely allocates who gets to answer by simple selection of an individual from the whole group of students or by selecting from those offering an answer (with their hands raised, for example). Thus the turn-taking system further reveals an orientation by participants to the organisational identities of others.

Christian Heath and Paul Luff (this volume) pursue an interest in the work of the auctioneer through an analysis of the distinctive turn-taking organisation in operation. In doing so they note how auctioneers address practical problems in managing the participation of large numbers of potential bidders through the deployment of the 'run'. It is not that parties to the encounter are somehow biologically encoded to 'perform' in these ways; they are not physically prohibited from speaking at certain times. It is rather that participants work with these practices of turn-taking to address distinctive practical and organisational concerns.

Furthermore it should be noted that these turn-taking 'systems' are actively sanctioned. There are expectations, indeed obligations, on parties to participate in particular ways within these systems. In meetings, people who do not conform to these practices may be sanctioned by the chair or by others in the meeting. In a similar vein, it has been noted that students expect teachers to provide feedback on their answers. As John Sinclair and Malcolm Coulthard has shown:

> It is deviant to withhold feedback continually, and we have a tape of one lesson where a teacher, new to a class, and trying to suggest to them that there aren't always right answers, does withhold feedback and eventually reduces the children to silence – they cannot see the point of his question. (Sinclair and Coulthard 1975: 51)

Of course, the formal provisions can be contested. Such arrangements impact on participants' opportunities for action and whether they may be able to 'influence' activities and individuals within some setting. In and through describable practices, people may try to overcome arrangements for participation (see Potter and Hepburn, this volume). At such moments detailing how people orient to the turn-taking provisions can reveal much about the concerns of those parties and the ways in which they are shaping the action.

Sequence as a resource for work

Understanding the sequential properties and implications of interaction can be a valuable resource not just for analysts, but also for organisational members themselves as part of getting a job done. Indeed Arthur Stinchcombe (1990) argues that an advanced understanding of 'ethnomethods' of interaction is an organisational requirement for certain roles (e.g. sales work). But how can we unpack the strategic use (whether implicit or explicit) of the sequential ordering of ordinary actions (see also Arminen 2005)?

Earlier in this chapter we discussed the idea of paired actions and the ways in which particular turns at talk project or shape potential next actions. The example drawn upon was the question–answer adjacency pair; it might be worth considering how questions and answers are put to work in different organisational settings. This can help to unpack the interplay between sequential features and distinctive organisational problems and contingencies (see also Raymond 2006).

One of the earliest studies in conversation analysis was undertaken by Sacks on telephone calls to an emergency psychiatric hospital (reported in Sacks 1992). The hospital was interested in how to get people to say their names because some callers would not provide them. Clearly one organisational strategy would simply be to ask the callers and thereby

make their name an explicit topic. But this would often be countered
with the question 'why?', and the answer to that question could then be
countered with an excuse of one sort or another. Things could become
awkward and distract from the business at hand, business that often
involved very distressed callers in need of significant personal and
organisational support.

Sacks analysed the opening moments of these calls and found some
recurrent patterns. As noted earlier, a greeting begets a greeting (e.g.
hello – hello), but in addition, Sacks also found that the form of the
greeting would often be adopted in the response as well. So, if the call-
taker provided their name, the caller would routinely respond in their
greeting with their name as well:

A: Hello, this is Mr Smith, may I help you?
B: Yes, this is Mr Brown.

There is no explicit demand or request for a name, and yet the caller
provides it. Sacks found that if callers did not give their name at this
juncture, they would usually not provide their name when asked later.
So a strategy that can be adopted to get someone else's name is to give
your own – and indeed this is a noticeable and recurrent feature of all
greetings. It would seem that 'greeting plus name' establishes particular
prospective constraints upon the next action. This is, of course, something the interested reader may wish to test out.

Sacks also considered methodic practices that could be applied by
callers to withhold their name and thereby escape sequential constraints.
Consider a further instance:

A: Hello this is Mr. Smith, may I help you?
B: I can't hear you.
A: This is Mr. Smith.
B: Smith.

In this fragment, the turn 'I can't hear you' works to 'skip' a turn. It
moves past the slot where the caller may deliver their own name and the
greeting becomes bound up with issues of mishearing. The sequence
ends with the caller re-stating the name of the call-taker ('Smith'). There
are now no sequential grounds for the caller to offer their name without
topicalising its production.

In these data, we cannot access the 'mind' of the caller or assess his or
her 'intentions', but this is not necessary for what we are doing. What

we can say, very concretely, is that on this occasion 'I can't hear you' skips a turn such that the caller has no clear opportunity to give his or her name. The caller may not have planned to withhold his or her name, but it *worked* this way and could work again. So it can be seen as a strategy that could be used by a caller to withhold his or her name without having to actively go against sequential constraints set in train by 'Hello, this is Mr. Smith.'

If we turn the same sort of analytic sensibility to the study of other work and organisational settings, we can find a variety of ways in which questions can be used to do organisational work. For example, Boden (1994) discusses how asking questions in a meeting can delay or even resist the need to provide evaluative assessments of ideas and suggestions. Dalvir Samra-Fredericks (2003b) discusses how questions in a series can be used to pursue agreement. Colin Clark, Paul Drew and Trevor Pinch (2003) discuss how salespeople can initiate questions in order to then affiliate with potential customers' responses as ways of building rapport. These examples focus on how questions are deployed in organisations and how understanding their form can help us to reflect on the business at hand. However, more generally, they indicate the ways in which we might interrogate the most basic building blocks of interaction to reflect on interactional solutions to the practical problems of any job of work.

Interactional/institutional asymmetries

Within many settings of organisational conduct there are asymmetries revealed in the form of interaction that arises. For example, there are often asymmetries between parties to the encounter with regard to the specialist knowledge and languages that they are able to invoke. There are often asymmetries with regard to participants' differential experience of the organisational practices and procedures relevant to the activity. There are also asymmetries in the access that different individuals have to information about each other. These can be crucial to the ways that the encounter unfolds.

Take, for example, Jack Whalen, Don Zimmerman and Marilyn Whalen's (1988) study of a fateful call to the emergency services in the USA. From the beginnings of the encounter, the caller and call-taker began to argue, resulting in an ambulance not being dispatched until the caller's stepmother had died. There were various accounts that arose in the aftermath to explain what happened, mainly relating to the stress both parties were under. However, Whalen, Zimmerman and Whalen present a powerful argument that at least part of the reason for the troubles can be found in the asymmetrical access of parties to the nature of the organisational procedures at hand.

They suggest that the caller and call-taker were orienting to a different type of 'service encounter'. The caller is orienting to the service as if it is similar to the service offered by a taxi or pizza company: i.e. if you request it, you will get it, and it will just be a matter of specifying the order and the delivery address. However, in taking calls, the emergency services face organisational problems in identifying hoax callers and also in ranking calls in terms of medical priority. Thus the organisation requires a valid and immediate reason to dispatch an ambulance and call-takers routinely ask for information about the medical problem prior to dispatch. In the case at hand the caller does not seem to expect this interrogative sequence of questions, just as you would not expect 'why do you want a pizza?' when you call the local pizzeria. As the caller begins to resist this line of questioning, it adds delays into the call as the call-taker attends to the caller's growing frustrations. This distracts from the business at hand and it alters how subsequent turns are heard and managed.

The delays that ensue in dealing with the call are not simply conversational delays but delays in service delivery that have disastrous implications for the caller and his stepmother. Thus, at least part of the explanation for the troubles that emerge is tied to asymmetries with regard to knowledge of the organisational procedures. As the caller does not work within with the organisational script there is a deepening misalignment between organisation and client. By studying less dramatic, but more commonplace, encounters, Robert Moore, Jack Whalen and Cabell Gathman (this volume) pursue these interests in asymmetrical access to organisational procedures. They demonstrate how staff and customers work through and indeed align lay and professional accounts used to describe orders in a copy shop.

Another sort of asymmetry that arises within call centre work relates to the differential access that caller and call-taker have with regard to the information systems in use by the call-taker. Simply put, the caller cannot see the texts and technologies that the call-taker is using to handle the call. A good example can be found in research on telesales staff by Whalen, Whalen and Henderson (2002) which shows how the asymmetry in access to the material setting of the worker can be used as a resource for staff in organising their work.

Like many other occupations, call centre workers display professional competence through interactional proficiency. However, given the nature of the job, the call-takers need to produce a 'hearably' competent call as customers have no more than the call-taker's voice to decide if they are dealing with the business at hand efficiently. The achievement of 'smooth' and seamless calls can display competence, and call-takers work to avoid 'clunky' moments in the interaction – awkward pauses, requests to 'hold on' and the like. This is made more difficult due to the fact that call centre staff are typically simultaneously managing computer-based information retrieval and entry while on the phone. Thus to produce a competent call and to work through the computerised script, the call-taker needs to master keyboard, mouse, software, paper documents (policies, phone numbers and the like), pens/notepaper and headset. The more experienced call-takers attend to these demands of call-taking by arranging their desks to ensure that relevant tools are ready to hand. Furthermore, within the course of a call, they learn to search for information in *anticipation* of likely next actions or requests from customers, such that they have the information to be able to provide a timely response.

This provides a flavour of the ways in which institutional asymmetries are reflected in and shaped by interactional asymmetries of various kinds. Clearly we cannot be exhaustive in this regard, but we have used our discussion of 'turn-taking', 'sequence organisation' and 'interactional/institutional asymmetries' to consider how occupational and organisational concerns can be located in the details of interaction. These provide a methodological resource with which to interrogate audio and video data. They are not 'findings' that are to be applied again and again to new settings, but should be viewed as analytic seams to mine.

From 'work talk' to 'body work'

The foregoing discussion has focused mainly, at least in terms of examples, on the treatment of audio data. However, the majority of studies in the present volume draw on visual data as well. Video data exhibits an additional 'density' (Grimshaw 1982) in that the empirical record now includes not only talk, but gesture, movement and the material environment of texts, tools and technologies in and through which the action is organised.

The ways in which we interact with others are fundamentally impacted by the ways in which we physically orient towards other people and the objects and technologies that are to hand. Take, for instance, the car journey. We are all aware that during trickier driving moments, such as negotiating a roundabout or a troublesome junction, conversations with drivers become less fluid. The embodied activities of the driver in negotiating the road are intertwined with the ways in which the conversation unfolds. It is no different in the workplace, where the use of a computer screen or a paper document can often mediate organisational and moral accountabilities. It seems critical, then, to consider ways in which 'tools of the trade' are practically deployed in the production of work, and the only way to capture such details, as they unfold moment by moment, is through audio/video recordings.

In organisation studies there has been much interest recently in the embodied character of work (see Dale 2000; Casey 2000). The approaches that we are outlining provide one means for taking seriously the embodied properties of work and organisation. As many of the papers here and elsewhere show, the production of organisational practice in face-to-face settings fundamentally co-implicates talk and the body (see C. Goodwin 1995, 2000; Heath 1986; Heath and Luff 2000; Hindmarsh and Pilnick 2007; Llewellyn 2008; Alby and Zucchermaglio 2006; J. Whalen, Whalen and Henderson 2002 amongst others; and Hindmarsh and Heath 2007 for a recent review). Thus the papers in this volume treat talk and the body as a package, not as separate 'channels'. For example, David Greatbatch and Timothy Clark (this volume) powerfully demonstrate how the study of story-telling in organisations is significantly enhanced by taking seriously the ways in which the verbal and the visual are co-implicated in a story's telling.

These studies are still fundamentally concerned with sequence. Indeed it is critical to note that bodily conduct gains its determinate sense by virtue of its sequential placement in the unfolding activity at hand. The same movement can on different occasions constitute very different actions, and so it is vital to recover how 'the body' is treated by participants themselves. This is demonstrated by Jon Hindmarsh and Alison Pilnick (2007), who studied highly skilled collaborative work in a medical setting. They analysed stretches of action that were almost entirely silent, but where each contribution was nevertheless sequentially organised, for example in the sense of attending to the implications of a prior glance, gesture or some noise (such as the 'beep' from an alarm system).

This interest in embodied practice should not be treated solely as an analytic concern. Understanding embodied conduct is fundamental to the ways in which organisational members experience and attend to organisational concerns. For example, Clark and Pinch (this volume) show how sales staff are acutely aware of the significance of different forms of bodily conduct in assessing customers' interest in products and their need for assistance. Similarly Heath, Luff and Marcus Sanchez Svensson (2002) discuss the ways in which surveillance staff 'read' the bodies of passengers depicted on CCTV images to identify and assess problems, difficulties and deviant behaviour that occur beyond the screen. Hindmarsh (this volume) extends this line of research by exploring the ways in which members of the public read the conduct of professionals in contributing to the collaborative production of a service, in this case dental health care.

As our 'car journey' example suggests, bringing the body into analyses of work also demands an attention to the physical contexts in which the bodies interact. The sense and significance of a bodily movement is intelligible for participants and analysts alike only in relation to its physical context (C. Goodwin 2003; Heath and Hindmarsh 2000). A movement is always away from one feature of the environment and towards a different feature and can be deeply consequential for the delicate co-ordination of work tasks. Therefore the complexity of the analysis is further heightened by the need to take seriously not only the bodies depicted in the data, but also the texts, tools and technologies with and around which those bodies are working.

Recovering organisational details

The concern with organisational detail and the data-driven approach that is adopted here encourages the use of 'transcripts' to focus the analytic gaze and to enable the analyst to unpack the sequential character of the activities at hand. One of the more noticeable features of this kind of work is the use of a range of bespoke transcription symbols to represent talk and also bodily conduct. Most forms of transcript in qualitative research tend to remove the 'noise' in the encounter – the hesitations, the use of 'err' and 'umm', the intonation and the like. However, given the concern with the details of interaction and the ways in which action is produced moment by moment these features are critical for sequential analysis.

To discuss the key features, consider the following data transcript, which is drawn from a study of a telecommunications control centre (see Hindmarsh and Heath 1998). The standard transcription orthography adopted was developed by Gail Jefferson (1984b). Like any transcription system it reflects the nature of the concerns and interests of the analyst, and so the concern with the sequential organisation of action drives the ways in which action is re-presented through these transcripts. As a result the transcript is designed to present the temporal production of talk (and potentially other conduct). So the talk runs down the page, line by line, and each line is given a line number (for ease of reference) and associated with the speaker (in Figure 2.1, C for 'Chris' and P for 'Phil'). Furthermore, pauses in talk are charted to the nearest 0.1 of a second. Mini-pauses of less than 0.2 of a second are indicated by '(.)', and latched utterances are linked by equals signs. To further reflect the temporal production of the talk, (portions of) words that are elongated are indicated by colons and in other cases angle brackets surround talk that is produced more quickly.

There is no call for the minutiae of speech production to be recorded in the way that some linguistic or speech therapy analyses would necessitate, but some simple features are indicated. Rising and falling intonation are marked by up and down arrows, louder talk is underlined or, in the extreme, capitalised. Quieter talk is surrounded by degree symbols. For reference, a full description of these symbols can be found in Jefferson (1984b).

The transcription of visual conduct is even more complex. Standard analytic practice involves the production of 'data maps' in which changes in gaze, gesture and other bodily/visual features are charted in relation to the production of talk (see Heath and Hindmarsh 2002; Heath, Hindmarsh and Luff forthcoming). This enables the analyst to unpack the temporal organisation of the conduct and thus to begin to explore the potential sequential associations between actions. However, for presentational purposes these are extraordinarily opaque. Therefore most chapters in this volume, and in the field more generally, use illustrative video 'frame-grabs' to reveal key visual features associated with different segments of verbal conduct.

```
 1  C:  Hello^ Rick^ ((on phone))
 2      (0.8)
 3  C:  Hang on a minute, I'll
 4      just put you on hold.
 5      don't go away.
 6      (1.0)
 7  C:  go on. [1]
 8      (3.7)
 9  C:  Brussel::s::
10      (0.6)
11  P:  yes? [2]
12      (0.6)
13  C:  Brussel-
14      (0.2)
15  P:  twenty one.=
16  C:  =Brussels Keybridge::
17      (0.3)
18  P:  twenty one.=
19      (1.0)
20  C:  uh-er, ss::i- wha-
21      (0.2)
22  P:  six oh two one. [3]
23      (0.2)
24  C:  oh^ six oh two one.
25      (.) yeah. [4]
```

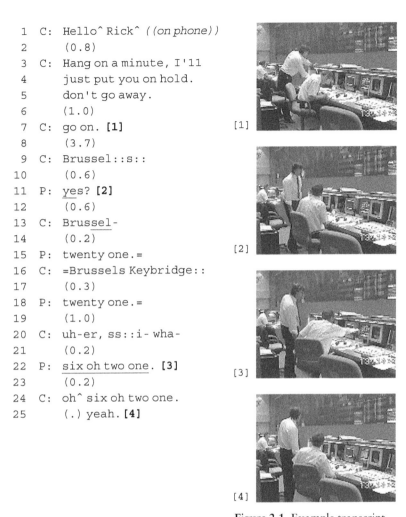

[1]

[2]

[3]

[4]

Figure 2.1. Example transcript

It should be noted that these transcripts are by no means a replacement for the recorded data but rather encourage the analyst to get to know the data in some depth. In watching a video clip for the first, second, third or even tenth time, the density of the record resists a full and systematic appreciation. At the outset it is easy to gloss what might be going on, and yet the value of the record is that it facilitates a more detailed understanding of these moments of interaction than field observation – this is where the practice of transcription is invaluable. Transcribing to this level of detail demands a serious attention to the

temporal relationships between actions, which can be used to explore
the sequential associations.

Take, for example the case presented in Figure 2.1. At the start of
the extract the two colleagues are engaged in entirely independent and
individual activities – Chris on the phone and Phil recording events in
the log-book – but as the extract progresses they move into a close
collaboration in identifying material relevant to the remote caller. We
are able to recover the ways in which subtle transformations in Chris'
talk and bodily conduct conspire to demonstrate his engagement in a
search both to the caller and to Phil, conduct that draws Phil into the
activity. Furthermore it is possible to reveal how both Chris and Phil
re-shape each contribution to the encounter in the light of the prior
one – Chris in demonstrating continued confusion over subsequent
turns (lines 13, 16, 20) and Phil in re-designing his contributions to
attend to these confusions (lines 15, 18 and 22). It ends with Phil
pointing to the relevant information on screen as he explicitly states
the number sought for and then Chris physically turns away to mark the
end of the search and to continue the call in 'isolation' from Phil. Thus
the video record enables the analyst to recover the interactional
resources (both verbal and bodily) in and through which Phil recognises
the activity in which Chris is engaged, begins to assist him and tailors
that assistance in light of Chris' emerging conduct. In this way the
transcript helps to chart movement from the individual to the collaborative and back again.

Conclusion

There are an array of approaches to the study of practice in contemporary organisational studies. Many of these take very seriously the
ways in which organisational actions are situated and the contingencies
that shape their production. Usually these approaches, whether in
sensemaking, practice-based studies or the organisational discourse
programme, focus on observational or discursive data of everyday
organisational conduct. They are overwhelmingly concerned to unpack
the work practices that underpin the achievement of organising and
organisation. So in these ways (and others) they share some significant
concerns with analytic work informed by ethnomethodology and conversation analysis. However the studies in this volume proceed in a way

that contrasts, sometimes sharply, with standard approaches to practice in organisation studies.

A key aspect of the distinctiveness of these studies is grounded in their recognition of the importance of the sequential properties of social interaction. For the authors in this volume, sequence is at the heart of their analytic endeavours – to unpack (and not just assume) matters of context, to ground analytic claims in interactional details and to prioritise and indeed demonstrate the participants' perspectives. Researchers new to this approach are often horrified by the seemingly masochistic level of detail at which organisational conduct is transcribed and analysed. However, the concern to attend to this level of granularity is reflected in the clear orientation of organisational members to this level of detail. Members themselves are sensitive to a pause following a request as indicative of potential rejection, a gesture as potentially undermining agreement and the rest. Moreover, and just as importantly, this level of organisational detail reveals much about the nature of the business at hand and the ordered properties of the setting. As such, the sequential analysis of interactional details delivers distinctive materials for understanding work and organisations.

PART II

Studies

3 A kind of governance: rules, time and psychology in organisations

JONATHAN POTTER AND ALEXA HEPBURN

Introduction

In the past fifteen years researchers in conversation analysis and discursive psychology have developed novel conceptions of the relationship between organisations, practices and individual psychology (Boden and Zimmerman 1991b; Drew and Heritage 1992b; Edwards and Potter 1992; Hepburn and Wiggins 2007a). They have built an approach to human conduct in institutional settings which is distinct from those traditionally offered in the disciplines of sociology, psychology and organisation studies. This distinctiveness comes from an analytic focus on records of actual organisations at work, supported by new recording technology and new representational forms that enable a more immediate engagement with human practices than is offered by questionnaires, interviews or ethnographic field notes and observations. At the same time it is derived from a rigorous focus on the orientations and constructions of organisational members as these are displayed in interaction itself (rather than reported post hoc in questionnaires or interviews).

In the field of organisational studies these approaches provide one powerful answer to calls to 'open the black box' so as to understand the 'actual behaviour' of organisations such as boards of companies (Huse 2005) and one way of moving 'beyond agency theory' in empirical work on companies (Pye and Pettigrew 2005). Although conversation analysts and ethnomethodologists have shown a sporadic interest in the nature and organisation of meetings and topics that have traditionally been the purview of organisation science, with the exception of Deirdre Boden's (1994) book on the 'business of talk' this has rarely come

Some parts of this chapter previously appeared as: J. Potter and A. Hepburn (2007), Chairing Democracy: Psychology, Time and Negotiating the Institution, in J. P. McDaniel and K. Tracy (eds.), *The Prettier Doll: Rhetoric, Discourse and Ordinary Democracy*, Tuscaloosa, AL: University of Alabama Press, pp. 176–204.

together in a sustained empirical programme (but see important contributions from M. A. Atkinson, Cuff and Lee 1978; C. Baker 1997; Boden 1995; Cuff and Sharrock 1985; Housley 1999, 2000; Huisman 2001). Recent moves to develop this connection have come from Dalvir Samra-Fredericks (2004a, 2005a).

In this chapter we will illustrate the kind of analysis that conversation analysis and discursive psychology can support through a detailed consideration of a single organisational event. We will use this to pick up and explore a set of current themes – time and control, authority and resistance, rules and practices – and to consider in particular the way in which organisational activities can be displayed, learned and resisted as they unfold in time and re-work the nature of time.

The analysis offered will be microscopic, but not as a contrast to macro social science – rather it is microscopic as it aims to capture the level of detail and organisation that the parties themselves demonstrably find relevant. Conversation analysis and discursive psychology have both shown the need to address interaction, and the value of doing so, at a level of granularity that can attend to individual lexical items, intonation, overlap and other features of talk and embodied action that speakers themselves attend to. These features can be rendered analytically tractable by the use of a combination of Jeffersonian transcription (see Jefferson 2004) and digital audio and video that can allow repeated inspection of conduct. This level of granularity does not detract from the focus on institutional organisations; rather, work in these traditions has shown precisely that it is required for a sophisticated grasp of institutional order. This kind of detail does not simply live inside broader structures, like an ant colony lives in a tank; rather it is a part of the constitution of broader structure. And the past decade of work in this tradition has produced a large body of empirical work that illustrates this programme in a range of different settings.

Rules and plans; institutions and psychology

In the course of this chapter, we will focus on how the orderliness of a particular organisational setting – a school board meeting – is built, and resisted, and the systematic resources used for both of these things. In organisations actors are making their world at the same time as they act within it, constituting and re-working institutional procedures from the inside. One area where this is visible is the operation of rules in organisations and their relation to practices. The traditional social science picture has rules as templates that guide and constrain practices (Bogen 1999). However, the perspectives that we have drawn on provide important correctives to this picture.

In philosophy, Ludwig Wittgenstein (1953) in particular pressed for a much more complex picture of the relationship between rules and actions. For example, he stressed that rules require further interpretive work to allow decisions about whether any particular case is rule following or departing. He undermines arguments that the orderliness of social life can be understood as a consequence of following encoded templates such as rules. The point is not that rules of some kind are not important for the orderliness of conduct and for organisational patterning; it is that they are not sufficient to produce such orderliness, and that their relevance does not flow in a simple unidirectional manner between rules and practices.

In sociology the ethnomethodological tradition has developed this perspective most fully. Harold Garfinkel (1967) highlighted the practical and ad hoc way in which individual actions are bought into line with, or shown to break, particular rules. Lawrence Wieder's (1974a) famous study of the operation of a 'convict code' in a halfway house for drug rehabilitation highlighted a range of subtle and locally situated activities done by 'telling the code', which cast doubt on the idea that the code could be used as a straightforward explanation for the actions of the convicts.

Let us spend a moment considering Lucy Suchman's (1987) ethnomethodological work on plans (which have often been taken to have the same explanatory privilege as rules). She suggested that, although plans are often treated as the crucial determinant of actions, they are in practice only a weak resource. Indeed, their apparent importance may be more a consequence of a Western bias towards rationality than a reflection of their actual causal potency. For a plan to operate it needs to have specified connections to the relevant features of settings and the contingencies within settings. However, as Wittgenstein pointed out with rules, this will mean an (impossibly) large set of further specifications. Suchman built a different view of plans, one which emphasised their role as resources for projecting and reconstructing courses of action in terms of prior intentions. The consequence of this view is that 'the prescriptive significance of intentions for situated actions is inherently vague' (Suchman 1987: 27). Crucially this vagueness is not a defect when compared with full specification; rather it is precisely what makes plans useful for their projective and reconstructive tasks – they can be applied to an indefinite number of situations in adroit and locally specific ways.

Suchman illustrated these ideas through an analysis of the prosaic and familiar interaction with and around photocopiers. This brought into sharp relief the basic tension between the orderly plans and outcomes that are specified in the manual and embodied in the menu system, and the messy trial-and-error considerations that appear in operators' talk. The operators (often) get to where they need to be in the end, producing their bound and double-sided documents, but their actions on the way are ad hoc. They use the menus, but they provide local interpretations of their sense. They refer to a range of background considerations and reconstruct the orderliness of what they do as they go along, often in terms of goals and plans. Even in a system as apparently straightforward as that of a photocopier there is no simple set of rules embodied in the manual that directly produces orderly operator conduct. That conduct does have order; but the manual is not sufficient for understanding it.

As David Bogen (1999) has noted, workers using classical conceptions of rules have used a procedure that abstracted the nature of these rules from an observation of practices, and then treated these practices as the orderly product of following these very rules. This form of explanation is sustained by a particular cognitivist picture of rules and practices rather than being adequately empirically supported. All of these critical points encourage caution over the use of rules to explain action. Yet this does not suggest that rule formulations are not an important and consequential topic of study. Indeed, this will be an important element of our example in this chapter, where we consider the operation of a meeting and the way rules and rule formulation appear within the talk of that meeting.

As well as ethnomethodological conversation analysis we will be drawing on a discursive psychological perspective. The key point here is that we will be considering psychological matters from the point of view of participants. That is, we will be looking at the way psychological states are displayed and formulated and the way psychological categories are used in practice. For example, Derek Edwards (2005) looked at the way speakers display subjective investment in a complaint or undercut that subjective investment by using categories such as 'moan' or 'whinge'. Practices such as complaining manage both an 'objective side' – the complainable matter in the world – and a 'subjective side' – the speaker's hurt, investment, intentions and so on. Interaction is organised to manage both the subjective and objective simultaneously (Edwards 2007). One of the features of managing the 'subjective side' is that it may be part of the management of organisational practices (Edwards and Potter 2001; Potter and Hepburn 2003; see also Samra-Fredericks 2004a). This will be highlighted in the analysis that follows; for some of complex issues that arise when considering cognition in action see Jonathan Potter and Hedwig te Molder (2005).

Barbiegate, meetings and social relations

The materials that we will work with come from a specific public controversy and, in particular, one meeting within that controversy. The precise nature of this controversy is not crucial to our general observations, although it perhaps accounts for the strong views expressed. A highly simplified version of events has a third-grade school girl in Colorado submitting an experiment to a school science fair that involved asking people which of two dolls, one black and one white, was prettier. The experiment and its results were considered problematic and withdrawn from the fair. The girl's father complained and the school board met to discuss the controversy. The controversy grew and came to national prominence. (For a range of different analyses and evaluations of the heated debate, including our own, see papers in Tracy, McDaniel and Gronbeck (2007).)

We were invited to contribute an analysis of the collection that included a set of school board meetings, newspaper reports and other materials. Interestingly the transcript we were given of the pivotal school board meeting where David Thielen, the girl's father, set out his complaint about the actions of the school started at the point where he begins to speak. However, when we looked at the video recording we had been given there was a brief untranscribed section where the chair of the school board introduced the meeting. This perhaps reflected that this was mere administrative chatter before the real business of the meeting. Indeed, for many the real interest was in the speech by one individual about freedom and oppression, for which the apparatus of traditional rhetorical analysis might be deemed most suitable.

However, as John Heritage and David Greatbatch (1986) have shown, it is important to understand even formal speeches in terms of their dialogical and recipient-designed features. Moreover, for us the school board meeting itself is a potential organisational setting rather than a frame for an abstract participant's position on the controversy.

One of the valuable features of these materials is that their recording is part of the data itself. The school board meetings were shown on the local community cable channel, and the record that was available for research was produced for that purpose. There was, then, no specific researcher reactivity. The camera is part of the event and the version it transmitted is a version for the community. The participants may therefore orient to the recording, but in a way that is endogenous to the event rather than researcher-inspired (Speer and Hutchby 2003). Furthermore, because it is a low-budget community channel there is only one camera and the transmission is not edited. These features made the video record an excellent data source.

In choosing to focus on the one school board meeting rather than the broader set of materials and specifically on the opening and closing of this speech rather than the speech itself, and the various potential historical and sociological contexts that might be invoked through historical study or social theory, we have taken a sometimes controversial analytic stance. Nevertheless, it is one common (but not universal) in conversation analytic and discursive psychological studies (compare Schegloff 1997 with Billig 1999). There are complicated issues here and we are not going to explore all of them (see Hepburn and Wiggins 2007b, for a recent summary). However, the point here is that if we want to understand the operation of this school board meeting we should take this as an issue that may be equally relevant for the participants (although they may have different access to and perspectives on this question). The key analytic point is that we will work with the interaction to watch the structure as it is built and re-built by the participants themselves.

A manual for chairing

What kind of thing is the social organisation of a school board? Whatever else it is, this social organisation is something built, managed, undermined and enforced in the local setting. Part of this is undoubtedly supported by the physical layout of the meeting with the board

Figure 3.1. The Chair

Figure 3.2. David Thielen

president sitting behind a raised desk at the front of a room (Figure 3.1) and the speakers from the floor speaking from behind a podium and addressing the president with the audience behind them (Figure 3.2). The issue of how to describe participants over the course of analysis is a subtle one, raising fundamental issues around analysts' versus participants' understandings. Person reference is interactionally charged in a range of ways (Schegloff 2006; Lerner and Kitzinger 2007; D. R. Watson 1997). Indeed, this is itself an issue of organisational politics. Whose characterisations of events should prevail? Should we as social researchers offer a technical specification or should we attempt to work with the categories and displayed understandings in the material? Thus although we have used the descriptive category 'Chair' rather than 'president' – as this reflects a conventional understanding of the business conducted by this actor in this interaction – it is important to avoid doing analysis by fiat simply in the selection of categories. Here the category 'Chair' will be treated as provisional and subject to further re-specification. Part of our interest will be in how the job of 'chairing' is accomplished.

The physical features of the scene are supplemented by the technological features. Both president and speaker are provided with microphones built into the furniture (i.e. a table for the president and the podium for the presenter). This underscores who the significant speakers are by, for example, making their speech clearly audible over background audience noise. Inspection of the video tape also shows that this is a well-attended event. Most of the chairs are full – the room feels busy. People appear to be listening attentively. It is a live organisational setting – speeches are being made to an audience both present and virtually present via the television transmission.

Let us start by considering the seventy or so lines of transcript before the 'speech' starts. The tape edit cuts off the first moments of the Chair's introduction. We have used standard Jeffersonian transcript (Jefferson 2004) and supplemented this with some basic indications about non-vocal activities. Video of the whole piece is available via the Loughborough Discourse and Rhetoric Group Website. We reproduce it in its entirety to give a sense of its fluidly unfolding nature. Ch is the Chair, DT is David Thielen and Va is Various anonymous audience members.

Extract 3.1

```
 1  Ch:  . . . any: issue you wan' to:, (0.5) u:m
 2        (.) we only have a coupla ground             turns to right
 3        ru:les:, the first and the most important
 4        i:s (0.6) er:: that you have to: um (1.0)    turns to left
 5        s:tart and complete your: comments within
 6        two minutes, (0.6) u:m                       turns to right
 7        (0.8) ↑Sa:ndy how'r we doin' on our: (0.3)   gazing to right
 8        on our TIMEr tech- (.) technology.
 9        (0.7)
10  Ch:  Good.= £I noticed at the                      nods, looks down
11        la:st one that er (0.4) .hhh
12        the: EGG timer was just     not quite        looks right
13        as precise as we needed.£
14        (0.5)
15  Ch:  [ (I) s(h)e(h)nse, ]
16  Va:  [((Quiet laughter))]
17        (0.3)
```

```
18  Ch:  Some people                                     smiles
19        would get about forty              turns to middle
20        five seconds and o'r people
21        get (0.2) four or five minutes
22        [cos of the way those things work so.]     looks down
23  Va:  [          ((Laughter))              ]
24        [ (0.6) ]
25  Va:  [((Quiet laughter and mumbling))]
26  Ch:  Ah: thanks: er:                        looks right
27        an we appreciate that, (0.6)          looks down
28        U:M: (0.8) s:o
29        I ↑am gonna try duh- e-                 looks up
30        (0.2) I-I don' wanna
31        be er- (0.2) er: (.) a ↑ty↓rant up here
32        but please try to keep your comments to
33        two minutes:, (.) er we do have a lodda
34        speakers tonight, (.) .hhh (.)
35        an' I am required by board policy to finish
36        all the speaker:s (0.4) er within an hou:r.
37        (.)
38  Ch:  Which I think we can do,               looks down
39        ↑if everybody (.) .hh (.)
40        u:m (.) abides by the rules.      looks up then right
41        (0.3)
42  Ch:  So:: er lemme call you up here
43        five at a time¿                        looks down
44        (0.2) .hh a:nd um (1.1) now we'll get ↑started.
45        First of all David The:lan, (.) then John
46        Ketling, (0.6) Esme Patterson, (0.7) Kate Morley,
47        (.) and Lauren Heger.                    looks up
48        (2.9)                                      nods
49  Ch:  Come on up.                  gestures towards self
50        (9.1)
51  Ch:  S'alright.
52        (1.3)                        camera cuts to DT
53        (I'm sorry one)             leans over podium
54        (2.5)              DT picks up notes, walks round
55        ((inaudible))          to other side of podium
56        (0.3)                          arranges notes
57  DT:  °Five minutes°                   looks at Chair
58        a:nd- >so I didn't-< (1.2)          looks down
59        I planned for five          tilts head to side
```

```
60          minutes and I'm sorry so I:'m gonna      looks at Chair
61          have to I guess (0.3)                      looks right
62          rush through this.                       looks to chair
63          (0.3)                                       looks down
64   Ch:    Well I'll be gennle.                    DT looks at Chair
65          (.)
66   Ch:    Bu:t* ah: (.) .hh (0.2) >ah w- i-<        DT looks down
67          it's been two minutes for quite a       DT looks at Chair
68          whi:le so do the best                     DT looks down
69          you ca:n to: er (0.5)
70          stick to that.                              DT looks up
71          (0.7)                                      DT looks down
72   DT:    U:m (0.9) My daughter did      hands in counting motion,
73          a science fair experiment like many    looking at Chair
74          others.
```

As a first take on this material let us consider the way chairing a meeting may be a dilemmatic activity. One of the themes in discourse work, particularly that associated with Michael Billig, Derek Edwards and others (Billig et al. 1988; Edwards and Mercer 1987), is the centrality of dilemmas to the operation of social institutions. In their work on 'ideological dilemmas', they note that institutions are often characterised by dilemmas over, for example, control and freedom, regulation and spontaneity, and formality and informality. Rather than seeing these dilemmas as problems to be solved for the smooth running of an organisation, they suggest quite the reverse: that they provide resources for sustaining that running. Take education, for instance. It is common to distinguish two kinds of educational ideology. A 'traditional' ideology focuses on learning set outcomes and following rules; a 'progressive' ideology focuses on developing pupils' own potential and helping them come to their own understanding of the world. Although these two seem opposed, work in this tradition highlighted the way these two ideologies are *simultaneously* drawn on as teachers manage classes and encourage pupils to reach particular outcomes. As Alexa Hepburn (2003) shows, what appear to be tensions and problems between ideologies in the abstract can be flexible resources in practice.

Chairing dilemmas

Let us explore this idea with the Barbiegate materials. We will focus first on the introductory remarks from the Chair. Analysis may seem micro or even trivial at times – but we are after the lived specifics of how this institution is subtly built by its participants; and not always built in ways that are designed for transparency. The videotape starts during the Chair's opening remarks, which include points about procedure – these are points about what should happen in what way, and in what order.

First, note that the structuring of what goes on in this setting is not being treated by the Chair as something that will happen automatically. Rather, various procedural elements are described, such as the time allocated to speakers. At the same time it is clear that the Chair is not attempting to describe the complete 'institution' of the school board beforehand – there are likely to be a wide range of taken-for-granted things that are brought to the situation (about how interaction works, about what kinds of things are likely to go on at meetings and so on). Moreover, as Wittgenstein argued with respect to rules and practices, the task of describing all of that would be indefinite and counter-productive. Thus those procedural elements that are described may be so because they specify things that are either unique or unpredictable; or they may be described because they have been areas of difficulty in the past, or are expected to be areas of difficulty on this occasion, or because they are departures of some kind.

Secondly, let us consider how this introduction is done. It has a number of interesting features. Take the Chair's very first words:

Extract 3.1.1: The rule

```
1  Chair:     . . . any: issue you wan' to:, (0.5) u:m
2             (.) we only have a coupla ground
3             ru:les:, the first and the most important
4             i:s (0.6) er:: that you have to: um (1.0)
5             s:tart and complete your: comments within
6             two minutes,
```

Consider the delivery of these opening words. Already we can see features that suggest the management of dilemmas of control in this institutional talk. Apart from the reflexive content of the talk on how the interaction will proceed, note the delivery, with its pauses and errs and ums. These occur most strikingly on line 4, prior to the delivery of the 'first and most important' rule, suggesting some kind of caution or trouble with the delivery of that rule. In conversation analytic terms this is a form of self-repair, a word search (Schegloff 1979). These features have been found, for example, in the openings of market research focus groups (Puchta and Potter 2004); and they contrast with degree-awarding speeches and other formal and cere-monial occasions that do not have the same emphasis on shared involvement (J. M. Atkinson 1982).

The hesitancy and the informality work against hearing the 'ground rule' about time limits as authoritarian and impersonal.

Laughter and authority

A further element that contributes to the management of the dilemmas surrounding control can be seen in the next selection, which continues from the previous one.

Extract 3.1.2: The joke

```
 7  Chair:    (0.8) ↑Sa:ndy how'r we doin' on our: (0.3)
 8            on our TIMEr tech- (.) technology.
 9            (0.7)
10  Chair:    Good.= £I noticed at the
11            la:st one that er (0.4) .hhh
12            the: EGG timer was just not quite
13            as precise as we needed.£
14            (0.5)
15  Chair:    [ (I) s(h)e(h)nse, ]
16  Various:  [((Quiet laughter))]
17            (0.3)
18  Chair:    Some people
19            would get about forty
20            five seconds and o'r people
21            get (0.2) four or five minutes.
22            [cos of the way those things work so.]
23  Various:  [ ((Laughter)) ]
24            [ (0.6) ]
25  Various:  [((Quiet laughter and mumbling))]
26  Chair:    Ah: thanks: er:
27            an we appreciate that, (0.6)
```

One of the things that Claudia Puchta and Potter (2004) noted in the way market research moderators opened focus groups was that they often used laughter. Laughter does not have to involve the more

elaborate joking that goes on here, but can be part of managing
delicate actions. For instance, Gail Jefferson, Harvey Sacks and
Emanuel Schegloff (1987) describe the way that laughter can be used
in the pursuit of intimacy, and Jefferson (1984a) shows how laughter
can serve as a display of making light of one's troubles by a troubles
teller. Hence laughter and humour can be used to 'soften' troubling or
critical actions.

First note the way here the Chair addresses Sandy by her first name
(a feature of interaction between familiars) and using the folksy and
inclusive 'how'r we doin' (not 'how are we doing', 'how are you doing'
or 'is the timer working?') when asking about 'our timer technology'
(again the inclusive 'our'). This sets up the ironic, indeed bathetic
contrast between the 'timer technology' and the 'egg timer'. The contrast is underscored in the delivery and intonation – 'TIMEr' is emphasised with increased volume, while 'tech- (.) technology' is stumbled
over somewhat and given some emphasis (line 8). Similarly the 'EGG
timer' is emphasised by increased volume (line 12). The second element
of the contrast is also delivered in a 'smiley voice' that, combined
with the volume increases, sounds as if the speaker is on the edge of
laughing. This hearably cues its non-serious nature and perhaps
encourages the laughter that follows in line 16. More extended laughter
follows the playful unpacking of 'not quite as precise as we needed'
following the contrast with forty-five seconds to four or five minutes in
lines 23 through 25.

The point about this ironic and humorous construction here is that it
manages the Chair's emphasis on improved accuracy in timekeeping (in
comparison to previous sessions). The tensions between control and
democratic participation are softened. Control is stressed, yet the
authority that goes along with that is softened.

Dilemmas and rules

We see the Chair doing further work with this dilemma in the next
extract, which again follows directly from the previous one.

Extract 3.1.3: The disclaimer and the rule

```
28  Chair:    U:M: (0.8) s:o
29            I ↑am gonna try duh- e-
30            (0.2) I-I don' wanna
31            be er- (0.2) er: (.) a ↑ty↓rant up here
```

```
32              but please try to keep your comments to
33              two minutes:, (.) er we do have a lodda
34              speakers tonight, (.) .hhh (.)
35              an' I am required by board policy to finish
36              all the speaker:s (0.4) er within an hou:r.
37              (.)
38  Chair:     Which I think we can do,
39              ↑if everybody (.) .hh (.)
40              u:m (.) abides by the rules.
41              (0.3)
```

Consider line 29, where the Chair's initial utterance emphasised his own role in performing some action 'I ↑am gonna try duh-' – most probably 'try to keep everyone to time' is repaired. The disclaimer 'I-I don't wanna be er- (0.2) er: (.) a ↑ty↓rant up here' (lines 30–31) follows this cut-off, and explicitly attends to the emphasis on his own role that was created by that initial utterance. This is then re-formulated as a polite request 'please try to keep your comments to two minutes' (lines 32–3). By repairing his prior utterance, the Chair attends to the potential for his actions to be heard as (over)controlling and this is managed with the disclaimer.

There is another similarity here with the start of market research focus groups, where a similar issue of control is being managed. A highly recurrent practice is for the moderator to say what the focus group is *not* (it is not a test, it is not like a school, it is not somewhere where there are right or wrong answers). That is, the relevant and troubling alternative is disclaimed. This is precisely what happens with the Chair's disclaimer. Tyranny is highlighted as a relevant problem category where rules are being imposed; that is *not* what is going on here.

Rules in practices

Let us stand back for a moment and consider again the broader issue of rules and practices. What we have here is not rule-bound activity in a simple way. At least, it may or may not be such a thing but it is not clear what evidence could settle the matter, or whether any evidence could (see Bogen 1999). However, we do have locally produced and reflexive rule formulations. The Chair glosses what the rules of the organisation are. However, note the delicate way the Chair does this. He builds a separation between himself and board policy. Rather than acting as an agent of authority, administering it to others like some more or less benign Judge Dredd, he is *himself* constrained by it: 'I am required by board policy to finish all the speaker:s (0.4) er within an hou:r.' (lines 35–6). He separates the constraining action of the 'board policy' rules from his own goals or desires – the emphasis on 'am required' counters the possibility that he may have a free hand in this. Although he does not explicitly say that he would like speakers to take longer, the explicit separation makes available such a possibility. We can see here an arena in which the classic sociological structure–agency divide is produced for the practical purposes of managing the Chair's accountability.

There is another important element to the Chair's construction of rules. Directly after his request that speakers must finish within two minutes he offers the description 'we do have a lodda speakers tonight' (lines 33–4). In this interactional slot this description is hearable as an *account for* finishing within two minutes. That is, the Chair moves beyond an emphasis on rules (without, however, deleting such an emphasis). Instead he emphasises a timescale will not only be *practical* (giving everyone time) but will also be *fair* (giving everyone a voice). Put another way, for the participants to disagree with such a request, for example, by bidding for extra time, might undermine this practicality and fairness. It is striking that even when considering the discourse of fascists or those arguing against ethnic advancement, argumentative commonplaces stressing practicality and fairness are commonly employed (Billig 1978; Wetherell and Potter 1992).

This point is further underlined by the Chair with his conditional on lines 38–40: 'Which I think we can do [finish within an hour], ↑if everybody (.) .hh (.) u:m (.) abides by the rules'. Note the display of hesitancy before the delivery of 'abides by the rules', again showing a possible softening of the rule formulation (through delaying it and showing attention to its delicacy). Note also that this utterance provides an environment where someone wishing to press for something different may be heard as wishing for special treatment at the expense of others and/or an extension of the length of the meeting. By this point, the Chair has built (one element of) the working of this organisation by using resources from lexicons of bureaucracy, of practical common sense and of a moral/political sense of fairness.

Time, rules and resistance

All this interactional work on the part of the Chair does not necessarily ensure that the time rule is followed. It may set up an environment where deviation is tricky, but people have a wide range of resources for resisting the imposition of strictures of this kind. Another way of looking at this is that this kind of organisational setting is produced conversationally, and as different analysts have shown conversation is an arena of contingency. One turn may set up conditions for what comes next, but it does not determine what comes next (Heritage 1984; Sacks 1992). Conversation is highly orderly, but not in the way a car engine is orderly. Turns of talk typically occasion a range of relevant options. One of the points of our analysis of the specifics of this interaction is to catch both the building of constraints and the resistance to those constraints. Moreover, we can see the parties' construction of versions of this process as either democratic or authoritarian. That is, the parties themselves are performing their own political analysis of the interaction they are a part of.

We will consider both the start and end of David Thielen's (henceforth DT) contribution to the interaction. This extract, again, follows on from the previous one.

Extract 3.1.4:   The minutes

```
42  Chair:    So:: er lemme call you up here
43            five at a time¿
44            (0.2) .hh a:nd um (1.1) now we'll get ↑started.
45            First of all David The:len, (.) then John
46            Ketling, (0.6) Esme Patterson, (0.7)
47            Kate Morley, (.) and Lauren Heger.
48            (2.9)
49  Chair:    Come on up.
50            (9.1)
51  Chair:    S'alright.
52            (1.3)
53            (I'm sorry one)
54            (2.5)
55            ((inaudible))
56            (0.3)
57  DT:       °Five minutes°
58            a:nd- >so I didn't-< (1.2)
```

```
59              I planned for five
60              minutes and I'm sorry so I:'m gonna
61              have to I guess (0.3)
62              rush through this.
63              (0.3)
64   Chair:     Well I'll be gennle.
65              (.)
66   Chair:     Bu:t* ah: (.) .hh (0.2) >ah w- i-<
67              it's been two minutes for quite a
68              whi:le so do the best
69              you ca:n to: er (0.5)
70              stick to that.
71              (0.7)
```

There are a range of interesting features of this stretch of interaction. Let us focus in particular on some features of the exchange between DT and the Chair.

The earliest thing that DT can be heard saying on the audio is 'five minutes' (line 57). It is quiet, but that is probably because he was still moving into range of the microphone. Most likely he had already said 'I planned for five minutes' and now repeats himself when the microphone allows him to be heard over the room noise (lines 59–60) when it becomes clear that people cannot properly hear. He continues, saying that he will be forced to 'rush through' his speech (he shuffles through the notes while saying this in a visual display of how the orderliness of his talk will be disrupted). DT's talk here is built in a way that manages two things simultaneously.

First, note the way DT formulates the hurried nature of his speech as a product not just of his own preparation of five minutes' worth of material, but also of the time rule ('I planned for five minutes and I'm sorry so I:'m gonna have to I guess (0.3) rush through this' lines 59–62). In particular note the finessed way the constraint from the rule is constructed – 'so I'm gonna have to I guess rush through this'. What the 'I guess' does is present the link between the rule and effect on his speech as something contingent. It projects the possibility of new information or actions changing the state of affairs. In effect it places the Chair in the position of being able to undo the problem or of sustaining the rule with its negative consequences. Note the way DT looks at the Chair in lines 60–2 – this highlights his potential relevance as a next speaker. So although DT begins with an apology, he is subtly attributing the problem elsewhere. It is not simply his fault but the fault of the school board's (now constructed as) autocratic time rule. He does not say, formally and explicitly, that he is being unfairly treated, but it is one way of hearing what he is saying that he has made available.

Inexplicit though DT's actions are, the Chair shows that he understands them. That is, he orients to the responsibility that is being placed on his own actions by suggesting that those actions will be 'gennle' (line 64). This softening is combined with both a reassertion of the rule and the statement that the rule has been in place for 'quite a whi:le'. This picks up and counters the implication that DT is being treated unfairly, or specifically denied what anyone could expect in these meetings, or what he personally could reasonably expect, in terms of time. Again, in terms of dilemmas of control and co-operation the Chair manages this by both the soft construction of his control (gentle) and the reassertion of the rule as longstanding. More broadly DT and the Chair negotiate the nature and legitimacy of these institutional arrangements as they unfold. This is not an abstract and theoretical negotiation over participation and organisational structure, and how it can be sustained or denied. Instead, it is a locally managed, rhetorically situated negotiation, rooted in the practical politics of everyday life (Wetherell and Potter 1992).

Psychology, perception and time

So far we have noted in passing the role of a range of 'psychological' categories and attributes – planning, being sorry, guessing, being gentle. We have tried to make explicit some of the practices that they play a role in. One of the things that discursive psychology has focused on is the way that psychological categories are oriented to actions (Edwards and Potter 2005; Edwards 2007). Some of this work has looked at the use of psychological predicates and ascriptions (Edwards 2006; Potter and Puchta 2007). Other work has looked at more indirect psychological orientations and issues. For example, Charles Goodwin has done a number of studies that consider 'perception' as part of practices such as air traffic control and oceanography (C. Goodwin and Goodwin 1996).

We are now going to leap forward in the current materials, ignoring the fascinating speech that DT makes (see Potter and Hepburn 2007;

and other chapters in Tracy, McDaniel and Gronbeck 2007 for more). Loosely speaking we focused above on how DT's presentation was opened; now we are going to focus on how it is ended. Our general point will be to reveal the complex, situated, conflictual work of both opening and closing. We will continue the line numbering to indicate the missing material.

Extract 3.2

```
162  DT:   .Hhh (0.3) we bemoa:n the lack of
163        children going in to            sound of alarm
164        ↓science especially women and camera pans to DT
165  DT:   minor ities.=
166  Ch:   =Is- is that- (0.2) the timer?
167        (0.4)
168  Ch:   Kay (.) u:m: (0.3) TAKE about another
169        thirty seconds °Mister Thielen.°
170        ((2.6))                  DT shaking head, arms wide
171  DT:   I'm sorry this was so: wrong in so
172        many ways. .Hhh (0.4) it was censorship
173        pl(h)ain and si(h)mp(h)le. Hh (.) .hh was
174        this ap↑propriate for elementary schoo:l,
175        (0.2).h >e↑lementary kids as young as
176        kindergarteners in< ~Sa(h)lma Alabama
177        mar ched u(h)p~ (.) .HHH
178        ~ag(h)ainst ↑wh(h)ite police officers with
179        [ german shepherds ] and fire hoses~.
180  Ch:   [((clears throat))]
181        (0.5)
182  DT:   And yet (.) we cannot ask (0.3) our children of
183        the sa:me age (.) .hh to address (0.2) or be
184        willing to be expo:sed to (.) racial issues
185        here.
186        (0.3)
187  DT:   After tho:se kinds of things wenn o:n.
188        (0.2)
189  DT:   .Hhhh this was sweeping it under the rug
190        ↑not cos the children're uncomfortable
191        with it but because the a:dults in an a:ll
192        white staffed elementary school.
193        (0.6)
```

```
194  DT:   This violates s:ix: (.) out of the thirty
195        bullets in your strategic plan'n beliefs
196        behind it.
197        (0.5)
198  DT:   That's twenny percent of them.
199        (0.5)
200  DT:   .Hh (.) an this h's opened up the schoo:l
201        district to serious legal liability.
202        (0.3)
203  DT:   Where you have clearly violated the ri:ghts
204        to free speech: (.) this [ is   what   I   w's ]
205  Ch:                            [((clears throat))]
206  DT:   to:ld by: >an attorney with the American
207        civil liberties union< .HHH[H th]at you
208  Ch:                              [Okay]
209  DT:   clearly violated her civil rights because she
210        was (.) u:m (0.3) this was done because of*
211        race.
212  Ch:   We- (.) we get [ your ] drift mi-
213  DT:                  [(and)]
214  Ch:   mister thielen: (0.3) thanks very much.
215        (0.3)
216  DT:   Um (0.2) I (0.2) am sorry that to the boa:rd
217        >issues this serious are< not worth (0.9)
218        a couple more minutes.=            **walks away**
219  Ch:   We:ll a number of us have spent quite a bit
220        of time on the phone with you Mister Thielen
221        but (0.3) ANYway why'n't you take
222        (0.5) er the poster board with you.
223        JOHN KETling?
```

Let us start by considering the Chair's practical display of 'hearing' in the context of the continued negotiation of the rules of timekeeping and, more broadly, the distribution of voice that is central to organisational participation.

The hearing

The timer goes off precisely two minutes and one second after the start of DT's speech (this two minutes does not include their negotiation about time). The timer is relatively quiet, but clearly audible on the recording (during line 163). At the point at which the timer goes off the video pans away from a poster that DT has placed in front of his podium and back on to DT's face. This suggests that the camera operator is orienting to the timer, moving to DT's face to catch his reaction for the television audience.

We are particularly interested here in the delay between the timer sounding and the Chair's display of hearing. The Chair has waited until what conversation analysts would call the end of DT's turn construction unit (TCU) before showing that he has heard the timer (Schegloff 2007). That is, he waits for a place where orderly speaker transition between turns could occur. This does four things.

First, it is less invasive than cutting in when the timer goes off, so it avoids an overly intrusive interruption. Note, though, that there is good interactional evidence that the Chair expects DT to continue, despite the prosodic and syntactic evidence that this part of the utterance is completed. It is often a feature of this kind of public speaking that closing and continuing intonation plus pauses are retained, despite the lack of formal need for them – perhaps it makes speeches sound more interestingly conversational (J. M. Atkinson 1982). That said, no doubt DT can also hear the timer and may be expecting to be interrupted. In any event, the Chair comes in noticeably early before the next TCU (line 166) heading off any possible continuation that DT might produce.

The second thing that the Chair's question – 'Is- is that- (0.2) the timer?' (line 166) – does is that it allows DT the opportunity to orient to the timer himself, either more or less explicitly. He can do that, for example, by answering the question. There is no evidence that he does this, although he is not visible on the recording at this stage. He does not note the timer's noise verbally, and he certainly does not stop when it is first audible on line 163.

The third thing to note is that the Chair presents himself as responding to the timer, but doing so in a casual and flexible way. This flexibility is underlined by the concession of 'about another thirty seconds' (lines 168–9) – the imprecision signalled by the use of 'about' displays the Chair as not overly concerned by the timer rule. This relates to the fourth point about the indirectness of the Chair's actions. Rather than saying 'your time has run out' or 'you must stop' his voiced display of possibly not hearing the timer ('is that the

timer?') both allows DT the opportunity to police himself and produces the Chair as someone not using the timer in a rigid and autocratic manner; indeed, he is precisely not being a tyrant as he has
already indicated.

Standing back again, the two parties have continued their delicate
and indirect negotiation of the rules concerning time. The Chair has
continued to manage the dilemmas of authority and democratic participation with indirect and conciliatory moves. Yet DT's resistance has
earned him more time and, maybe, further helped display himself as a
victim of school board actions.

The drift

Let us consider a final part of the sequence to see how this negotiation
over time and authority plays out. Here when the Chair clears his throat
on line 205 DT has been speaking for two minutes and fifty-six seconds
from the start of his speech. Of course, a throat clearing could just be a
throat clearing (just as within psychoanalytic therapy a cigar may
sometimes just be a cigar), but its clear audibility suggests that it has
been done for the microphone; there is no sign of the Chair trying to
mask it. And such throat clearing is, of course, a conventional way of
drawing attention to something.

Towards the end of the sequence we can see the Chair making three
increasingly explicit attempts to bring DT to a close. The first, on line
205, is the throat clearing that we have already noted. The second is on
line 208. The Chair says 'okay'. This is close to the transition relevant
place after 'union' where DT is rushing through and doing an inbreath
with extra volume, both displaying his claim to continue holding the
floor. By saying 'okay', a receipting turn, the Chair is reflexively constituting DT as having completed. Nevertheless DT produces what he
says next as a continuation (constituting the Chair as interrupting rather
than receipting). This occasions a third and most explicitly terminal
turn (lines 212 and 214).

The Chair's turn is hearably critical. How does it achieve this?
Part of what is going on can be understood from the sequential order
of things – after the accusatory turns at the end of DT's speech (lines
203–11) it is hard not to hear the Chair as having a slot for a rebuttal
or account. Put another way, the accusatory turn generates an environment where all the parties (DT, the other people there, the local

television viewers, and us as overhearing analysts) are likely to inspect whatever comes next for its role in rebutting, accounting and so on. Furthermore, we can speculate that the Chair is indirectly admonishing DT for going on too long, perhaps trying to get more than his organisationally appropriate due time. Yet he does not directly respond to the material in DT's final turns, but makes a more general response. His formulation 'drift' may indicate that the details are unimportant and/or unclear. Moreover, as an idiom it does not require specification of what the meaning or purpose of DT's speech is that has been 'got.' It does not show a specific understanding that might be open to contest, using up more time.

The sequence as a whole ends with a pair of turns that escalate the dispute even further. DT may be responding to the critical nature of the Chair's turn. He expresses disappointment ('I (0.2) am sorry that to the boa:rd >issues this serious are< not worth', lines 216–18). This is combined with a construction of what has produced the disappointment. This construction is contrastive – the seriousness of the issues (line 217) is set against the very small value placed on them by the board ('not worth (0.9) a couple more minutes.' lines 217–18). One of the central themes in discursive psychology is the way constructions of mind and constructions of reality are produced to sustain particular actions, and how the one plays off against the other (Edwards and Potter 1992). This is a compact example of this in action. By constructing his psychological state as 'sorry', he builds the solidity of what is generating that mental state – the actions of the board forcing him to curtail his speech. DT's 'psychological' response supports the seriousness of the board's flawed response; the harsh nature of the response provides a warrant for his psychological response. Each plays off against the other. DT here produces the board as arrogant and presents himself as undermined and excluded. This re-works the institutional procedures as strategic and pernicious rather than generic. Its legitimacy becomes a sham.

At this point the Chair does something interesting. Let us stand back a bit before considering it. As we have already indicated, there has been a lot of dispute in discourse studies about the nature of context, and how it should be analysed (Billig 1999; Schegloff 1997, 1998b; Wetherell 1998). Many issues here are not easily resolved and depend on the broader aims of the research. Nevertheless a conversation analytic and discursive psychological approach urges caution about claiming the relevance of contextual particulars without a careful analysis of how such particulars are oriented to, or how they become relevant, in interaction. One way of being cautious like this is to consider context as an issue for participants. What contextual features are invoked or constructed in the course of interaction? This is, of course, pervasive. Throughout his speech, for example, DT is working on a version of the relevant context for his actions. Indeed, he constructs both a locally relevant version of his daughter's science project, and a grander narrative on the nature of prejudice and the nature and history of science. He draws, as people do, on all the world-building potential of talk.

What is notable on this occasion is that in response to DT's criticism of the board, the Chair constructs a fragment of context. He describes time spent on the phone to DT by board members ('us') prior to the meeting. This does two things. First it suggests, in the face of DT's contrary claims, that he *has* been given time and *has* been taken seriously. Secondly, it implies that the Chair has been acting properly by not revealing this until it becomes relevant to DT's criticism.

It is worth noting the detailed construction of the Chair's claim. A range of work in ethnostatistics and quantification rhetoric have started to outline some of the ways in which quantification is produced to rhetorical effect (Gephart 1988; Potter, Wetherell and Chitty 1991). While DT's claim is a minimizing one with its 'couple more minutes', the Chair's 'number of us' (line 219, note the emphasis on number) and 'quite a bit of time' (lines 219–20) is both vague and at the same time maximising. The power of vagueness of this kind is that it makes the claims hard to contest (Drew 2003; Potter 1996). More broadly, the different versions on offer paint different visions of DT's involvement with the democratic process, emphasising that he has been either indulged or frozen out.

Psychology – institution – interaction

In our analysis we have tried to show how the particularity of what is going on, with all the specifics of sequence, repair, intonation and so on, is fundamental to the analysis. The style of analysis used here draws on both conversation analysis and discursive psychology. A key feature is that it treats neither organisational structures nor psychological states as prior to, and separate from, the interaction (Hepburn and Wiggins 2007b). Rather, we have tried to show how both structure and psychology become interactionally live in the fine specifics of these materials and how they can be made analytically tractable through a close study of the materials. In terms of classic sociological debates over the primacy of agency and structure, these things become practical issues for the participants as they attempt to build, and resist, the causal power of structure and manage their own and others' agency. Psychology here is something to be accomplished, as is organisational structure. Participation is supported, managed and constrained through different practices. Can the Chair maintain control and reassert institutional procedures without being treated as tyrannical or authoritarian? Can David Thielen develop his critique of the school board's actions with respect to his daughter's project without being treated as racist or reactionary? To understand what this organisation is here as it emerges in the course of these few minutes we have had to pay attention to these concrete practices. If that is true in this one case it may be true more generally in organisation studies, and this will mean some major theoretical and methodological movements.

4 | On the reflexivity between setting and practice: the 'recruitment interview'

NICK LLEWELLYN

Introduction

In recent years there has been a much discussed 'turn to practice' within organisation studies (see Jarzabkowski 2004; Boczkowski and Orlikowski 2004; Alby and Zucchermaglio 2006; Nicolini 2007). This has raised questions about how to theorise and empirically access practice, in ways that reveal the interplay between knowledge and ordinary work activity (Gherardi 2001: 132–5; Gherardi and Nicolini 2002b). Such questions and interests have simultaneously, though largely independently, been pursued in a body of ethnomethodologically informed research, which is also committed to a 'practice-based theory of knowledge and action' (C. Goodwin 1994: 606). Such themes are apparent in studies of 'situated actions' (see Suchman 1987) and the 'choreography' of ordinary work practice (J. Whalen, Whalen and Henderson 2002). A key concern of 'workplace studies' (see Luff, Hindmarsh and Heath 2000; Heath, Luff and Sanchez Svensson 2002) has also been the interplay between knowledge, learning and ordinary work practice (see Hindmarsh and Pilnick 2007). Despite common interests, the points of connection between these literatures have been minimal.

The present chapter explores one way in which ethnomethodologically informed research might inform the 'practice turn' within organisation studies, via an illustrative study of interaction during graduate recruitment interviews. The chapter explores how the practice of recruitment is a product of, and simultaneously a resource for, ordinary interaction during job interviews. What Graham Button calls 'interview orthodoxy' (Button 1992) is reproduced through interaction, but it simultaneously allows actors to resolve practical problems such as 'what next' and 'why this now' (Garfinkel 1967). The chapter presents a distinctive way of recovering practice 'in flight' (Garfinkel 1986), what practitioners use to practically accomplish their 'judgmental and interpretive work' (Suchman 2000: 30) and, indeed, how candidates find themselves within 'the interview'.

Knowledge *in* and *of* practice

This chapter presents an analysis of conduct during recruitment interviews. It is centrally concerned with practical ways in which candidates and interviewers display (to one another) their appreciation of the setting and its 'organised ways' (Garfinkel 1967). The demarcation 'recruitment interview' is approached as something to be discovered through analysis that focuses on how people orient to what Button calls 'interview orthodoxy' (Button 1992). As with all interaction, the setting's guiding conventions and norms cannot be made entirely transparent in prefatory comments and explanations. As they are produced, the actions of the interview do not come with explanations of how they embody and display interview orthodoxy. Candidates have to 'learn on their feet', how this or that utterance or gesture might form part of the setting (Garfinkel 1967). In different ways, parties have to search for 'the interview' as they are going along.

By the term 'interview orthodoxy' Button (1992) refers to the guiding premise or auspice within which it is possible to witness 'an interview is going on'. During 'recruitment interviews' candidates act and are treated in ways that would be neither normal, nor on occasion tolerated, in 'informal' settings (Sacks, Schegloff and Jefferson 1974). But such treatment is locally understandable, in both practical and normative terms, via interview orthodoxy. Put simply, this recognises that interviewers are testing and rating candidates, that there is an ulterior motive 'behind' the action (Button 1992). This is more than a simple analyst's description of the setting. It can be called an 'orthodoxy' to the extent that it informs how participants build and grasp situated activities. In keeping with ethnomethodological study policies, 'the setting' is understood as both a product of interaction and a resource for crafting and recognising interactional moves.

The key image of 'the recruitment interview' is of something which is never still or entirely transparent, but has to be continually *searched for* and *discovered* in the details of unfolding courses of action. The argument is not that social structural settings such as 'interviews' should be reduced to talk (Schegloff 1991). But, for some stretch of conduct to be recognisable as 'a job interview' it will have to be built that way by participants on each and every separate occasion. Social settings do not simply happen; they have to be practically reproduced. For their part, social actors have to be practically (though not necessarily consciously or discursively) attentive to the ebb and flow of account-ability and relevance; they have to be able to find 'where things are going' and 'what people are trying to do' as action unfolds.

Practically, this can be accessed in terms of a back-and-forth move-ment between actions in their immediate sequential environment and a setting's 'guiding presuppositions' (Garfinkel 1967; Schatzki, Knorr-Cetina and von Savigny 2001). In institutional settings utter-ances and gestures 'acquire particular implicativeness because [they can be seen] as devices for accomplishing interactive work which is made relevant by the setting' (Walker 1995: 103). The setting, as an objectively presumed fact of organisational life, becomes a resource for the moment-by-moment management of interaction (M. R. Whalen and Zimmerman 1987). Local occasions of order require that people act on various *ways of knowing* the implicativeness of this or that utterance at that point. This is not so much knowledge *in* practice as knowledge *of* practice. Precisely because participants' knowledge (of what some utterance might be doing) has to be dis-played and made public, the analyst has a unique resource (Sacks, Schegloff and Jefferson 1974). Knowing does not have to be reduced to a cognitive phenomenon because such processes are public and witnessable, to participants and to analysts alike.

By focusing on practical ways in which interviewers and candidates orient to interview orthodoxy the chapter recovers both the profes-sional practice of 'the interviewer' and indeed the *work* of being a 'candidate' (Suchman 2000: 30). Quite what this work entails, in and of itself, remains somewhat unspecified within the literature. Of parti-cular interest is how both parties orient to candidates' talk as an object of assessment. For example, in the materials candidates spent a good deal of time talking about their past experiences travelling and work-ing abroad, captaining sports teams, organising university societies and so forth. But these discussions were not casual. They were built and 'oriented to' with respect to an ulterior motive. This raises a series of intriguing questions. How did interviewers accomplish their basic organisational task and rate candidates, based on these discussions? How were candidates' stories of their past experiences produced so as to document their competencies and the extent of their achievements? By exploring such processes, we gain insights into how interviewers and candidates 'worked' the interview schedule. As we shall see, the work of evaluation was not simply a private affair, between the interviewer and the scoring form. It permeated the moment-by-moment flow of activity within the setting. Candidates themselves were actively involved.

Recruitment interviews and the study

The recruitment interview is a largely overlooked setting whose central orthodoxies have yet to be analytically treated (but see Button 1992). A largely functionalist literature has explored what happens 'within' the interview. Familiar topics have included 'impression formation and management' (Snyder and Swann 1976; McDonald and Hakel 1985) and 'relational control' (Tullar 1989). Critical literatures have emphasised the disciplinary character of human resource management practices (Townley 1993) and have located 'the interview' as a site for indoctrination (Bergström and Knights 2006). But within both literatures 'the job interview' is deployed merely as convenient shorthand (Barley and Kunda 2001).

The present chapter follows Button's (1992: 229) lead in arguing that 'what makes an interview recognizable ... is not the sign on the door, nor just the gathering together of certain people. It is rather what those people do, and how they structure and organize their interactions with one another, that achieves for some social settings its characterizability as an interview.' In one of the few studies to directly address the practice of the recruitment interview, Button described a thoroughly bureaucratic format. This consisted of a series of predetermined questions, with slots for relevant answers (see Button 1987, 1992). Candidates could not ask interviewers to elaborate, so as to determine what a particular question was 'getting at'. Interviewers did not ask 'follow-up' questions that would inevitably display how they had understood the candidate's prior answer. Via interactional practices some degree of standardisation was secured in the name of equity and fairness. No single candidate was helped more than any other.

The interviews that were recorded for the present study looked quite different. By way of background, they took place in the organisation's headquarters in London and were the second stage of the firm's graduate recruitment process. Candidates had been selected following initial interviews and aptitude tests. To progress to the third and final stage, candidates had to negotiate one-to-one interviews, which are the data for this study. Interviews lasted for roughly forty-five minutes and were conducted by one of three different interviewers. They followed a similar format. Following an initial exchange of greetings, interviewers offered and then requested brief biographical statements. Candidates were asked how they had prepared for the interview, then to discuss instances where they had 'motivated a team', 'displayed team-working skills' or 'occupied a leadership position'. Following this, candidates were asked to discuss, at length, a pressing matter or matters of the day, such as 'the environment', 'technology' or 'the European Union'. Such discussions took place under the auspice of 'finding out how [candidates] think'. Finally, candidates were asked if they had questions.

As they performed the various tasks of the interview candidates were numerically and qualitatively assessed by interviewers. Access was granted to these scoring forms, candidates' application forms and their *curricula vitae*. Candidates were assigned numerical scores for 'academic ability', 'experiences, activities and qualities' (work experience, gap year plans) and 'depth and breadth' (hobbies, responsibilities, achievements). There were ten points for each section; thus thirty was the highest possible score. Candidates needed to score over eighteen to progress to the next phase of the recruitment process. The 'level of abstraction' reached by candidates, when discussing a topic of current affairs was also rated on the following scale Δ+, Δ, Δ−, ά+, ά, ά−, β+, β, β−. The following assessment appears in an interviewer's report, which included the final decision: 'signs of ά on both LOA [level of abstraction] topics but not convincing on either, for example ...'.

Answers as objects of assessment

In a descriptive sense, candidates' talk *really was* being numerically assessed and evaluated. They were scored out of thirty. But the task of assessment was not merely a matter for the interviewer and the scoring form. It also informed how the ordinary actions of the interview were assembled and understood turn by turn. For example, interviewers routinely assessed candidates' talk, both upon completion and in the midst of its production. This raises the question of what interviewers used to establish successes and failures; what stocks of knowledge were practically deployed, for example, to find absent achievements?

In this chapter two examples are considered which provide some insights into this matter. In the first, the candidate is talking about his time spent on an expedition in South America organised by the company World Challenge. In the midst of his talk, the interviewer intervenes to establish how you 'get on to' such an expedition. This would seem to be searching for an achievement of some kind. The interviewer is publicly and accountably disappointed to learn it is 'just' (line 2) a matter of paying money.

Extract 4.1   [EA2. 251. Neg/Ach]

```
1  C:      ... expensive to go on
2  IR:     but that's it, y'just pay money
3          and you're on?
4          (.)
5  IR:     okay
6          (.)
7  IR:     huh fair enough ...
```

In this case the interviewer 'orients to' the sense that getting on an expedition should be more than a matter of paying money. A norm is introduced, not abstractly, but in and through the design and placement of the interviewer's turn at talk. The 'just' in 'you just pay money and you're on' (lines 2–3) implies that paying is a minimal condition (Drew 1992). The 'unamused laughter' ('huh') that comes before 'fair enough' also suggest the interviewer is not impressed. Of course, it would be perfectly possible to say 'fair enough' in ways that sounded genuine. In this sequential environment, however, it is clear that the interviewer in fact does not think it is fair enough that you 'just pay money and you're on'. Rather this is being problematised. At a very early stage in the analysis, we start to sense how the market value of candidates' past experiences is not fixed, but interactionally determined via the imposition of frameworks for practically finding merit and achievement.

This was a recurrent type of intervention, which saw interviewers searching for achievements. Consider one more case below, where the candidate has been talking about his time working in an Australian

mine. The interviewer inquires how the candidate found the work.
The candidate states that it was via a family relation.

Extract 4.2   [EA2. 93. Neg/Ach]

```
 1  IR:   and how did you set that up?
 2        (0.2)
 3  C:    oh this was through a: relative
 4        of mine (.) who huh came to visit
 5        ((sequence omitted)) he is the manager of
 6        the mine ((sequence omitted))
 7        (0.4)
 8  IR:   okay (0.2) fortuitous
 9  C:    he huhu offered me the job so huh
10        (.) I was rather lucky there
11  IR:   yeah, indeed
```

In this case also, it would seem the interviewer's question (on line 1) is
searching for some kind of achievement. The candidate is not especially
attentive to this, in the sense he does not 'admit' he got the job via a
relation. He simply presents the detail. He is then found to have been
'fortuitous' (line 8). The interviewer orients to the job as a gift rather
than something won. The candidate goes along with this way of representing his good 'luck' (line 10). For good measure, the interviewer
agrees with the candidate ('yeah indeed', line 11).

In this setting, candidates were assessed for the extent of their
achievements and accomplishments. This raises questions about how
achievements and interests can be witnessed and practically rated.
How can one candidate's experience backpacking across Bolivia be
compared with another's experience working in an Australian mine?
Through what bodies of knowledge and forms of expertise can interviewers make such determinations? In these extracts we get some
insights into resources interviewers used to practically resolve such
administrative dilemmas and thereby work the interview protocol.
Interviewers found occasions where successes and achievements *should*
appear, against which the absence of achievement at particular points
can be rendered noticeable and accountable.

The analysis now moves to consider a second way in which candidates' past achievements and accomplishments became relevant. At
some moments, interviewers either downplayed or appeared inattentive to candidates' successes or the gross relevance of the fact that

candidates were 'being rated'. They did not cast a judgement, as above, but brought such matters into question, allowing eager candidates to drive home the scale of the achievements.

In Extract 4.3, the candidate has been asked how he 'motivates people'. He talks about his time spent organising the university choir, stressing his efforts to build up attendance, which resulted in a choir with twenty-five members. The interviewer pursues the issue of having twenty-five, saying it is 'just about enough' (line 1).

Extract 4.3   [EB4.49.Fish/Pos]

```
 1  IR:   and twenty five is huh just about enough
 2        isn't it, [for a:.
 3  C:              [well, in my first year someone tried
 4        to run a choir with eight ((sequence omitted))
 5        twenty five was actually pretty massive
 6        (.)
 7  IR:   okay okay
 8  C:    it filled the length and the width of
 9        the room ((sequence omitted))
10  IR:   okay so it worked very well, very good (0.4)
11        well that's plenty on the kind of life skills
```

Of course, the formulation 'just about enough' may have been a simple mistake, a curious detour into the world of choirs and their composition, rather than an explicit attempt to 'fish' for more information. The key point, though, is that such formulations can be heard to have a particular implicativeness in this setting (Walker 1995). The candidate clearly hears it not as a general point about the composition of choirs, but as an utterance that is inattentive to the matter or scale of his achievements. The candidate replaces 'just about enough' with the formulation 'pretty massive' (line 5). He then adds a further detail, that the choir filled 'the length and the width of the room' (lines 8–9). The interviewer then clearly orients to not a clarification about choirs, but a clarification about the extent to the candidate's achievements when he says 'okay so it worked very well, very good' (line 10). The talk has been (re-)tethered to the central premise of the interview: that what should be at stake are the candidate's achievements.

In the following materials, the target of assessment shifts to the *quality of the answer*, which was the main focus of Button's study

(1992). How well is the candidate answering the question? This raises questions about resources participants use to recognise inadequate 'answers' and 'answering'. Questions are also raised about the implications of such displays, what they might accomplish.

In Extract 4.4, both parties orient to a problematic answer. The candidate participates in the assessment of her own discourse. She has been asked what decisions she finds hard to make and 'struggles' to find an answer. In the early parts of the extract she is not weighing up alternative ways of answering; she is having trouble finding anything to say. This is not an account of her cognitive state, but of her conduct. The initial delay is accounted for via a range of interactional devices. Pauses of roughly equal length are interspersed with 'hmm' (line 4), 'tsk' (a 'tut', line 6), a failed turn beginning ('I think huh', line 8) and an exceptionally prolonged outbreath or sigh ('hhhhh', line 8). The candidate says 'interesting question' (line 10), which retrospectively orients to the question's difficulty.

Extract 4.4 [EB3.63. Neg/Answering/I&C]

```
 1  IR:   what do you find to be the most kind of- difficult
 2        kind of decisions that you have to take
 3        (3.0)
 4  C:    Hmm
 5        (3.5)
 6        tsk
 7        (3.0)
 8        I think:huh: hhhhhh
 9        (2.4)
10        °interesting question°
11        (1.4)
12  C:    the thing is there's so many different types of
13        decisions ((smiling voice)) it's hard to like (.)
14        point out (one thing) I think huh the most difficult
15        types of are the ones where you think like the short
16        term solution would be easier but you know that the
17        long term solution would be better than ( ) huh
18        if you have huh (0.4) huh: hhhhh a scenario where like
19        the short term would be much easier but you know that
20        you know that it's not going to come out right (.) or
21        against a scenario where you take the long term
22        perspective and you know that in a way it is you're
```

```
23          taking risks but it is going to come out right
24          ( ) hhh
25  IR:     I- I know what you (.) me:a[n but could you=
26  C:                             [y e a h ((breathy))
27  IR:     =gi[ve me an example?
28  C:         [I know I'm trying to like ((laughing sigh))
29          (.)
30  IR:     I thought you were hehe
31          (1.4)
32  C:      I guess I can do it! I can do it back to where I
33          worked two summers ago ((sequence omitted for 48.0))
34          like cost-risk analysis sort of thing
35          (.)
36  IR:     mmh okay okay that's a really good example
37          ((sequence omitted)) I'm very comfortable with that
```

As the candidate 'finally' begins to build an answer (around line 14) she continues to orient to the problematic nature of her own talk, at one point producing a sigh ('huh: hhhhh') of just over three seconds in length (at line 18). Whilst the candidate's talk could have been practically managed as a perfectly adequate abstract answer to an abstract question, she publicly orients to its imperfect character. Such displays are interesting not just because they orient to the performative logic of the setting, against which the delayed beginning of an 'answer' may be seen as a performative 'failing', but also because of the sequential implications of such displays. Most obviously, they might extract some degree of help or support from the interviewer.

This is precisely what happens here. The interviewer intervenes, on line 25, to highlight the *vague* character of the answer to this point ('I know what you (.) me:an but'. At one level, this is a most benign intervention. Whilst the candidate's turn *is* being problematised, the interviewer both claims to know what the candidate means and supplies a 'way out'. He suggests that she might discuss an example.

Notice how the candidate orients to this intervention and perhaps to the possibility the interviewer is supplying help. First of all, the candidate does work to establish ownership of knowledge pertaining to her own troubles (see Heritage 2005: 196). When he intervenes, the interviewer is not telling the candidate anything she does not already

know. In this sense, perhaps *he is not helping*. Prior to the completion
of the interviewer's 'I know what you (.) me:an but' (line 25) the
candidate re-enters the sequence to say 'yeah' (line 26). Before the
interviewer asks for 'an example' (line 27), the candidate seems to see
where this is leading and says 'I know I'm trying' (line 28). The interviewer goes along with this way of interactionally constituting the
'olive branch' he has handed the candidate ('I thought you were',
line 30). When she finally finds a way of answering, this is something
she has done, free of help and assistance.

Mild interrogation

In Extracts 4.1–4.4, candidates' achievements and the quality of
their answers were clearly at stake. From all possible relevancies
that might be bound up with talk about world travel, choirs or working for a mining firm, we saw how that talk was implicated by a
logic of assessment and evaluation. In this section we also see interviewers searching for information that would help them evaluate
and assess candidates. But the analysis now shifts a little to consider
an additional practice that 'comprised the routine work' of the interviewers (Suchman 2000). Here we see interviewers adopting an interrogatory stance towards candidates' talk to evaluate the robustness
of their arguments.

Throughout the present materials, interviewers would challenge
candidates and get them to expand, explain and justify their points.
The data is littered with mild interrogatory sequences. In the initial
example presented below, the candidate has been asked how he motivated members of the athletics team he was captaining. Rather than
accepting the candidate's response, the interviewer probes a little
further.

Extract 4.5 [EB2.76. Integ/'Motiv']

```
1  C:    ... in that way
2        (.)
3  IR:   so you got them together (.) just once
4  C:    huh it was more huh each person
5        individually in a way, before huh
6        before their individual events
7  IR:   okay okay but how much before, you
```

```
8        mean five minutes before or
9        (.)
10  C:   well huh talking to them the week
11       before or and then huh it depended
```

It is worth considering the resources and reasoning deployed by the interviewer, through which he accomplishes his judgemental and interpretative work (Suchman 2000). First, on line 3, the interviewer formulates the candidate's turn, suggesting he may have spoken to the athletics team 'just' once beforehand. Through this formulation, the interviewer seems to introduce a norm, which implies this might have been insufficient, 'once might not be enough'. The interviewer is searching for the merit of the candidate's approach, drawing on practical knowledge of good practice. Following the candidate's response, the interviewer does this again. He says 'but how much before, you mean five minutes before' (lines 7–8). Again, a normative imperative seems to be introduced, via the 'but'. It would be a mistake to agree ('yes, five minutes before'). At the very least, more information is required. In this extract, the interviewer does not simply allow the account to unfold, as would have happened in Button's (1992) data. Rather he invokes normative criteria designed to render the candidate's approach amenable to assessment.

It was common for interviewers to probe in this way, not just in search of candidates' achievements or competencies, but also to access their reasoning. This was most apparent during the section of the interview where candidates were invited to talk about some topic of the day, such as the environment or the European Union. As they were talking on such topics, interviewers would gently challenge candidates to defend their arguments. Distinctive sequences were produced, with opposition often quickly giving way to praise. Such challenges were akin to little tests for the candidate to pass.

Consider an initial example, where the candidate has been talking about the UK's national lottery. He is talking in general, without a clear end in sight. In the midst of the candidate's answer, the interviewer intervenes to challenge the candidate's position (at lines 5 and then 9).

Extract 4.6 [EA2.300. TT/Integ/Rebut]

```
1  C:   ... and it's can get addictive huh and
2       this is obviously not good to spend
3       vital money on the lottery
```

```
4           (0.4)
5   IR:     aha (.) so why do they do it?
6           (.)
7   C:      why do they do it (0.4) huh well, because it's
8           a dream ((continues)) give people dreams=
9   IR:     =so that's good then, cause it gives people dreams=
10  C:      =but it's false isn't it, cause the chances
11          of winning are very small
12  IR:     yeah, okay. (.) what else
13          (.)
14  C:      huh (.) well, I think
```

The candidate had argued that the national lottery is addictive and that the 'lower classes' spend too much money on it. The interviewer asks 'why they do it' to which candidate says because it 'gives people dreams'. The interviewer then turns the argument around. She re-casts having dreams as something that is 'good' (line 9), and this goes against the candidate's position. The types of resources interviewers used to constitute their professional practice are being unpicked gradually, via a close interest in work activity. Easily enough the candidate rebuts this manoeuvre, arguing the dreams are 'false' because the chances of winning are so small. As was characteristic, the interviewer both accepts the point ('yeah, okay') and then invites the candidate to return to the task at hand, talking in general about the lottery ('what else', line 12).

These clearly were not arguments in the conventional sense. What mattered was not so much *what* candidates were arguing for or against, but rather *how* they were answering, their ability to develop and defend a position. This is most obvious, empirically, on occasions where candidates' rebuttals were actively welcomed.

Extract 4.7   [EB5. 103. TT/Rebut+Assess]

```
1   I:      when you say ((continues)) but I'm
2           thinking of, for example, Nigeria
3           where you could I think have made the
4           same argument and that really hasn't
5           been effective
6           (0.2)
7   C:      yes, tsk (0.2) I don't, I don't think
```

```
8        Nigeria, I don't think you could put
9        Nigeria and South Africa into the same
10       exactly the same sort of brackets, I mean
11       ((continues for approximately 6 seconds))
12       and I think that will help a lot
13       (.)
14  IR:  okay, that's really good, (.) now suppose
```

In this case the candidate rejects the interviewer's argument (lines 7–12) stating that Nigeria and South Africa are not really comparable. Upon its completion, the interviewer positively assesses the candidate's response (line 14). He orients to the candidate's talk as a performance to be rated, rather than a rebuttal to be contested. Again, it is not just that candidates' talk *is* amenable to assessment and evaluation; we are seeing how this relevance permeated the moment-by-moment constitution of practice. How both candidates and interviewers tethered their own and the other's conduct to the 'setting's organised ways'.

Interview orthodoxy as a resource for practice

Up to this point the analysis has discussed mostly how, from a host of possible relevancies, delayed turn beginnings, talk about working in an Australian mine and rebuttals were brought within the auspices of a logic of assessment and evaluation. In fairly obvious ways, it would be unsettling and problematic were actors to continually invoke such a logic in casual conversation, say, when discussing what a person did at the weekend ('really, just that') or where they went on holiday ('you just paid and then went, huh, fair enough'). The argument now shifts a little, to suggest that certain recurrent practices were witnessable and observable via interview orthodoxy, which supplied resources for grasping what was going on *at that point*. Two examples are considered, where interviewers refused to produce clarifications and where candidates were pushed to the point of 'drying up'.

On occasion interviewers would withhold clarifications, somewhat like the practice described by Button (1992). On such occasions, talk was to be laid out in a very particular way, with *the candidate* taking charge of its direction. This happened in two main places, either after interviewers had asked for some general talk on the environment or the European Union (see Extract 4.8) or following general requests for more 'topic talk' (see Extract 4.9).

Extract 4.8   [EB1. 132. TT/CL/WH]

```
1  IR:    could you analyse the
2         wider implications of the
3         concern for the
4         environment
5         (0.2)
6  C:     wider implications, in
7         what sense?
8  IR:    =in any sense you like
9  C:     in any sense that I like,
10        huh,
```

Extract 4.9   [EA1. 258. TT/CL/WH]

```
1  IR:    what else
2         (3.0)
3  C:     i:n terms o:f
4  IR:    in terms of anything you can
5         think of
6         (.)
7  C:     sport (.) huh
8         (4.2)
```

In neither case above does the interviewer go along with the project of the candidate's prior turn. In the extracts the interviewer does not clarify the 'sense' (Extract 4.8) or 'terms' (Extract 4.9) that are apparently puzzling the candidate. The institutional character of these sequences perhaps becomes most obvious when we try to imagine comparable examples in ordinary conversation. Imagine the first three turns in Extract 4.9, for example, unfolding in light of the question 'what did you do at the weekend'? This would be strange indeed. Such a device is perhaps only imaginable as a way of testing someone. It suggests a clear asymmetry, that one party is entitled to line up 'hoops' for the other to jump through. In the data, in neither case do candidates face any difficulty understanding what is going on. In no obvious ways do they find the device to be either uncanny or disruptive (Garfinkel 1967). What is established, and reflexively recognised, is the instatement of a particular practice, which demands candidates assemble their talk without direction.

Secondly, consider a harsher practice. This involved interviewers pushing for more and more talk, to the point the candidate had nothing left to say. In Extract 4.10 the candidate has been asked to speak in general about the role of 'sport in society'. It takes approximately four minutes for the candidate to run out of things to say.

```
Extract 4.10   [EA1. 276. 'Dried up']
 1  C:    an. it's a source of entertainment as
 2        such (.) huh::
 3        (0.6)
 4  C:    tsk, hhh ((sigh))
 5        (4.6)
 6  C:    I'm huh °having problems°
 7        (8.5)
 8  C:    °I've dried up°
 9        (3.5)
10  C:    °that's basically it°
11        (1.2)
12  IR:   perhaps think about how ...
```

In this case, the interviewer overlooks the sequential and normative implications of the candidate's repeated 'calls for help' and his explicit admission he has nothing more to say (on lines 8 and 10). Only at line 12 is the candidate given a lifeline. But this sequence is neither norm-less nor a reflection of the interviewer's lacking competence. Whilst the candidate may not have enjoyed this stretch of conduct, he has no obvious difficulty locating how the action forms part of the 'setting's organised ways' (Garfinkel 1967). On line 6, when he says 'I'm having problems', he is alive to the contextual relevancies in play. He is being tested and is failing. When he claims to have 'dried up' (line 8), the candidate draws upon familiar grammar for precisely these kinds of difficulties. The candidate publicly and accountably orients to his own deficiencies and not the unreasonableness of the interviewer's conduct. Once more, we see how candidates orient their conduct to interview orthodoxy, on this occasion in the midst of defining their own institutionally specific problems.

The tyranny of interviewer knowledge and judgement

In different ways, the chapter has been concerned with what interviewers use to constitute their professional practice. In Extracts 4.1
and 4.2, this included a sense of when and where 'achievements'
should appear in stories about work experience and world travel.
In Extract 4.5, the interviewer drew on knowledge about preferred
tactics for motivating people. Even the socio-political comparability
of Nigeria and South Africa has come into play. At one level all these
interventions were arbitrary. In Extract 4.1, the interviewer could
have overlooked the candidate's good fortune and focused on positive
aspects of the experience. How many times (and when) you need to
speak to an athletics team in order to motivate them is also not an
exact science. A key matter, once interviewers produce these kinds
of next actions (question-answer-next action), would seem to be the
constraints they establish. Do candidates have the opportunity to
counteract the apparently arbitrary imposition of interviewer
knowledge?

Just one case is examined in Extracts 4.11a and 4.11b. The candidate
has been asked to suppose he was in position of considerable influence
within an organisation; what would the main environmental issues be
and how would he manage them? As he comes to a close (lines 2–4), and
then again in lines 6 to 8, the candidate argues that corporate and
environmental interests can co-exist in harmony. This is flatly rejected
by the interviewer, who then asserts a position; he crosses a particular
line and by so doing starts to 'answer' his own question.

Extract 4.11a   [EB1. 163. TT/Counter-assert]

```
 1  IR:   are you sayin[g
 2  C:                  [the right corporate decision
 3        can also be the right social, environmental
 4        decision huh managing the impact of operations
 5        (.)
 6  IR:   okay, that's huh again sounds nice huh but
 7        it's, it doesn't quite come out like that=
 8  C:    okay
 9        (.2)
10  IR:   I mean if you take brent spa as an example huh
11        that certainly wasn't- whether or not it was the
```

```
12        right decision or not you could argue about
13        but I'm certain it wasn't what came out, so how
14        would you set about managing for example
```

Notice that the interviewer not only asserts a position; he also presents his view as *unarguable*. In his terms, at the time the decision about Brent Spa was made 'you could argue about' it (line 12). In retrospect, though, it is unarguably the case that corporate and environment interests did not coincide in the case of Brent Spa.

Extract 4.11b

```
15  IR:   opposition to your ideas
16        (.)
17  C:    well in in your corporate role you have ((sequence
18        omitted)) but that minimises the impact
19  IR:   sure I understand that
20  C:    okay
21  IR:   but how are you gonna manage that in respect of
22        people who don't accept that you've actually
23        achieved that ((sequence omitted))
24  C:    that's really the best you can do, and huh,
25        you're, there's never gonna be an airtight
26        situation, where you're not gonna get opposition,
27        it's just impossibl[e, there are too many
28  IR:                      [mhm]
29  C:    competing views and factions so huh under the
30        ((sequence omitted))
31  IR:   so that's that's fine okay so that really completes
32        the how does Howard think bit okay
```

In response, and in a short space of time, the candidate moves from arguing that there is no conflict between corporate objectives and environmental concerns to arguing that there will never be agreement, that it is 'impossible' (line 27). In this case, there is a stronger element to the interviewer's intervention. He seems to mean it. The candidate finds himself inclined to re-work his position.

In this data we sense the power, even tyranny, of the recruitment interview, which arises from the interviewer's ability to silence their own role in shaping the trajectory and the content of candidates' talk. In ways that seem indisputable, the interviewer plays a considerable role in shaping both what the candidate is able to say and how. But when he concludes this stretch of interaction by saying 'so that really completes the how does Howard think bit' (lines 30–31), it is without irony. His role in shaping the answer is silenced. In Button's data, this separation of talk and context was achieved (albeit imperfectly) via strict turn-taking procedures. Through them, interviewers were placed 'outside of the candidate's talk so that it might be objectively examined' (Button 1987: 170). In the present study, the objectification of the candidate was achieved through other means, namely via the technology of the scoring form.

Discussion

This chapter has examined the reflexive interplay between recruitment practice and interaction during job interviews, not abstractly, but through the analysis of actual episodes of work. It has been concerned not just with knowledge *in* practice, but also with knowledge *of* practice, how people display (to one another) their sense of the entitlements, relevancies, logics, expectations and styles, relevant for the task at hand; how people tether their conduct to the organised ways of recruitment; how people produce themselves as organisational subjects moment by moment.

Rather than thinking of knowledge as an object possessed by individuals or organisations, it has been understood here as something that people *do* with and for one another (Nicolini, Gherardi and Yanow 2003). Analytic attention has shifted to real-time activity in order to grasp knowledge as a publicly accountable property of ordinary conduct. Knowledge of practice has been analysed *in use*, as parties are engaged in the business of 'working' the setting. Rather than dualistically separating 'knowledge and action', 'thought and deed' and 'mind and body' (Chia and MacKay 2007), they have been considered together. The chapter has presented a way of getting close to action, which is increasingly valued within practice-based literature. Despite this newfound emphasis (Jarzabkowski 2004: 544), there have actually been few practice-based empirical studies that analyse practice as things are underway, in motion or being done (but see Alby and Zucchermaglio 2006; Nicolini 2007; Hindmarsh and Pilnick

2007). The chapter has presented one way of resolving a tension between theoretical framings, bound to images of fluidity and motion and what remain comparatively static empirical studies.

Ethnomethodologically informed studies are concerned with public and shared ways in which people display their knowledge of the practical and moral components of action and setting. They seek an *empirical-analytic* warrant for this or that demarcation. For the present study, it has been meaningful to speak of 'the recruitment interview' because the action itself seemed to be produced in and through 'interview orthodoxy' (Button 1992). Everything that happened seemed to be implicated by this. For example, interviewers could say 'you're doing fine'; 'clarification' could be understood as 'help' and withheld (Extracts 4.8 and 4.9) or it could be unwanted (Extract 4.3); the presence/absence of achievement was grossly relevant (Extracts 4.1 and 4.2); the delayed onset of any answer became a novel kind of problem (Extract 4.3); candidates, pushed to the point of drying up, found their own failings in the unfolding silence (Extract 4.10). In such data, there would seem to be good evidence in support of the demarcation 'interview'. This is perhaps most available comparatively, when we think what such sequences might look like, practically and normatively, if they were produced during casual conversation (Sacks, Schegloff and Jefferson 1974).

The approach taken is distinctive. It can be contrasted with what Robert Chia and Brad MacKay suggest is the dominant view embedded in practice-based social theory, whereby analysts study the 'patterned *consistency* of actions emerging from ... interaction rather than on the micro-activities of individual ... agents' (Chia and MacKay 2007: 224). Of course, such an approach does have merit. In the present data we have sensed how candidates from institutions embedded in the class structure of British society (the Universities of Oxford, Cambridge and Durham, the London School of Economics and so forth) drew upon an accumulation of appropriate life experiences (world travel and working aboard) to ease their way into employment with a large multi-national firm. There are clearly alternative ways of grasping the patterned nature of these data. The crux is this. What such approaches do is give the job of witnessing 'patterned consistency' to the analyst. What ethnomethodologically informed studies seem to show is that social activities are themselves already orderly and organised not for analysts, but for members. In the first place, discernable patterns and patterned consistency are things ordinary members recognise during the flow of ordinary activity. Indeed, it is only because members are able to see how some action might form part of the setting's organised ways that orderly scenes of work are held together and sustained. The practice of recruitment is simultaneously a product of interaction and a kind of template against which conduct can be reflexively grasped and managed.

By tracking such processes second by second, the analyst can gain unprecedented access to the operation and character of situated knowledge. In organisation studies, the 'practice turn' has led scholars to develop a newfound interest in easily missed forms of expertise as they are embedded in ordinary work (Gherardi and Nicolini 2002b). But such studies have stopped short of dealing with recordings. With such materials in hand, it becomes possible to develop a new level of insight into the knowledgeability of actors. This in turn can throw up some interesting insights, for instance concerning practical ways in which actors participate in their own apparent subordination.

Clearly, the premise that talk is being assembled 'for other reasons' furnishes interviewers with possibilities that do not arise in ordinary conversation. On occasions candidates found themselves in potentially demeaning circumstances, most apparent in Extract 4.10 where the candidate 'dried up'. In this extract, and generally, if challenged the interviewer could account for their conduct in relation to interview orthodoxy, i.e. as an attempt to see how the candidate coped with this type of interactionally generated pressure. Possible ways in which A might shape the conduct of B expand dramatically. Indeed, it was argued that this is precisely how the candidate (in Extract 4.10) located the action, as a 'working example' of interview orthodoxy. In this way the candidate experienced his own failings.

In that example, and at no other point in the data, does the candidate try to step outside this framework. Indeed, it is not clear how this would be possible, in the same way that even those who claim to be uninterested in 'fashion' will inevitably make a 'fashion statement' of a kind each day. Even if a candidate refused to 'jump through the hoops', perhaps by questioning the relevance of talking about 'sport in society' for a job in petrochemicals, that refusal could itself be taken to document the kinds of personal characteristics and traits that were being assessed. 'The interview' is thus akin to a total institutional framework for interaction (Goffman 1961).

Of course, such processes were not always oppressive. On other occasions, candidates – much more so than interviewers – did work to actively (re-)establish the relevance of the central premise of the interview (see Extract 4.3), when talk seemed to drift from the matter of their achievements and accomplishments. On other occasions, candidates confronted problems they could overcome easily enough, e.g. 'difficult questions' (Extract 4.4) and 'mild interrogation' (Extract 4.6), leading to positive assessments of their performance. Overall, then, interview orthodoxy generates a distinctive field of *possibilities* for supportive and fairly oppressive interventions, by explaining, justifying and making the rationality of those interventions apparent. The setting's core features – the interviewer's power, the fair treatment of the candidate and institutional identities – are all tethered to, and reproduced through, practical ways in which actors orient to the setting's central premise.

5 | *The situated production of stories*

DAVID GREATBATCH AND TIMOTHY CLARK

Introduction

At a general level storytelling is a pervasive feature of everyday discourse both within and outside organisations. Existing research on organisational stories indicates that they are not simply frivolous diversions that seek to amaze and entertain the recipients. Rather they may serve a number of important functions for organisations, which include socialising new organisational members by articulating the culture of an organisation; assisting with the development and verbalisation of visions and strategies; helping develop points of similarity within disparate and dispersed organisational groups; sustaining and legitimating existing power relationships as well as providing opportunities for resistance against them; and acting as collective organisational memory systems (Boje 1991, 1995, 2001; Boyce 1995; B. Clark 1972; Gabriel 1991, 1995; Moeran 2007; Mumby 1987; Wilkins 1983).

Whilst previous studies have produced important insights into various aspects of storytelling within organisations, a common failing has been their focus on the analysis of textual recordings of stories rather than an examination of their *in situ* production. It has generally been assumed that a story's original meaning and purpose, as conveyed when it was initially told, is apparent from an analysis of a textual record of this event. With notable exceptions (e.g. Boje 1991, 1995, 2001), storytelling has not been viewed as a situated communicative act. This is surprising given that, as David Boje (2001) demonstrates, studying storytelling episodes as situated communicative acts, which are shaped not only by storytellers but also by story recipients, is critical to understanding their form, function and reception.

In this chapter we show how conversation analysis can be used to study storytelling as a situated communicative act and to shed light on how the performative impact of stories may vary significantly when they are told on different occasions. This involves a comparative analysis of two storytelling episodes in which a speaker tells the same story to two different audiences. The speaker, Daniel Goleman, is a highly successful presenter on the international management lecture circuit and one of an elite group of management speakers referred to as management gurus. Management gurus are purveyors of influential management ideas such as 'excellence', 'culture change', 'learning organisation', 'business process re-engineering' and, in the case of Daniel Goleman, 'emotional intelligence'. In addition to writing best-selling management books they disseminate their ideas in live presentations to audiences of managers around the world (Huczynski 1993; Jackson 2001; T. Clark and Salaman 1996, 1998). As perhaps the highest-profile group of management speakers in the world, they use their lectures to build their personal reputations with audiences of managers. Many gain reputations as powerful orators and subsequently market recordings of their talks as parts of audio- and DVD/web-based management training packages. A key element of their success is seen as the stories they tell (T. Clark and Salaman 1998; Huczynski 1993). Stories therefore help build and sustain their reputations with audiences well beyond the initial popularity of a book.

The storytelling episodes analysed in the present chapter are drawn from two commercially available video recordings of lectures given by Goleman. The chapter begins with a brief review of the literature on storytelling in organisations. It then shows, through a comparative analysis of two occasions on which Goleman tells the same story, how stories are shaped with respect to and by the interaction between the speakers and audience members and how their meaning and performative impact may vary significantly when they are told on different occasions. The analysis builds on our previous conversation analytic research on speaker–audience interaction in the context of both management and political oratory (Greatbatch and Clark 2002, 2003, 2005; Heritage and Greatbatch 1986). The chapter concludes by drawing out some of the theoretical, methodological and substantive implications of this approach for research on stories in management and organisation studies.

Storytelling as a communicative act

A review of the literature indicates that researchers have adopted a variety of approaches when collecting organisational stories. Some studies have searched for examples of organisational stories in the academic literature and historical accounts of organisations (B. Clark 1972; Martin *et al.* 1983; Mumby 1987). Others have tape recorded conversations and interactions in a number of formal and informal contexts within organisations in conjunction with notes derived from participant observation (Boje 1991; Gabriel 1995; Smart 1999). Further methods have included experiments (Martin and Powers 1983) and surveys (McConkie and Boss 1986; Wilkins 1984). Finally, a number of researchers, in addition to collecting stories from a range of documentary sources, have used unstructured interviews in order to identify stories that are circulating within a variety of different types of organisations (Gabriel 1995, 2000; Moeran 2007; Wilkins 1983).

However, regardless of the approach adopted, Boje (1991, 1995, 2001), drawing on the earlier critique of the anthropological and folklorist story literature by Robert Georges (1969, 1980), has argued that studies of storytelling within organisations have adopted what he terms the 'stories-as-texts paradigm'. Whether the research has been extensive or intensive, based on surveys, experimental methods, questionnaires, interviews or archival/documentary research, stories have been treated as objective data disconnected from their original telling. They are viewed as nothing more than texts with little attention given to the natural context in which the stories are told. Consequently, as Boje (1991: 109) notes, 'the textual content, rather than the storytelling event, is the focus of study'. Drawing on arguments from the folklore literature, the point he makes is that the full meaning of a story is assumed to be discernable from a detailed analysis of a textual record of the words used by the teller. However, he argues, this fails to include a number of elements that combine to create a storytelling performance and ignores the active influence of the recipients. This point is well captured by Georges (1969: 316) when he writes of the dominant folklorist approach to collecting stories that 'these texts constitute nothing more than a written representation of one aspect of the message of complex communicative events'. So, when stories are treated as texts they are disembodied from their original telling within the specific context and organisation, with the consequence that their significance as performed entities is lost. Thus, without examining storytelling in its natural context we cannot be certain how the specific characters, plot elements, narrative structure and emphasis work separately and in conjunction with one another to underpin the achievement of the telling of the story.

Even when stories are collected through ethnographic methods involving conversations, such as in formal and informal interviews, researchers do not regard this as a particular storytelling event that differs from that within the organisation. Rather the performative contexts of the interview and the organisation are treated as identical. Yet, as Yiannis Gabriel (1995: 496) argues, the nature of a story is modified through repeated tellings in that at each telling 'some elements are discarded, others are incorporated or elaborated ... each text may then travel, undergoing further elaborations with each recital'. Nevertheless, the underlying assumption in much prior research of organisational storytelling is that the informant is reproducing as precisely as they are able a story that they may have previously recounted to their organisational colleagues or heard told. Again this criticism mirrors that made by Georges when he writes with respect to folklorist research, 'Most researchers tend to regard storytellers as carriers of specific stories or kinds of stories and conceive the principal duty of the storyteller as reproducing or re-creating, as "accurately" as possible, individual stories he has heard from others, while those who hear these stories from him will in turn "pass them on", again, as "accurately" as possible, to others.' From this point of view researchers of organisational stories similarly view interviewees/informants/storytellers as having a special ability to 'reproduce or recreate [a story], insofar as is possible, with word-for-word consistency from telling to telling' (Georges 1969: 323). Despite Yiannis Gabriel's (1995) point that stories vary in important ways from one telling to another, stories are assumed to have an unchanging quality regardless of the specific context within which they are told.

This approach in turn assumes that the mode of communication adopted by the storyteller is that of sender and that of the audience is passive recipient. Storytellers and audiences do not therefore actively participate and so mutually influence the telling of an unfolding story.

However, given the situated production of stories it cannot be assumed that the same story is told in an identical way to different audiences. This latter observation echoes with Gail Jefferson's (1978: 219) argument that 'stories are sequenced objects articulating with the particular context in which they are told. For example, storytelling can involve a story preface in which the teller projects a forthcoming story, a next turn in which a co-participant aligns themselves as a story recipient, a next in which the teller produces a story, and a next in which the

story recipient talks by reference to the story.' Given that in conversations stories emerge from turn-by-turn talk, informants may select one
story from a range of possible alternatives and adjust their rendition by
emphasising certain features over others to meet the locally occasioned
circumstances of the research interview (Kirshenblatt-Gimblett 1975).
Furthermore, whether the researcher is aware of it or not, their own
verbal and non-verbal reactions to the unfolding story will influence any
particular rendition.

   In this chapter, we demonstrate the importance of studying storytelling as a real-time communicative act by comparing two storytelling
episodes in which the management speaker Daniel Goleman recounts
the same story to different audiences during lectures given on the
management lecture circuit in the United States. Using the approach
and findings of conversation analytic studies of storytelling in talk-in-
interaction (e.g. C. Goodwin 1984; Jefferson 1978; Sacks 1974, 1992),
we track each storytelling episode as it unfolds in real time. Our analysis
exemplifies the problems with the 'stories-as-texts' paradigm in two
interrelated ways. First, it shows how the same story is presented and
interpreted in different ways in the two lectures, even though the wording is very similar. Secondly, it shows how the meaning and significance
of the story are negotiated between the storyteller and story recipients
on a moment-by-moment basis as the storytelling episodes unfold, and
how paralinguistic and kinesic cues, which are rarely, if ever, considered
in storytelling research in organisation studies (Boje 1991, 2001), play a
key role this process.

Analysis

Daniel Goleman is the author of the best-selling book titled *Emotional
Intelligence* (1996). This spent over a year on the *New York Times* best-
seller list. Prior to that he was a science journalist and wrote for pub-
lications such as the *New York Times*. On the basis of the success of
Emotional Intelligence he has become a frequent and highly regarded
speaker on the international management lecture circuit. The story that
is focus of our analysis is told on two different occasions. The first
telling, in Lecture 1 ('Emotional Intelligence: A Cornerstone of
Learning Communities'), occurs in a dimly lit conference centre.
Goleman speaks for just over fifty minutes to an audience of more
than a hundred people from behind a podium. Occasionally he moves

away from the podium but never in front of it. The second telling, in Lecture 2, occurs a year or two later during a seventy-five minute speech ('Emotional Intelligence') to an audience of around a hundred people. The audience sits on a tiered structure arranged in a horseshoe shape. Goleman is able to wander the floor in full view, without any obstacles between the audience and himself. The setting is much brighter and more intimate and has a colourful backdrop. Apart from the nature of the auditorium and audience, a critical difference between these two lectures is Goleman's appearance. In the first lecture he is heavily bearded and wears glasses. In the second lecture he has trimmed his beard and does not wear glasses. The importance of this difference will become apparent when we discuss the analysis of the two tellings.

The story concerns Goleman's experience(s) on catching a bus in New York. Goleman depicts the bus driver's actions as exemplifying emotional intelligence in that he succeeded in energising passengers who were initially irritable and unsociable due, in part, to the hot weather. As Table 5.1 shows, the two renditions of the story are very similar in terms of both their structure and wording.

In each lecture Goleman tells the story, positively assesses the central character and then goes on to discuss the element of emotional intelligence that the story exemplifies. However, Goleman contextualises the

Table 5.1. *A comparison between the text of two versions of the same story*

Lecture 1	Lecture 2
Preamble	Preamble
The last element the fifth part of emotional intelligence is social skill which in a sense means handling emotions in relationships. Handling emotions in the other person. Well if you're really skilled that's what you're doing.	You see emotions are contagious. Emotions pass between us as part of every interaction. People who are really adept at social skill they know this. They use it, and they think better.
Story preface	Story preface
None	Now I am going to tell you the story that changed my life. It showed me that we are all part of each other's emotional toolkit (.) for better or for worse.

Table 5.1. (*cont.*)

Lecture 1	Lecture 2
Story	**Story**
I was once waiting for a bus on a hot horrible August day in Manhattan. The kind of day when it's so humid and awful and yucky that everybody's going round in a bubble like don't look at me, don't talk to me, don't touch me.	It was a really hot horrible, humid day in New York city, and everybody's walking around in a kinda of a bubble that says don't touch me, don't talk to me (Very light audience laughter) you know. Leave me alone I'm a little prickly and irritable today.
And I was standing there in my bubble waiting for the bus and the bus pulled up and I got on bubble intact. And the bus driver did something surprising. He spoke to me. He actually spoke to me. He said hi how are you doing. I was taken aback.	And I'm waiting for the bus with my bubble intact, (Isolated audience laughter) and it pulls up and I get on careful to bring my bubble with me and the bus driver does something really surprising. He talks to me. (Isolated audience laughter) He says hi how are you doing? It's great to have you on the bus. He really means it. (Isolated audience laughter) I'm shocked. (Light audience laughter)
And I sat down, and I realised that this bus driver was carrying on a dialogue with everybody on the bus. Oh you're looking for suits are yuh, well you know there's a great sale in this department store up here on the right, and did you hear about the movies in the centreplex here on the left, the one in cinema one isn't very good. I know it got good reviews but cinema three that's really good. And did you hear about what's opening up in this museum up here on the right. On and on and on like that.	I sit down and all of a sudden I realise this guy's carrying on a dialogue with the whole bus. Oh you're looking for suits are you. You know this department store down here on the right it's got a great sale on suits you should check it out. (Isolated audience laughter) Hey did you hear about this great Picasso show at the museum down here. On and on and on.

Table 5.1. (*cont.*)

Lecture 1	Lecture 2
And people would get off that bus and he'd say well so long it's been great having you. And they'd say yeah it's been great being on this bus. (Isolated audience laughter).	People'd get off the bus and he'd say so long it's been great having you (Isolated audience laughter) And they'd say it's been great being on this bus. (Audience laughter)
Storyteller's assessment	**Storyteller's assessment**
That man was an urban saint. (Audience laughter)	That man that man was an urban saint, (Isolated audience laughter) He was sending ripples of good feeling throughout the city.
Key lesson	**Key lesson**
You see (.) emotions are contagious. There is a hidden emotional economy that passes amongst us all, it's part of every interaction.	When I saw him I realised that we all have this power to make each other feel better or worse. And we have this power no matter what we do because it's how we do it that makes the difference

story in different ways in the two lectures. In the first lecture he uses the story to illustrate the fifth element of emotional intelligence, social skills, which he defines as handling emotions in relationships. In the second lecture, however, Goleman presents the story as depicting an event that changed his life. Here, then, the story is afforded significantly more importance than in the previous lecture. Whereas in the first lecture it was presented as an illustration, on this occasion it is presented as an account of an epiphanic experience, which was central to Goleman becoming an advocate of the theory of emotional intelligence.

Although the story is contextualised in different ways, the structure and wording of the two renditions are very similar. It is therefore noticeable that the audience responses in the two lectures differ in important respects. In Lecture 1 the audience listens in silence until the completion of the story, at which point a handful of people laugh in response to Goleman's description of the exchanges between the bus driver and his passengers. Then, following Goleman's post-story char-acterisation of the bus driver as an urban saint, a large number of audience members laugh out loud. The audience reactions to the story in Lecture 2 differ markedly from this. Here the conclusion of the story evokes collective audience laughter, whereas Goleman's characterisation of the bus driver as an urban saint evokes only isolated laughter – precisely the reverse of the situation when the story was told in the earlier lecture. Notice also that earlier components of the story evoke either laughter or isolated laughter, whereas before this was not the case. These differences result from the different ways in which Goleman relates the story paralinguistically and kinesically in the two storytelling episodes. Space considerations mean that it is not possible to look in detail at every aspect of this, so we will concentrate on the end of the story, as this is key to understanding its function on these particular occasions.

The extracts in Table 5.1 comprise decontextualised transcripts of the two renditions of the story, which are akin to the data used in many management studies of storytelling. In order to explain the different reactions of the audience members, however, it is necessary to consider the storyteller's paralinguistic and visual actions as his two renditions of the story unfold in real time.

Lecture 1

As Extract 5.1 shows, Goleman's reactions to the episodes of audience laughter that follow his story and his subsequent assessment of the central character differ.

Extract 5.1 [EI: 0.40.00]

```
 1  Gol:  hh On and on and on like that..hh And people
 2         would get off that bus (.) and he'd say well so
 3         long it's been great having you.=And they'd say
 4         yea:h it's been great being on this bus.
 5         (.)
 6  Aud:  h-h[-h-h  h hh[h-h
 7  Gol:     [That ma:n [was an urban saint.
 8                     [Smile face->
 9         (.) Smiles
10  Aud:  hhhhhhhhhh hhhhhhhhhh hhhhhhhhh-[h h-h
11  Gol:                                  [You see (.)
12         emotions are contagious. (1.4) There is a <hidde:n
13         emo:tional economy> that passes (.) amongst us
14         all:,=it's part of every interaction
```

Thus note that Goleman does not confirm the relevance of the isolated audience laughter which follows his story by ceding the floor. Instead he almost immediately proceeds to characterise the bus driver as an 'urban saint'. However, Goleman *does* confirm the relevance of the laughter which follows this assessment of the bus driver by remaining silent until this laughter starts to die away, at which point he starts to elaborate the aspect of emotional intelligence that the story has been used to exemplify.

Further light can be shed on this storytelling episode by considering Goleman's visual conduct as he concludes his story and then characterises the central character as an urban saint. This reveals that Goleman's non-verbal actions operate to emphasise his assessment of the bus driver's actions, rather than the story itself. They also illustrate how Goleman recounts the story without any indication that it is intendedly humorous. He does not announce that it is a humorous story, smile or use comedic/incongruous paralinguistic cues or gestures, all actions that are routinely associated with the delivery of humorous messages (Greatbatch and Clark 2003, 2005).

As Goleman describes the exchange between the passengers and the bus driver, he holds his arm out to the right, as his voice trails off to almost a whisper (Figures 5.1a and 5.1b). Neither his speech delivery nor his bodily actions suggest that some form of collective response from the audience would be appropriate at this point. On the contrary, both his tone of voice and his outstretched arm gesture indicate that he has yet to complete the current unit of his talk.

However, as Figures 5.1c–5.1f show, as soon as he begins to characterise the driver as an urban saint, Goleman's vocal and non-vocal actions combine to emphasise his message and thereby to make it stand out from the preceding speech materials. In addition to speaking more loudly and forcibly, Goleman forms his fingers into a pointing action (Figure 5.1c). He then rotates his arm and thrusts his outstretched finger(s) towards the audience (Figure 5.1d). Subsequently, Goleman lowers his arm so that by the time he completes his sentence he is pointing at the floor (Figures 5.1e and 5.1f).

Thus Goleman's tone and rhythmic delivery, together with his gestures, serve to mark out his characterisation of the bus driver as an urban saint as the punch line of the preceding story. It is his post-story

And they'd say
yea:h it's
been great

Figure 5.1a

being on this bus.

Figure 5.1b

That man
(Isolated audience
laughter)

Figure 5.1c

assessment rather than the story per se that he emphasises both vocally
and non-vocally, and which he delivers as his key message in this
segment of the lecture. Moreover, in contrast to the preceding talk,
Goleman's facial expression and paralinguistic actions are also consistent with the delivery of a humorous message, for he adopts a 'smile

was an

Figure 5.1d

urban

Figure 5.1e

Saint.

Figure 5.1f

face' – characterised by the upper lip being drawn back and the corners of the mouth raised slightly, a slight puffing of the cheeks, brightening of the eyes and creases under the eyes (Pollio, Mers and Lucchesi 1972) – and a 'smile voice' – characterised by a noticeable increase in the frequency and pitch of the speech (Shor 1978; Tartter 1989), which

Audience laughter

Figure 5.1g

Audience laughter

Figure 5.1h

You see
emotions are
contagious...

Figure 5.1i

imbues his talk with a 'cheery resonance' (Lavin and Maynard 2001: 467). Goleman also broadens his smile as he falls silent following the post-story assessment.

As can be seen in Figures 5.1g–5.1i, Goleman confirms the relevance of audience laughter not only by ceding the floor/remaining silent until the laughter starts to die away but also through his bodily actions. As the audience members laugh, Goleman turns away from them, walks to the lectern and glances at his notes (Figures 5.1g and 5.1h). Then, as the audience laughter fades, he turns back towards the audience members, raises his arm and points towards them as he starts to distil out the key lesson of the story (Figure 5.1i).

In this case, then, Goleman uses the story as an example of the fifth aspect of emotional intelligence. He delivers the story in a 'serious' frame before shifting to a humorous frame and evoking laughter as he delivers a positive assessment of the bus driver's actions.

Lecture 2

By the time of the second lecture Goleman was no longer wearing spectacles and had trimmed his beard. These are significant changes to his facial appearance because they meant that the audience members would be able to see his eyes and mouth more clearly than in the past; consequently his facial expressions would be more clearly visible than on previous occasions. This was perhaps linked to the fact that Goleman had also honed his style of public speaking, adopting a much more energised, animated, forceful and vital style of public speaking than in his previous lecture, including the use of more pronounced facial expressions.

As noted earlier, in this lecture the conclusion to the story evokes collective audience laughter, whereas the assessment of the bus driver evokes only isolated laughter – the reverse of what happened in Lecture 1. As Extract 5.2 shows, Goleman treats the occurrence of laughter following the story as relevant by pausing until the laughter starts to die away.

Extract 5.2 [EI2 – 30:16]

```
1  Gol:   On and on and on. (0.3) People'd get
2         off the bus (.) and he'd say so long
3         it's been great having you
4  Aud:   h-h-[hh h-h=
5  Gol:       [And they'd say it's been great being on this bus.
6  Aud:   hhhhhhhhh[h –h- h- h- h h h
7  Gol:            [That man that man was an urban saint?
8  Aud:   h-h-h-h- [h-h
9  Gol:            [He was sending ripples of good feeling
```

```
10          throughout the city. (0.6) When I saw him (.)
11          I realised that we all have this power (0.2) to make
12          each other feel better or worse. (0.2) And we have
13          this power no matter what we do (.) because it's how
14          we do it that makes the difference
```

As can be seen, the wording of the conclusion of the story and the subsequent assessment of the bus driver are virtually identical in the two lectures. What is key to understanding the delivery of the story on this occasion is the way in which Goleman shifts the emphases that he places on different elements of the storytelling episode. In this case, he places much greater emphasis than before on the concluding element of the story. Rather than channelling audience attention towards his characterisation of the bus driver as an urban saint, he presents the end of the story as a focal assertion and succeeds in evoking collective audience laughter in response to it.

Consider Figures 5.2a–5.2e. In contrast to the first lecture, Goleman both highlights his depiction of the way in which passengers in the story responded to the bus driver as they got off the bus ('And they'd say it's been great being on this bus') and projects the relevance of audience laughter upon its completion. Thus, as he begins to quote the passengers, he leans towards the audience, arms at his side (Figure 5.1a). Then, he lifts up both forearms before thrusting his hands downwards as he says 'great' (Figure 5.2b). As he completes the paraphrase he lowers his hands (Figure 5.2c) so that by the end of the story they are at his side, as he stands smiling at the audience (Figure 5.2d). Together with his animated tone, these actions not only convey the nature of the passenger's reactions to the bus driver, but also imbue the story with a more humorous tone than was the case in the first lecture. As the audience members laugh, he stands, relaxed, arms at his side, smiling at them without speaking and giving no indication that a resumption of his speaking is imminent, thereby confirming the relevance of the laughter (Figures 5.2d and 5.2e). Then, as can be seen in Figures 5.2f–5.2i, as the audience laughter starts to fade, he leans forward slightly towards the audience, thrusts out his left leg towards them, lifts his forearms to chest level, and cups his hands as he characterises the bus driver as an urban saint.

And they'd
say yeah

Figure 5.2a

it's been great

Figure 5.2b

being

Figure 5.2c

Goleman's paralinguistic and visual conduct, as he characterises the bus driver as an urban saint, differs from the first lecture in two important respects. First, in contrast to the first lecture, as he completes this post-story assessment of the bus driver, Goleman's paralinguistic and visual conduct does not suggest that completion of the post-story assessment will also represent completion of the message he is in the process of

on this bus.
You know.

Figure 5.2d

Audience laughter

Figure 5.2e

That ma:n

Figure 5.2f

delivering. Thus, whereas in Lecture 1 his gestures were consistent with message completion (recall how he lowered an outstretched arm/finger so that by the time he completed the post-story assessment he was pointing at the floor), in this case Goleman stands poised to continue speaking. Moreover, whereas in the first lecture he voiced his assessment with falling intonation, on this occasion he delivers the assessment

that man was
an urban

Figure 5.2g

Saint?

Figure 5.2h

Isolated audience
laughter

Figure 5.2i

with rising intonation. This suggests that further talk may be imminent and that the message-in-progress is yet to be completed.

The second difference between the two renditions of the post-story assessment of the bus driver is that in Lecture 2 Goleman does not signal humorous intent by smiling and, although a handful of audience members do laugh, the overwhelming majority remain silent. Moreover, in contrast to the first lecture, Goleman subsequently gives no indication whatsoever that laughter is a relevant response at this juncture. Instead, he proceeds almost immediately to explain *why* the driver was an urban saint and how the driver's actions provided him with a revelatory insight into the importance of so-called emotional intelligence. Thus, Goleman does not present his post-story characterisation of the bus driver as an urban saint as the humorous punch line of the story, as was the case in his previous lecture; instead he embeds it in a 'serious' account of the lesson he learnt from the events he described in his story.

In summary, Goleman's paralinguistic and visual actions serve to formulate the story and post-story assessment in very different ways in the two lectures. In the first lecture, Goleman channels the audience's attention towards, and evokes audience laughter in response to, his post-story characterisation of the bus driver as an urban saint. However, in the second lecture he adopts a different tack. Specifically, he invites (and subsequently confirms the relevance of) collective audience laughter in response to the final element of the story, before shifting to a 'serious' footing as he depicts the bus driver as an urban saint during the course of delivering a broader message which (1) contextualises the driver's actions in terms of the theory of emotional intelligence and (2) identifies the wider impact the driver's actions had on his own thinking. In other words, it is the story itself that is framed as humorous, rather than the storyteller's post-story assessment of the central character's actions. Thus, in the first case, the story is embedded in an argument structure in which it is positioned as a prefatory component preceding a punch line, which comprises the storyteller's assessment of the central character's actions; in the second case the final element of the story itself is formulated as the punch line, while the post-story assessment of the driver's actions is embedded within a 'non-humorously' formatted message which distils the lesson to be learnt from the story.

These differences in Goleman's paralinguistic and visual conduct are due at least in part to the fact that he uses the same story in different ways in the two lectures. In the first lecture, Goleman uses the story merely to illustrate a dimension of emotional intelligence, whereas in the second lecture he presents the story as depicting an epiphanic moment in his life. This is a significant shift in emphasis, with the story now being presented as leading to his 'conversion' to the set of ideas concerning emotional intelligence that he is conveying to this audience. The story is no longer just an example; it is an account of a life-changing revelatory experience. By presenting the final element in the story as a punch line, and inviting audience laughter at that point, Goleman highlights and emphasises the remarkable quality of the incident (Greatbatch and Clark 2002, 2003, 2005). He also imbues the events depicted in the story with more significance than was the case in the previous lecture because on this occasion he does not channel the audience's attention towards his post-story assessment of the bus driver. Goleman's vocal and non-vocal actions thus place greater emphasis on the actions of the bus driver and his passengers than was the case in the previous lecture. This perhaps serves to underline the epiphanic aspects of the storytelling episode in this lecture. The performance-based aspects of the storytelling episodes are thus key to understanding the specific functions of Goleman's 'urban saint' story when he recounts it in the two lectures.

Discussion

Despite Boje's (1991) cogent critique, the 'story-as-texts' approach continues as a major stream in storytelling research in organisational studies. Thus, for example, recent studies of storytelling within organisations have adopted such an approach, drawing on stories gleaned in interviews and participant observation (e.g. Gabriel 1995, 2000; Moeran 2007). Our analysis of Goleman's rendition of the same story on two different occasions underlines the problems with the 'stories-as-texts' paradigm, which treats stories as entities removed from their performative context and which conceptualises storytelling as a process in which the meaning is fixed (by the teller) and remains relatively stable and static across tellings. A decontextualised transcript of a story may give a very different impression of the production and reception it received from the audience when told live. As we have seen, a story (or component of a story) that looks serious on paper may receive a humorous response from members of an audience or vice versa. Moreover, the same story may be used and interpreted in different ways on different occasions. The performance-based aspects of storytelling episodes – especially paralinguistic and visual cues – are thus key in relation to understanding the functions of stories. We cannot therefore assume that the nature of the events recounted in a story has a fixed and final significance. Stories may be presented, interpreted and received in different ways, even though the wording may be very similar or even identical.

In addition to illustrating the importance of paralinguistic and kinesic actions in storytelling episodes, this chapter also shows how stories emerge through a process of interaction between storytellers and story recipients. The literature on storytelling in organisation studies as a whole fails to systematically examine the impact of storyteller/recipient interaction on story content, delivery and function. Thus, for example, little if any consideration is given to how the delivery and content of stories are shaped in response to the immediate reactions of recipients, or how storytellers elicit displays of approval from recipients, or how recipients' reactions are evoked, co-ordinated and managed. Even those studies that have focused on audio/video recordings of real-world story-telling episodes have overlooked storyteller/recipient interaction, involving instead either textual analysis of decontextualised transcripts or speaker-focused analyses, which do not consider how stories unfold in real time and emerge out of a process of interaction between storytellers and recipients (e.g. Greatbatch and Clark 2003, 2005).

In this chapter we have illustrated how stories are embedded within and arise out of interactions between speakers and listeners, and how this is key to understanding the significance and *in situ* meaning of stories, the extent storytellers and recipients display shared understandings of stories, when and where story recipients respond and so on. Thus, for example, our analysis of the storytelling episodes involving Goleman underlines that collective laughter is not simply a spontaneous reaction to stories whose content is self-evidently humorous, but rather is often evoked by storytellers through the use of a range of verbal and non-verbal practices. By varying his visual and paralinguistic conduct, Goleman stresses and invites collective laughter in response to different components in the two storytelling episodes. Goleman's paralinguistic and visual actions do not merely embellish and enliven his narration of the story; they are key to establishing the story's *in situ* meaning and significance, and projecting and co-ordinating appropriate collective audience responses on each occasion. Furthermore, what our analysis indicates is that whether a story is good, bad, successful or unsuccessful is not due to a number of essential and stable ingredients (Gabriel 2000; Taylor, Fisher and Dufresne 2002). Rather the various elements that combine to create the 'aesthetic experience' (Taylor, Fisher and Dufresne 2002) and underpin any subsequent evaluation of a story are themselves *in situ* accomplishments. As we have shown, differences in the use of paralinguistic and kinesic cues influence the immediate reception of a story and may therefore influence any future views as to its effectiveness.

Considering the interactional dimensions of storytelling also reveals the importance of story recipients' conduct during the course of story-telling episodes, and the ways in which stories represent joint accomplishments, involving both storytellers and story recipients. In the cases considered in this chapter, audience members are not passive recipients of a story whose meaning is straightforwardly determined and trans-mitted to them by the storyteller. This becomes especially apparent when we consider how audience members display competing under-standings of the urban saint story and Goleman's post-story assessment of the bus driver's actions, and how the storyteller subsequently tacitly accepts some displayed understandings but not others. In the first lecture, only a handful of audience members laugh upon completion of the story, whereas most, if not all, laugh following the storyteller's subsequent assessment of the central character. While the storyteller (Goleman) tacitly disconfirms the relevance of the isolated laughter following the story by proceeding immediately to produce the assess-ment, he tacitly confirms the relevance of laughter following the post-story assessment by ceding the floor until the laughter starts to die away. In the second case, most audience members laugh following the story, whereas only a few laugh following the storyteller's post-story assess-ment. Here, in contrast to the first lecture, the storyteller treats the occurrence of audience laughter following the story as relevant, by ceding the floor, but tacitly disconfirms the relevance of laughter follow-ing the post-story assessment by continuing to speak after the first few beats of laughter (rather than, for example, remaining silent in expecta-tion that the isolated laughter will lead to full laughter). All of this occurs in real time, as the story emerges out of the moment-by-moment actions and reactions of the storyteller and story recipients on two separate occasions. The status of the story and the post-story assessment as humorous or non-humorous is negotiated *in situ* and is not embodied in the words used by the speaker. The completion of the story and the post-story assessment involve the use of almost identical wording on the two occasions, with the differing interpretive frameworks and reactions resting on the storyteller's use of different paralinguistic and visual cues.

The key message of this chapter is that the nature, meaning and significance of stories (and specific incidents within them) are achieved *in situ* and that paralinguistic and visual cues play an important role in this process. Approaches that analyse stories using decontextualised transcripts are therefore misconceived. It is only by studying stories in natural contexts, as they emerge in real-time interactions between story-tellers and story recipients, that we can grasp their roles and significance in organisational (and other) settings. Conversation analysis is ideally suited to this task of studying stories as joint accomplishments in naturally occurring talk-in-interaction.

6 | Orders of bidding: organising participation in auctions of fine art and antiques

CHRISTIAN HEATH AND PAUL LUFF

Introduction

Auctions provide an institutional solution to the pricing and exchange of goods and services of uncertain value. In turn, auctions raise a number of social and organisational issues and problems that have to be resolved by participants themselves in and through interaction (Maynard 1988). For example, an auction of fine art and antiques consists of a gathering of a large number of people, in some cases several hundred, all of whom may have an interest in purchasing the goods on sale if the price is right. The lots in which participants are interested and the price they are prepared to pay is largely unknown, both to fellow buyers and to sale room personnel. The auctioneer has to deploy an organisation that enables the potential contributions of multiple participants to be identified, elicited and co-ordinated so that the price of the goods can be maximised in a transparent manner and sold to the highest bidder. The success of the auction, the valuation and exchange of goods, is dependent upon the participants' belief and trust in the process – that no personal interest or connivance, on behalf of or by the auctioneer, vendor or buyer, has falsely influenced the price and the eventual ownership of the goods. In other words, the neutrality of the auctioneer and the auction house

We would like to thank all those auctioneers, assistants and buyers who so willingly allowed auctions to be observed and recorded and who more generally helped with the research. We would also like to thank Stephen Patten, Karin Knorr Cetina, Douglas Maynard and Dirk vom Lehn for their helpful comments and ideas concerning the observations and issues addressed in this paper. We would also like to thank Jon Hindmarsh and Nick Llewellyn, who provided very helpful comments and editorial suggestions. The research of which this paper forms a part is undertaken as part of an UTIFORO, a project funded by the Engineering and Physical Sciences Research Council. An earlier version of this paper was published in the *British Journal of Sociology*.

and the integrity of bids – that they are real bids representing actual demand – are critical to the process being, and being seen to be, fair (C. W. Smith 1990).

Despite the substantial corpus of research in economics and econometrics (see for example Klemperer 2004; Menzes and Monteiro 2005; Krishna 2002), as Haidy Geismar (2001: 28) suggests, there is a 'dearth of sociological writing about auctions'. There are a number of important exceptions, in particular Charles Smith's (1990) insightful ethnography of the construction of value, but in large part economic sociology has neglected the auction notwithstanding its importance to the operation of a broad range of markets in contemporary society. Putting to one side a lack of substantive interest in auctions, these brief yet highly contingent moments of social interaction would seem to demand an analytic focus that differs from much economic sociology with its emphasis on formal institutional structure, state regulation and inter- and intra-organisational relations (see for example W. E. Baker, Faulkner and Fisher 1998; DiMaggio and Louch 1998; Swedberg 1997; Uzzi 1997; White 1981). In this regard, Jens Beckert's (2007) recognition that markets involve complex problems of co-ordination and constitute 'arenas of social interaction' points to the sociological importance of the situated accomplishment of markets, and yet, like a broad range of other, highly insightful studies of economic activity (for example Biggart and Delbridge 2004 and Fligstein 1996), directs analytic attention to institutional forms and socio-political structures and arrangements.

Over the past decade or so we have witnessed the emergence of a growing corpus of studies of markets as cultures (Abolafia 1988, 1996), a corpus of research that has begun to address 'concrete organised markets' and re-specify the socio-economic foundations of exchange. These studies and the theoretical and programmatic debates that serve to underpin and elaborate their significance recognise the centrality of 'social interaction' to the contingent production and reflexive constitution of particular markets (for example Abolafia 1988, 1996; Callon 1998, 2005; Knorr Cetina and Bruegger 2002; C. W. Smith 1990; Woolgar 2004). They also place agency, or as Michel Callon (2005) suggests 'agencement', at the heart of the analytic agenda; indeed Callon argues that the 'the exploration and description of different forms of agency, as well as the analysis of their (possible) diffusion, constitute an immense project ahead of us' (2005: 4).

Despite these commitments, one can see the ways in which particular theoretical and conceptual distinctions draw analytic attention away from the analysis of how human agency is manifest within situated action and interaction. For example, Mark Granovetter's (1985) highly influential work on the social organisation of economy, in particular the laudable concept of 'embeddedness', serves to powerfully promote inter-connectedness and inter-relationality at the expense of the investigation of the situated specifics of how talk and interaction sustain particular types of market. In turn, the conception or model of social interaction found in, or presupposed by, a range of ethnographic studies of markets treats co-ordinated, collaborative action as embodied in, and deriving from, common understandings or distributed cognitive states that can become, as Mitchel Abolafia (1998) and Callon (2005) suggest, institutionalised. Unfortunately, the practices in and through which participants themselves accomplish and co-ordinate their actions and activities in concert with each other in practical market situations, situations in which agency is exercised, articulated and revealed, are disregarded by virtue of the models of the social action that underpin, or are presupposed by, these studies. By relegating the situated and the interactional, they disregard the socially organised competencies and skills, the practices and reasoning, the orders of action, that serve to accomplish and sustain forms of market activity.

In this paper, we seek to demonstrate that the analysis of economic action as a 'form of social action' (Swedberg 1997) and the commitment to treating markets as 'processual systems' (Knorr Cetina and Bruegger 2002) drive analytic attention towards the details of social interaction and the ways in which markets are configured and sustained through social actions and activities including talk, gesture and bodily action. Drawing on video recordings of auctions of fine art, antiques and objets d'art, augmented by field work, gathered in the UK and abroad, we address the ways in which auctioneers deploy and articulate an organisation that selectively enables participants to legitimately compete for particular goods and thereby transparently determine their value and their ownership. We focus on auctioneers and the practices upon which they rely to establish a social and interactional arrangement for bidding and the ways in which they identify, discriminate and encourage bidders, organising active 'economic agents' within the practical accomplishment of rapidly passing moments of market activity. We address the ways in which auctioneers, in concert with buyers, establish and sustain an order of bidding, organise and reveal the participation of buyers and accomplish the authentic, transparent and trustworthy exchange of goods.

Ordering bids

In our data there can be up to three hundred people at an auction at any one time, many of whom are potential bidders for any of the objects that come up for sale. There may also be a number of people who have booked telephone lines with the auction house to enable them to bid on particular lots through sales assistants and others who have registered to bid through the internet. In most cases, the auctioneer is unlikely to know with any certainty who wishes to bid for a particular lot or the price they are prepared to pay. At its most basic, the auctioneer, in co-operation with bidders, has to implement an organisational arrangement whereby the potential contributions of multiple participants, many of whom might wish to bid if the price is right, are organised through an orderly sequence of turns, where those turns, to draw on Harvey Sacks, Emanuel Schegloff and Gail Jefferson (1974) are 'valued', literally in this case.

It is worthwhile considering one or two examples. Extract 6.1 is drawn from a sale of important Old Master pictures at a leading London auction house. The painting in question is widely considered one of the two 'sleepers' of the sale: a previously unknown masterpiece that is likely to achieve significantly more than its catalogue estimate of £20,000–£30,000. The auctioneer introduces the lot and attempts to open the bidding at £15,000. For convenience, and to preserve the anonymity of the participants, we have simplified the transcripts and represented bidding by numbering particular bidders in the order they enter the bidding, for example B.1 for bidders based in the room or SA.1 for the sales assistants representing those bidding over the telephone. We have also indicated when bidders withdraw.

Extract 6.1 (abbreviated)

A: Lot Twenty Two (2.1) Argh:: Lot Twenty Two (1.0) The
     studio of Anthony van Dyck (2.1) a:::n::d (2.1) <fif-
     teen thousand to open it (0.3) At fifteen thousand
     pounds. (0.3) [B.1] At sixteen thousand I see,
     already. At sixteen thou:sand in the room. At sixteen
     thousand pounds: (0.2) At sixteen, standing. [B.2]
     Seventeen thousand
        (.) [B.1]

A: Eighteen thousand
     (0.2) [B.2]
A: Bidding? Nineteen thousand
     [B.1]
A: Twenty thousand
     (0.2) [B.2]
A: Twenty two thousand
     (sequence omitted)
A: Forty two thousand
     (0.2) [B.2]
A: Forty five thousand
     (0.2) [B.1]
A: Forty eight thousand
     (0.4) [B.2]
A: Fifty thousand
     (0.2) [B.1]
A: Fifty five thousand
     (0.4) [B.2 withdraws]
A: At fifty five: thousand. Standing at fifty five thousand
     [B.3]
A: Sixty thousand
     (0.2) [B.1]
A: <Sixty five thousand>
     (0.3) [B.3]
A: Seventy thousand
     (0.2) [B.1]
A: Seventy five thousand
     (sequence omitted)
A: Ninety thousand
     (1.2) [B.1 withdraws]
A: At ninety thousand now::. On my right (.) > At ninety
     thousand on my right. At ninety thousand pounds (0.5)
     Coming in lots of places.
     (0.2) [SA.1]
A: Ninety five thousand (.) with Susan
     (0.5) [B.3]
A: One hundred thousand
     (2.3) [SA.1 withdraws]
A: >At one hundred thousand pounds<
     (0.3) [B.4]
A: One hundred an ten thousand
     (1.2) [B.3]

```
A:   One hundred and twenty thousand
     (4.2) [B.4]
A:   One hundred and thirty thousand
     (2.3) [B.3]
A:   *One hundred an forty thousand
     (4.2) [B.4 withdraws]
A:   *At one hundred an forty thousand (2.3) One hundred, an
     forty (0.5) <thousand pounds: (3.4) In the room
     (0.5) and selling it
     (0.2) [SA.2]
A:   One hundred an fifty thousand.
     (13.5) [B.3 withdraws]
A:   To Jane now (0.7) At one (0.2) hundred (0.2) an fifty
     (0.3) <thousand pounds: (0.3) Against you in the door-
     way (0.3) At one (.) hundred (.) an fifty (0.2) >thou-
     sand pounds (0.2) {Knock}
```

Irrespective of the values that potential buyers may have in mind, following the introduction of the lot and its description, bidding is organised in terms of a series of increments that rapidly escalate the price, in this case from £15,000. The increments remain stable through certain values, £1,000 until £20,000, then increments of £2,000, of £2,000 and £3,000, £5,000 and then £10,000. With only one bidder remaining, the painting is finally sold, on the fall of the gavel or hammer, at £150,000, ten times its opening price. The auctioneer announces each bid after it has been made, for example 'sixteen thousand I see already'. He then seeks a next bid and announces the bid when it is made: for example 'seventeen thousand', indicating an increment of £1,000. It is the auction house that ordinarily determines the incremental structure so that once a second bid is announced all those within the room know the values that will serve to escalate the price of the goods within a certain set of values. The pauses are occupied by the auctioneer inviting particular participants to bid followed by bidders indicating whether they are prepared to accept the next increment.

Once an incremental structure is established, it projects the series of prices that serve to escalate the price of the goods at least for a certain range of values. In consequence, following the announcement of the second bid all those present know at any point what it will take to advance the price of the goods. The value of each increment, and the incremental structure that is used for the sale of each lot, depends on the current price of the lot, and it is not unusual for the leading auction houses to detail the incremental scale associated with particular values at the back of the auction catalogue that accompanies the sale. Occasionally auctioneers may use a different scale or change the scale during the sale of a lot. For example auctioneers may split increments to encourage further bidding, or jump increments, to reduce the number of willing bidders. Nevertheless, in establishing an incremental scale, the auctioneer escalates the price of goods in a systematic and transparent fashion that does not favour, nor respond to the whim of, a particular buyer. It allows the price of the goods to be rapidly and efficiently escalated in values that are transparent to all those with an interest in the goods.

In Extract 6.1 a total of six different participants successfully bid. There are other potential buyers who attempt to bid but are excluded from contributing; for example at £90,000 the auctioneer states that bids are 'coming in lots of places'. The serial escalation of price does not involve numerous bidders, but rather the successive contributions of two participants. In receiving a first bid, the auctioneer identifies a second potential buyer, takes a bid at the projected next increment, and returns to the original bidder to invite the next bid. In Extract 6.1 we find a number of exchanges in which the bids of two potential buyers are juxtaposed: B.1 and B.2, from £16,000 to £55,000 (when B.2 withdraws), B.1 and B.3 until £90,000 (when B.1 withdraws), B.3 and SA.1 until £100,000 (when SA.1 withdraws), B.3 and B.4 until £140,000 (when B.4 withdraws) and finally SA.2 at £150,000 (when B.3 withdraws).

The escalation of price at auctions of fine art and antiques is based on the 'run'. The auctioneer establishes, or seeks to establish, *two bidders and no more than two bidders at any one time*. The principle is applied irrespective of the value of the object or the scale of the increments, whether it is £5, £5,000 or £500,000. With stable incremental scales, the run forms the foundation of the organisation through which auctions are accomplished in an orderly manner.

Establishing two bidders and no more than two bidders provides the auctioneer with a way of initiating direct competition between two principal protagonists. It also provides a resource for disregarding the potential or actual contributions of others that, if acknowledged, would disrupt the flow and rapid escalation of the price. As Extract 6.1 reveals, the participation of further bidders is postponed until one bidder withdraws. At that place the auctioneer undertakes a search to identify a new bidder to replace the participant who has just withdrawn. In Extract 6.1, one of the two bidders declines to bid at £55,000, at £90,000, at £100,000, at £140,000 and finally at £150,000. For instance:

Extract 6.1.1

A: Fifty five thousand
        (0.4) [B.2 withdraws]
A: At fifty five: thousand. Standing at fifty five thousand
        [B.3]
A: Sixty thousand

In the first four cases the auctioneer successfully identifies a new bidder. When the auctioneer fails to find a new bidder, the goods are sold if they have reached the reserve, that is, the lowest price that the vendor is prepared to accept. The transition of bidders at auction is localised to times when one bidder declines to make a further bid and the auctioneer identifies, and accepts a bid from, a new potential buyer.

One further point is worth mentioning at this stage. In establishing a run, the auctioneer not only projects a series of increments and distributes those increments between two specific bidders, but also establishes the pace and rhythm at which bids are elicited and voiced. The pace and rhythm of bidding vary between bidders, different types of auction and the auctioneer's ability to encourage potential buyers to respond to projected increments with dispatch, enabling the floor to be rapidly passed to the second bidder. The pace and the rhythm of bidding are of some importance. They can help sustain the involvement and commitment of bidders and more generally of participants, some of whom may spend many hours waiting for particular lots to come up for sale. They can also serve to enable participants, both buyers and auctioneers, to draw inferences concerning the willingness of particular bidders to remain in the run. It is not unusual, for example, when there is a small delay before an individual bids at the next increment, to find those in the sale room preparing to write down the selling price of a particular lot, or auctioneers beginning to look for a new bidder to replace the participant they anticipate will withdraw. In some circumstances the auctioneers will articulate the next bid more forcefully to encourage the participant to go a further increment, enabling the run to be sustained and goods to reach their reserve and be sold.

Revealing the source and integrity of bids

The ability of auctions to resolve the price and exchange of goods of uncertain value is founded upon the authenticity of bids: that bids are genuine contributions from potential buyers or their representatives and reflect actual demand for the goods in question. The conduct of auctioneers during the sale is critical in this regard, particularly the ways in which they invite, acknowledge and juxtapose bids; this is important in establishing people's belief and trust in the process and the eventual price that goods achieve.

In announcing bids, auctioneers go to some trouble to reveal the source of a bid. The entry of a new bidder, and the establishment of a run, frequently involves the auctioneer in revealing the location of the bidder in some cases by explicitly describing their position – 'back of the room' or 'front row', or the involvement of remote bidders as in 'with Jane on the telephone'. Even as the run develops over successive increments, the auctioneer, through bodily orientation, visual alignment and sometimes gesture, displays the source of each bid and, in seeking agreement to the next increment, will enable both the potential bidder and all those gathered in the room to see who has the opportunity to bid at that moment. Consider, for example, the first run in Extract 6.1. As he announces each increment, the auctioneer gestures towards the bidder, alternating between his left hand and his right with regard to the bidder's respective location within the room.

The ability of a gesture and the accompanying visual and bodily re-orientation of the auctioneer to unambiguously discriminate a

Nineteen thousand   Twenty thousand

Figure 6.1. The auctioneer gesturing towards the bidder (from Extract 6.1)

participant from the audience is dependent upon a practice that selects particular individuals at particular moments within the developing course of the activity. It enables participants to know when it is their turn within an organisational arrangement that severely constrains participation, in particular the opportunity to bid. The gestures, visual and bodily re-orientation that accompany successive announcement of increments serve to demarcate and display the timely contribution of specific participants and thereby reproduce the procedure, 'two and no more than two bidders at any one time'.

Bids from a member of the audience or via the telephone are not the only source of bids received by the auctioneer. Potential buyers who are unable to attend the sale may leave bids on commission with the auction house. These bids, the highest price that the buyer is prepared to pay for a particular lot, are documented on the sales sheets or auctioneer's book. Auctioneers use their own discretion to bid on behalf of the potential buyer until the lot is secured or the commission is beaten by a bid in the room or on the telephone. Less commonly known, at least outside the trade, is that auctioneers may also bid on behalf of the vendor up until one increment below the reserve. The convention is described at the rear of some auction catalogues and is a practice that is followed by many major auction houses dealing with fine art and antiques, including Sotheby's and Christie's.

Commission bids and bidding on behalf of the vendor raise an important issue concerning the integrity of sales by auction and the reliability of the price that goods achieve. Indeed, auctioneers are some-times accused of simply creating bids for their own convenience, and indeed commission bids and bidding on behalf of the vendor (a prac-tice that the state is currently attempting to outlaw in New York) are important resources for auctioneers. They provide the auctioneer with the opportunity to establish a run and escalate the price where there is only one bidder or in some cases where there is no bidder at all. Taking a bid 'from the chandelier', 'off the wall' or 'from the book' – that is, bidding on behalf of an absent buyer or the vendor, or occasionally on behalf of no one at all – plays an important part in establishing competi-tion and escalating the price in an orderly and systematic manner. Moreover, it is in the auctioneer's interest to escalate the price of the goods until they have reached their reserve and, if possible, well in excess of that figure. If the article does not sell, the auction house does not receive its fee or receives a reduced fee and, in general, the higher the price the article reaches the higher the commission received by the auction house (up to 25% of the hammer price paid by the vendor and the buyers' premium of between 10% and 25%). The reserve price and commission bids are documented on the confidential sales sheets or auctioneer's book that rest on the podium directly before the auctioneer.

Consider Extract 6.2. The auctioneer has a number of bids left on commission and three telephone lines have been booked – worked by sale room assistants. It is worth noting that, in accordance with the practice of this particular auction house, the incremental structure changes at £1,000. The auctioneer initiates the sale by announcing a bid of £900 and then looks around the room to find a participant prepared to bid. Bids on commission are shown by 'A' and positioned with their announcement by the auctioneer.

Extract 6.2

A: Lot One Sixty Five and (0.3) [A.] nine hundred is
     already bid with me. At nine hundred pounds, at nine
     hundred pounds and against the room.
       [SA.1]
A: Nine fifty. One thou<u>sand</u> [A.] with me. (0.3) At one
     thousand
       (0.5) [SA.1]
     Eleven hundred with Gina
A: Twelve hundred [A.] with me and against you.
       (1.4) [SA.1]
A: Thirteen hundred with Gina (.) I'm out. At thirteen
     hundred with Gina
       [SA.2]
A: Fourteen hundred with John
       (2.3) [SA.1]
A: Fifteen hundred
       (1.5) [SA.2]
A: Sixteen hundred. (3.0) No? Sixteen hundred it's John's
     bid at sixteen hundred. (0.8) {Knock}

The auctioneer takes the first, the starting bid, from a commission noted in the sales sheets. He announces that the bid is 'with me' and simultaneously turns towards and gestures at the sales sheets lying on the podium (see Figure 6.2). He then places the thumb and forefinger of his left hand erect on the page so that is visible to those in the sale room. With 'against the room' two sale room assistants attempt to bid on behalf of telephone buyers. He selects one of the two assistants, Gina,

'[SA.1 bids] Nine fifty'   'One thousand [A.] bids] with me'
gestures towards sale room   points at hand on book
assistant

Figure 6.2. The auctioneer indicating a bid from the sales sheet (from Extract 6.2)

gestures towards her and announces a bid of £950. He takes the next
bid off commission. With his thumb and forefinger still positioned on
the page, he announces 'one thousand with me' and points with his right
hand to his left that remains pointing at the sales sheet. He establishes a
run between the commission and a sales assistant, and as he announces
each increment, he gestures towards either Gina or the book. Prior to
announcing the bid of 'thirteen hundred', he removes his left hand from
the sales sheets and declares that he, the commission buyer, is out. He
then establishes a second run between Gina and a second sales assistant,
John, who secures the lot for his client at £1,600.

The auctioneer decomposes the commission, the maximum price that
the buyer is prepared to pay for the lot, into a series of increments and in
this way uses the commission to establish competition with buyers in
the room or, in this case, those on the telephone represented by sales
assistants. In taking bids from the sales sheets the auctioneer acts as a
surrogate buyer and, in each and every case, displays the source of the
bid as he announces the increment. He also gestures towards and points
at the sales assistants as he announces their bids, both as Gina competes
with the commission and as the two sales assistants finally compete with
each other for the lot in question. These successive announcements and

their accompanying gestures serve not only to reveal to bidders their current position, but also to display, to all those present, the source of the bid and the current price.

The ways in which bids are voiced and revealed, whether from the sales sheets, a buyer in the room or a remote participant represented by a sale room assistant, enable all those present to witness the successive and contingent articulation of bids from a seemingly independent source: independent of the interests and commitments of the auctioneer who voices the increments and 'mediates' the competition. In voicing the current increment, the auctioneer uses his visual and bodily orientation to invite the next bid, to acknowledge bids from particular participants and to render their contribution visible both to those in the run and to all those gathered in the room (see Heath and Luff 2007a). The gestures are designed to delineate and demarcate the bids and the source of those bids. They enable the audience to witness the progressive emergence of the price with regard to the actions of the protagonists, including in this case the auctioneer himself. The sales sheet or book is rendered visible to the bidders and the audience, in a sense for all to see, and treated as if it is a source of independent bids that the auctioneer is simply voicing on behalf of another. Even the withdrawal of the commission from the bidding is voiced and illustrated gesturally, enabling bidders, potential bidders and those in the room to see for themselves the state of play, as if the person who left the commission bid was there as an active participant in the room.

Establishing and preserving runs

Auctioneers do not take bids off commission or from the vendor at any place within the emerging sale of a lot, but rather organise bidding to enable certain combinations of bids to be taken at particular stages within the proceedings. Differentiating the source and selection of bids provides an important resource in eliciting contributions and establishing runs, as well as in enhancing the transparency and legitimacy of the process. Consider Extract 6.3.

Extract 6.3

A: Lot number: (0.2) Four Three Three (.) Four Three Three
        the lot number: now. Bidding here at one hundred pounds
        now.
            (.) [A.]

One ten <u>is there</u>.   One ten I'amd bid. One ten.   One twenty on commission now.

Figure 6.3. The auctioneer indicating a bid 'on commission' (from Extract 6.3)

A: A hundred pounds I'm bid straight away for <u>this</u>, at a
     hundred pounds:, (.) One hundred pounds (will do it)
     One hundred one ten (.) n<u>ow</u>:? (0.3) A hundred pounds
     only. One hundred pounds, one hundred pounds. One ten
     <u>now</u> quickly?
         (0.3) [B.1 bids; B.2 attempts to bid]
A: One ten <u>is</u> <u>there</u>. One ten I'm bid. One ten. [A.] One
     twenty on commission now. One thirty now:? One twenty
     still with me, at one twenty.
         [B.2 bids]
A: One thirty bid <u>there</u>: fresh bid, one thirty, one
     thirty. F<u>or</u>ty now:? (0.2) At a hundred an thirty pounds
     (.) bi<u>ds</u> there at one thirty. Do show if you happen to
     have an extra bid. At one thirty over there. {Knock}

The auctioneer takes the first bid from commission. With the
announcement of the first bid, he attempts to find someone within the
room willing to bid at the next increment. He rapidly repeats the current
increment whilst looking at different areas and individuals within the
room. As he voices the next increment, with 'one ten now quickly', two
people in the room raise their hands. The auctioneer announces 'one ten
<u>is there</u>' and points at one of the bidders. He repeats the increment and
then announces the next bid, 'one twenty'. Rather than seek to take a
bid from the other party in the room, the bid of 'one twenty' is once
again taken 'on commission', from the book. In announcing the bid, the
auctioneer gestures first towards himself and then the book on
the podium.

Despite having two participants bidding in the sale room, the
auctioneer creates a run between a commission, an absentee buyer
and a participant within the room. The commission enables a starting
bid to be announced and provides a vehicle through which the contributions of individuals within the room may be juxtaposed. Indeed, the

auctioneer disregards one of the potential buyers within the room to enable the price of the goods to be escalated with respect to the commission bid. He prioritises the commission over the contributions of a particular individual in the room at this stage and creates a run between an absentee buyer and one participant in the room. He selects the bidder in the room on the basis of first come, first served, B.1 raising his hand slightly in advance of B.2 during the utterance 'one ten now quickly'.

In this regard, it is worth adding that, on taking a commission bid at £120, the auctioneer turns to the individual who bid 'one ten' and invites him to bid at the next increment 'One thirty now:?' In other words, he attempts to sustain a run between the commission and the first bidder. The bidder declines and the auctioneer reiterates the current increment and the source of the bid. Rather than undertake a general search for a new bidder, the auctioneer turns to the bidder he excluded earlier and utters 'at one twenty'. He bids, and with the commission having reached its maximum, secures the goods at £130. In prioritising the commission from the outset, and in taking two and no more than two bidders at any one time, the auctioneer disregards the contributions of particular participants. He can then return to those participants to see if they are willing to bid at later increments and thereby ease the transition between the runs. It provides the auctioneer with a sense of who might be interested in a lot prior to actually accepting their bid(s).

Commission bids or bids on behalf of the vendor enable the auctioneer to initiate bidding and begin the sale of the lot even though there may be no one willing to literally 'show their hand'. In some cases, auctioneers will even produce a run based on commission and vendor bids alone until there is someone willing to bid within the room. Taking such bids enables the auctioneer to establish a sense of demand and a pace of activity and to encourage a sense of urgency amongst any interested parties, parties that may be reluctant to bid first. Creating a run or runs from the outset using commission bids, rather than introducing them at some subsequent stage, also contributes to the transparency of the process. It is not simply that there is an apparent order, or principle, underlying their production, but that the auctioneer is not seen to introduce bids in a seemingly strategic manner – to increase the price where a second bidder cannot be found.

With the run forming the foundation to the escalation of price at auction and the eventual sale of the goods, auctioneers use various techniques in order to sustain bidding, techniques that, for example,

are not infrequently deployed in cases where the reserve has yet to
be achieved and where there is little indication that new bidders are
preparing to enter the fray. A common practice is to offer to split the
increment as in 'I'll take twenty-five if it helps you' and at other times
auctioneers try to persuade, even cajole, the under-bidder to go one
more bid. Remarks such as 'don't let him put you off, madam', 'just
one more, sir, and you will knock him out' or more curiously 'it's only
money, sir; you can have plenty of fun with this' can prove surprisingly
successful in encouraging a further bid. More often than not, however,
auctioneers encourage or attempt to encourage further bids in a more
subtle and implicit fashion, at least initially, rather than cajoling a
participant to go a further increment.

Consider Extract 6.4 where the auctioneer makes a number of
attempts (most of which numbered alongside the transcript) to elicit a
further bid from the under-bidder. We join the following sale as the
auctioneer announces a bid at £1,700 and turns to the under-bidder to
invite her to bid the next increment (£1,800). Prior to the completion of
the figure 'seventeen' the under-bidder looks down towards her left and
the mouths the word 'no'.

Extract 6.4

A:	Seventeen
B.3:	*No (1.2)
i. A:	Sev:::enteen:: Seventeen (best to get it right).
	(.) That's fine (.) Seventeen at the moment
	(0.4)
ii. A:	No? Thank you madam (0.2) At seventeen then on the
	far left
	(0.4)
iii. A:	Last chance madam
	(0.2)
iv. A:	Seventeen hundred pounds:
	(1.2)
v. A:	No? (0.6) Yes? (.) [B. 3 bids] Eighteen hundred well
	done
A:	Eighteen hundred now thank you
	(.)
A:	Nineteen sir? (.) Nineteen hundred
A:	(Sorry) well done (.) Nice? (0.4) Nineteen. What
	do you want me to sell it quickly sir? Nineteen
	hundred on his phone. Nineteen:: hundred {Knock}

Figure 6.4. Pursuing a bid (from Extract 6.4)

Rather than look for a new participant to establish a run, the auctioneer provides the under-bidder with the opportunity to change her mind
and encourages her to make a further bid. He continues to look at her
and smiles. She looks up and returns his smile, and he produces 'Sev:::
enteen::'. With 'Sev:::enteen::' she once again declines to bid, producing
a negative or lateral head nod. He does not accept the declination, but
continues to look directly at her and reiterates the invitation to bid with
'Seventeen (best to get it right)'. She once again declines to bid, producing a negative head nod and turns away smiling. The auctioneer
initially accepts the declination and with 'That's fine (.) Seventeen at the
moment', turns from the under-bidder and looks for a new bidder.
Almost immediately he turns back to the under-bidder to have her
reconfirm her declination. Once again he looks for a new bidder turning
first to his right, including the sales assistants working the phones, and
then to his left. He fails to find anyone willing to bid and turns back to
the under-bidder and utters 'last chance madam'. She turns towards the
auctioneer but does not bid, and he once more looks around the sale
room repeating the current increment 'seventeen hundred pounds:'.
Once more failing to find anyone willing to bid, the auctioneer
returns to the under-bidder and with 'No? (0.6) Yes?', producing a
rocking, equivocal gesture, that successively offers the opportunity to
bid. She confirms 'Yes?', bidding the next increment, £1,800. The
auctioneer turns immediately to the second bidder in the run and
successfully elicits a bid at the next increment, namely £1,900.
Despite some resistance, the auctioneer successfully elicits a further
bid from the under-bidder and thereby sustains the run, adding a further
two increments to the sale price of the goods. The very ways in which
the under-bidder declines the initial and subsequent invitations to bid,
and her willingness to visually re-engage, enable the auctioneer not only
to have a sense that she may be ambivalent about withdrawing from the

bidding, but directly and personally to pursue her for a further bid. By responding to and displaying recipiency to the auctioneer (Heath 1986), the under-bidder subjects herself to the possibility of repeated attempts to elicit a bid, attempts that are visible and audible to the under-bidder, and witnessed by all those gathered within the sale room. In various ways, the auctioneer upgrades the opportunity, inviting, encouraging, even cajoling her to bid a further increment.

Unfortunately for the under-bidder, as in many instances, her additional bid elicits a further bid from the principal protagonist. In this case a relatively small amount is added to sale price of the goods, just £200 (allowing the goods to achieve their reserve), but in some cases where the auctioneer successfully encourages the under-bidder to go a further increment, £50,000 or even £100,000 may be added to the final sale price of the goods, significantly adding to the commission earned by the auction house.

Market activities: institutional forms and interactional organisation

Auctions provide an institutional solution to the pricing and exchange of goods of uncertain value. In turn they pose a number of problems and issues that have to be addressed within the practical accomplishment of the sale. As an institutional solution to a social problem, auction houses and auctioneers mediate exchange between vendors and buyers, providing a neutral and robust mechanism that does not favour particular interests or parties and enables demand to be transparently revealed and price escalated until sold to the highest bidder. As Charles Smith (1990: 90) suggests, 'the need to establish the legitimacy of price and allocation informs auctions from top to bottom'. While the reputation of particular houses, the ways in which they organise and promote sales, and the limited legislation that applies to the sale of goods at auction may contribute to the legitimacy of sales, auctions rely upon a body of socially organised practice that enables the fair and transparent valuation and exchange of goods to be systematically accomplished within these brief, recurrent, yet highly contingent, episodes of interaction.

These problems and issues are resolved by virtue of a social organisation, an interactional arrangement that selectively focuses participation whilst creating specific opportunities for anyone present (or represented) to bid for the goods in question. The organisation enables the auctioneer to establish competition between specific individuals whilst simultaneously rendering that competition, their participation, and the eventual sale transparent and witnessable to all those who happen to be present. The systematic escalation of price is accomplished through the creation of the run, in which bidding involves two and no more than two bidders at a time. It limits and localises the number of 'active' participants that might at any single moment affect the price of an object. Specific incremental scales render the escalation of the price visible and predictable, so that at any point a bidder and all those who are present know where things stand and what it will take to advance the price. The introduction of new bidders is localised to a point at which one bidder's withdrawal gives the auctioneer the opportunity to invite others to enter the bidding: first come, first served. The auctioneer (re-)establishes a run, until only one bidder remains. The articulation of each bid is designed to simultaneously acknowledge one party's bid and elicit the next, and to render visible to all those present the current price and the source of the contribution. In these and various other ways, an 'interaction order' is deployed that systematically escalates the price of goods until only one bidder remains, enabling the legitimate transfer of ownership.

These practices render the process visible, transparent, witnessed and witnessable: the sale is not only done, but seen and shown to be done, in an ordered, fair and accountable manner. Trust in, and the legitimacy of, the price and transfer of ownership of goods is accomplished in and through this interactional organisation, a body of socially organised practice that simultaneously structures and renders transparent the actions of particular participants.

As Gerald Reitlinger (1982) demonstrates, general trends in the value of particular goods mask significant variation in the price and value achieved for particular types of goods even within the same auction. In directing analytic attention towards the contingent and interactional organisation of the auction process we can begin to discover a range of situated, contextually relevant issues that bear upon the market's accomplishment and the outcomes it produces. Whilst we agree with Charles Smith that there might be little to be gained 'in believing that economics has much to offer sociologists interested in understanding real auctions' (1991: 1541), it may be the case that detailed studies of auction practice and interaction contribute to an understanding of economics and its findings. Consider for example the wide-ranging and insightful corpus of studies by Orley Ashenfelter and his colleagues concerned with auctions and in particular art auctions (see for instance Ashenfelter 1989 and Ashenfelter and Graddy 2002). These studies suggest that auction houses are generally truthful: there is a high correlation between the price received and the average of the auctioneer's high and low estimates. Our own research would suggest that it is problematic, analytically, to disassociate the estimate from the ways in which price is accomplished at auction. In the first place, a significant proportion of commission bids and, one suspects, bids from telephone buyers and those in the room are sensitive to, if not based on, the estimates documented by the auction house. Secondly, it is widely recognised that estimates, coupled with the reserve to which they are intimately related, play an important role in the ways in which auctioneers escalate the price and the trouble they will take to progress the value of the goods to a particular figure. As we have seen, auctioneers can successfully encourage further bids from reluctant participants and thereby significantly add to the value of particular goods enabling, in some cases, those goods to reach their reserve and thereby be sold. In other words, the very outcome of an auction, including the price that goods achieve, is highly contingent and dependent on the practices in and through which auctioneers elicit, juxtapose and co-ordinate bids. To corrupt John Maynard Keynes (1936), conventions in the ways of working may serve to reflexively constitute the very outcomes – in this case, the prices – that are anticipated.

More generally, it is not clear that the growing corpus of ethnographic studies of markets and the debates regarding the cultural embeddedness of economic behaviour, agency, participation, the economic constitution of economies and performativity (see for example Abolafia 1988, 1996; Callon 1998, 2005; Miller 2002; A. Barry and Slater 2002; Woolgar 2004) provide the conceptual or methodological resources to gain analytic purchase on the fundamentally social and interactional foundations of the activities that enable the exchange of goods. As Karin Knorr Cetina and Urs Bruegger (2002: 910) suggest in their discussion of cambist markets 'these sequences of utterances (and in this case gestures, bodily actions and the like) do not just convey information, but perform economic actions'. As Abolafia (1988) hints, all too often the idea of markets as cultures leads to an emphasis on the character and characteristics of institutional forms and sociopolitical processes and glosses the contingent accomplishment of market activity, and the resources, practices and forms of rationality on which it relies. In consequence, the institution, its characteristics and its culture bear the analytic burden with little regard to the ordinary action and interaction that underpins market activity such as an auction. In disregarding the interactional, the concepts and ideas that are central to much of the emerging sociology of markets – concepts and ideas such as agency, embeddedness, interdependence and the like – remain largely unexplicated, and the situated and contingent character of ordinary day-to-day operation of markets is rendered epiphenomenal.

It has long been recognised that institutional forms, social networks and macrostructures – the 'social orders of markets' (Beckert 2007) – emerge within, are dependent on and are sustained through social interaction. The 'interaction orders', to use Erving Goffman's (1983) term, and the social and endogenous organisations on which they rely, remain presupposed and largely unaddressed by studies of markets, and yet they form the very foundation to the activities and arenas of social interaction that enable their accomplishment. Like a small but growing number of recent studies (for example Knorr Cetina and Bruegger 2002; C. Clark and Pinch 1995a; C. Clark, Drew and Pinch 1994, 2003), we are concerned with discovering and explicating the ways in which institutional forms and structure emerge within and are sustained through social interaction. In this way we can begin to examine how fleeting moments of interaction serve to systematically accomplish markets and begin to reflect upon and re-consider some of the key concepts and ideas that underpin studies of markets. As Tony Lawson (1995) suggests, the analysis of markets and economic behaviour should entail in the first instance an 'elaboration of the human practices responsible'. Those practices are inextricably embodied, articulated and sustained in and through social interaction. As organisational arrangements, these passing moments of interaction are of some significance to contemporary economics and economies, as well as to studies of market behaviour and social institutions.

7 Some major organisational consequences of some 'minor', organised conduct: evidence from a video analysis of pre-verbal service encounters in a showroom retail store

COLIN CLARK AND TREVOR PINCH

Introduction

This chapter reports the results of an analysis of the ways shoppers regularly occasioned (or attempted to occasion) or avoided (or attempted to avoid) verbal encounters with salespeople in a retail store. These everyday events are of vital importance for retail researchers and practitioners as they not only precede and influence but also make possible the various economic outcomes (notably product sales) that comprise the very *raison d'être* of the type of retailers we examine. More specifically, our study reveals that the different kinds of pre-verbal encounter conduct the shoppers engaged in to accomplish these actions are underpinned with and managed through a complex, integrated framework of socially organised communicative practices that, along with the interactional 'rules', expectations, obligations and other situational factors which also inform these actions, comprise a highly economically consequential, underexplored and commonly misunderstood dimension of the retail shopping and selling process.

Our work builds on a growing body of research illustrating the fundamentally social and interactional basis of buying, selling and consumer conduct in real-life settings as diverse as street markets and TV infomercials (Pinch and Clark 1986; C. Clark and Pinch 1988, 1995a, 1995b), auctions and mock auctions (C. Clark and Pinch 1992; Heath and Luff 2007b), street entertainment and street vending (Mulkay and Howe 1994; C. Clark and Pinch 1995a; Llewellyn and Burrow 2008), telephone sales (C. Clark, Drew and Pinch 1994; Mazeland 2004), business-to-business selling (Mulkay, Clark and Pinch 1993; C. Clark, Drew and Pinch 2003) and retail and service encounters (Garfinkel and

140

Livingston 2003; B. Brown 2004; C. Clark 2004). In contrast to the more traditional methods researchers and practitioners usually employ to understand retail shopping and selling (surveys, interviews, direct observation, personal experience, focus groups, secret shopper studies and so forth),[1] the data base and methodology we have employed – the detailed analysis of real-life video recordings of retail shoppers' and salespeople's own evident interactional practices – provide perhaps the only way that the subtle conduct and the largely tacit, constitutive communicative processes we examine could ever be captured and properly appreciated. Indeed, as we shall see, our findings cast doubt on many of the shopper contact-related assumptions widely held by retailers as well as on much of the prescriptive advice that retailing companies, trainers and authors of 'How to' books tend to provide for the salespeople working in the type of store we studied. These data, this research focus and these research findings also provide a novel and systematically different foundation by which it is possible to more accurately (1) understand how and why shoppers and salespeople evidently behave in the ways they do; (2) determine the causes and consequences of their particular conduct; and (3) formulate practicable solutions to any problems that arise out of this conduct and the encounters these parties have with one another. In these respects our study also has direct relevance for researchers working in the areas of consumer product involvement and service quality and, more generally, for organisations seeking to better understand how their employees could interact more effectively with others, particularly members of the public.

(Mis)understanding retail encounters

In the predominantly prescriptive literature on retail selling there is an almost ubiquitous assumption that encounters between salespeople and shoppers begin from the point at which verbal contact commences between these parties.[2] However, by making this assumption – even though, intuitively, it has an 'obvious common-sense' ring of plausibility about it – the authors of this literature commit three fundamental errors. First, they tend to place more weight than appears justified on the importance of the first words a salesperson says to a shopper, claiming that, when wisely chosen, such words are likely to have a major influence on whether a shopper accepts a salesperson's approach and, ultimately, whether a contacting salesperson can persuade a shopper to make a purchase. For example, Yvonne Bodle and Joseph Corey (1977: 241) claim that 'The first five to ten words spoken to a customer are the most important words in a sale.' Many authors also argue that retail salespeople must avoid using clichéd, contact-opening utterances such as 'Can I help you?' when approaching shoppers and list the verbal gambits salespeople should employ to forestall dismissive, 'I'm just looking', types of shopper responses to occasion an encounter and to generate sales (e.g. 'Would you prefer that [i.e. the product the shopper is looking at] in the black or the silver colour?' – see e.g. Bodle and Corey 1977; Rogers 1988; M. Brown and Tilling 1997; Kennon 2006). In our data, however, these verbal gambits and, indeed, the salespeople's first words more generally had no discernible impact on whether a shopper accepted a verbal encounter initiated by a salesperson or subsequently made a purchase.

Secondly, this literature tends to ignore or pay only cursory attention to the verbal encounter-related activities that take place *before* any verbal contact occurs between a salesperson and a shopper. Occasionally, mention is made of the importance of a salesperson establishing eye contact with or smiling at a shopper prior to making a verbal approach (Bodle and Corey 1977; Rogers 1988; Kennon 2006), or 'sizing up' a customer by observing, for example, their clothing, the way they walk, their facial expressions or which particular merchandise they pause to look at or touch (Charters 1922; Rogers 1988). The main objective of a salesperson establishing eye contact or smiling is usually said to be that of conveying 'politeness' or 'confidence' (e.g. Kennon 2006: 40), informing the shopper that 'you know that they are there' (e.g. Rogers 1988), or generating a friendly, pleasant atmosphere (e.g. Bodle and Corey 1977: 241). Furthermore, the aim of such shopper observation or contact is typically stated to be to assist salespeople to achieve sales rather than to help them make better decisions about how, when or if a shopper should be approached. In our data, though, a great deal of crucially important encounter-related shopper activity – particularly the establishment of mutual eye contact with salespeople, and shoppers' displays of involvement with store merchandise – occurred before any verbal contact between these parties took place. This almost exclusively *bodily* conduct, the various manifestations and social organisation of which form the focus of our chapter, had a decisive influence on whether a salesperson and shopper ever established a verbal encounter with one another (and therefore whether a sale became possible) and the kinds of service quality perceptions the shoppers were likely to form about the store or the sales staff.

Thirdly, the assumption that persons are engaged in an encounter with one another only when they have started to talk with one another also rests on a fundamental misunderstanding about what actually constitutes an interpersonal encounter. This assumption flies in the face of a well-established sociological research literature, pioneered by Erving Goffman (e.g. 1959, 1963) and subsequently conducted by other researchers, primarily conversation analysts, via the analysis of recordings of the deployment of bodily conduct in naturally occurring interactions (e.g. C. Goodwin 1981; Heath 1986; Schegloff 1998a; Robinson 1998). One thing this research has demonstrated is that when people 'are in one another's presence, subject to the contingencies of mutual monitoring' (Goffman 1963: 13–30; Schegloff 1998a: 565) – that is, when they can see or hear one another and realise they may, in turn, be seen or heard by those other people – their conduct is liable to be influenced by those people, even though they may not verbally or formally be interacting with them or even able to see one another. As we will see, the shoppers and salespeople we studied were regularly in such 'non'-encounters with one another. Furthermore, the highly distinctive forms of pre-verbal encounter bodily conduct the shoppers engaged in embodied and projected systematically different types of socially and economically consequential shopper identities that were routinely undertaken with particular regard to the sales staff, even when no explicit recognition or acknowledgement of the latter's presence in the store was apparent.[3]

Data analysed

Our data comprise video recordings of one 9.00 a.m. to 6.00 p.m. working day's worth of naturally occurring shopping and sales activity involving 317 shoppers and 5 'roaming' sales staff in a UK showroom retail store.[4] Because there were important differences in the pre-verbal encounter conduct of the shoppers depending on whether they were on their own or in groups, we occasionally use the terms 'shopping units' (SUs) when referring to individual shoppers or shoppers in general, and 'multi-person shopping units' (MPSUs) when referring exclusively to shoppers in groups. We studied 253 SUs, of which 74 (29.2 per cent) made a purchase.

With respect to the particular subject of our study, these SUs comprised two types of shoppers – those who established a verbal encounter with a salesperson (i.e. where verbal contact was initiated by one party and accepted by another) ($n = 156$; 61.7%) and those who did not ($n = 97$; 38.3%). Each SU also tended to adopt and to maintain one of four distinct forms of pre-verbal encounter bodily conduct via which they displayed their different encounter-related and purchase/non-purchase related shopper identities, particularly when they were stationary and looking at store merchandise: (1) 'open-to-contact SUs' ($n = 61$) – who established a verbal encounter with a salesperson in what transpired to be a relatively straightforward and unproblematic way; (2) 'actively seeking contact SUs' ($n = 98$) – whose bodily conduct was characteristically the same as open-to-contact SUs except that they engaged in additional work on one or more occasions to establish a verbal encounter with a salesperson; (3) 'browsing SUs' ($n = 35$) – who neither actively sought nor tended to occasion a verbal encounter with a salesperson; and (4) 'actively avoiding contact SUs' ($n = 59$) – whose bodily conduct was characteristically the same as browsers except they engaged in additional work on one or more occasions to avoid verbal contact with a salesperson.

One finding which hints at the economic importance of the subject matter we examine is that only those SUs who established a verbal encounter with a salesperson made a purchase. On this basis we start by reporting (1) the various interrelated ways the verbal encounters between the salespeople and shoppers regularly were established or avoided and (2) the main social and communicative principles that enabled and underpinned these interpersonal accomplishments. We then provide additional evidence that affirms the fundamentally social and interactional basis of this shopper conduct. Finally, we outline the potential economic consequences of this conduct and, more generally, the implications of our findings for researchers and retailers.

Establishing and avoiding verbal retail encounters

The importance of mutual eye contact

In our data the activity that is commonly deemed to signify the beginning of a retail encounter – namely the first words that are exchanged between a salesperson and a shopper – was most often *not* the beginning of such retail encounters at all. Sequence 1 (shown in Figure 7.1), which shows one (shopper-initiated) way the salespeople and shoppers regularly established verbal encounters with one another, illustrates a common pre-verbal feature of these encounters and an important underlying organising principle via which many of these encounters were established and on other occasions avoided – that, ordinarily, mutual eye contact not only precedes, but also *ought* to precede, verbal contact.[5]

The arrowed shopper has just entered the store and is walking towards a salesperson (S) who is leaning on a sales counter examining a hand-sized computer. In Image 7.1.1 this shopper, who already has noticed the salesperson, is scanning the merchandise displayed along the left-hand wall of the store (from our viewpoint) and searching his pockets for what transpires to be a battery. While continuing his walk into the store, he glances at the salesperson (Image 7.1.2) before looking at other display goods nearer to and just behind the salesperson (see the shopper's gaze in Image 7.1.3). He then stops walking and stands about 1.5 metres away from the salesperson (Image 7.1.3). Approximately 0.5 second after doing so the salesperson raises his head – a move that, although we can only see the back of his head, appears to culminate in his looking at the shopper's face (Image 7.1.4). As this is happening the shopper turns his head towards the salesperson and, judging by the relative alignment of their heads and the focus of the shopper's gaze, they appear to establish mutual eye contact (Image 7.1.4). Half a second later the shopper lowers his head, breaking eye contact as he does so, and recommences walking towards the salesperson (Image 7.1.5). The salesperson then says 'Hello' – a greeting which the shopper returns. In Image 7.1.6 the shopper, now standing directly in front of the salesperson, presents a battery from his pocket, glances at the salesperson's face and asks 'Have you got a couple of those please? They're out of a calculator.'

In this sequence, and in the vast majority of the 156 verbal encounters that were established between a salesperson and a shopper ($n = 125$, 80.1%), such mutual eye contact preceded or, at the latest, occurred in conjunction with the first words spoken between these parties. This 'glance exchange' (Kendon 1990: 180) served as a means by which the salespeople and shoppers – like people in other types of face-to-face situations – reciprocated a first 'taking account' of each other's presence (Kendon 1990: 88), ratified their openness and willingness for

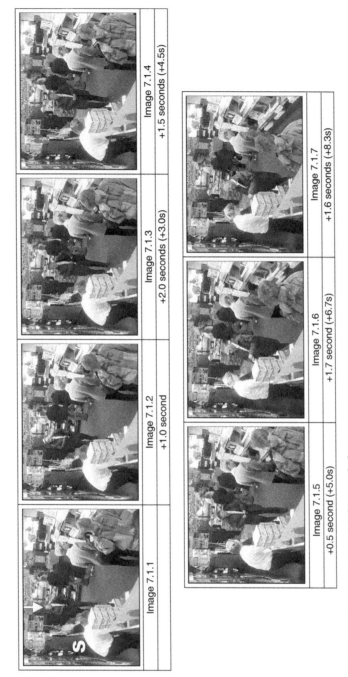

Figure 7.1. Sequence 1: establishing verbal contact

a verbal encounter (Goffman 1963; Kendon 1990: 202) and occasioned verbal encounters with one another.

But, typically, these verbal encounters were not only preceded by and ratified with mutual eye contact, there was much evidence that indicated they were also *conditional* upon mutual eye contact. That is, mutual eye contact was recurrently treated by the salespeople and shoppers as invoking an obligation on them to enter into a verbal encounter with one another and in this regard had a 'promissory' character (Goffman 1959: 14–15). Four observations lend support to this claim. First, in 122 (97.6%) of these 125 encounters the salesperson and/or shopper(s) broke eye contact almost immediately after mutual eye contact was established, as happens in Image 7.1.5. (Such mutual eye contact tended to last for well under a second.) The ensuing period of no mutual eye contact, which lasted at most for a few seconds, was typically spent by the shopper(s) or salesperson moving closer to and aligning themselves more squarely and frontally with one another, as happens during Images 7.1.4–7.1.7. These actions suggest that the salespeople and shoppers were treating their encounter as already being sufficiently established at this juncture to not immediately require any further visual confirmation or direct, encounter-initiating monitoring of the other party.

Secondly, the aforementioned 125 instances of mutual eye contact were in each case the first occasion, during these shoppers' visit to the store, that mutual eye contact took place between the salespeople and shoppers who established a verbal encounter with one another. Thirdly, aside from seven cases where a salesperson who was already engaged in a verbal encounter briefly acknowledged the presence of a shopper waiting to be served next, there were no occasions where a verbal encounter was not then established after a salesperson and shopper had exchanged mutual eye contact. Fourthly, the tendency for mutual eye contact to precede verbal contact also contrasted dramatically with the experiences of those SUs who did not have a verbal encounter with a salesperson ($n = 87$) as well as those encounters where contact was verbally initiated by a salesperson but was not accepted by the contacted shopper ($n = 10$). In the former cases no mutual eye contact with a salesperson occurred at any point during each SU's visit to the store.[6] In the latter cases no mutual eye contact occurred at any point before *or during* the salesperson's contact-initiating utterance.

In sum, the manner in which the vast majority of the verbal encounters were established between a salesperson and shopper, as well as the
actions and experiences of every one of the 97 SUs who did not have or
did not accept a verbal encounter with a salesperson – that is, for 222
(87.7%) of the SUs studied – strongly indicated there was an organising
principle underlying the encounter-establishing conduct of the salespeople and shoppers that mutual eye contact should be established
before or, at the latest, in conjunction with any verbal contact. As we
shall see, this fleeting, prefatory action and this apparently minor and
seemingly insignificant communicative principle had a major and economically consequential impact on the pre-verbal encounter conduct of
the shoppers we studied.

Nevertheless, there was an evident exception to this organising principle which manifested itself most starkly in the thirty-one (19.9%) verbal
encounters that were established – and established quite unproblemati-
cally – without prior mutual eye contact. In twenty-eight of
these encounters the contacted person's displayed level of involvement
with something or someone other than the person that had initiated
contact with them appeared to be the basis of why verbal contact had
been accepted and initiated without prior mutual eye contact. As we shall
show below, the particular types of involvement-attributable bodily
conduct, displayed by contacted persons and acted on by others, most
noticeably by contacting people, highlight another organising principle
that also underpinned the pre-verbal encounter conduct of the shoppers
and salespeople, particularly with respect to how and when their verbal
encounters were established and, in other cases, avoided.

Shopper and salesperson involvement

In Figure 7.1, as the salesperson and shopper move from being in a
situation of 'mere co-presence' to 'full-scale co-participation' (Goffman
1963: 102) and establish their verbal encounter, there are changes in their
bodily conduct with respect to (1) the object of their gaze; (2) the
orientation of their head/eyes, torso and legs/feet; (3) their proximity to
one another; and (4) their general bodily alignment to one another. These
changes not only embody the heightening level of interpersonal involvement between these parties, but they also provide an excellent example
of the prototypical features of 'low'- and 'high'-involvement bodily
conduct more generally. Compare, for instance, the low interpersonal

involvement of the salesperson and shopper in Image 7.1.1 (taken after the shopper has noticed the salesperson but before mutual eye contact is established) with their higher level of interpersonal involvement in Image 7.1.7 (taken at the end of the shopper's utterance 'They're out of a calculator', shortly after their verbal encounter has commenced). In Image 7.1.1 the salesperson and shopper are distant from one another and looking at (and thus currently involved with) different things. And although the shopper's torso and legs are oriented towards the salesperson, thereby projecting an involvement with that salesperson as a potential next involvement (Schegloff 1998a), these parties are not otherwise aligned to or involved with each other. By Image 7.1.7 the salesperson and shopper are standing closer to one another, and each person's head, torso and legs are in alignment, both with the principal elements of their own body and with the other person. Moreover, while only the shopper is looking at the salesperson, the latter is now displaying his higher current involvement with the shopper by looking at the battery the shopper has just presented to him.

Twenty-five (80.6%) of the thirty-one verbal encounters that were established without prior mutual eye contact were initiated by a salesperson, and twenty-one (84.0%) of these encounters were initiated while the contacted shopper was looking at merchandise displayed in the store.[7] One reason why these shoppers may have accepted verbal contact and the contacting salespeople may have initiated verbal contact without prior mutual eye contact was the high level of involvement the shoppers displayed, via their bodily conduct, not directly to a salesperson but, rather, to the product(s) they were looking at before the contact-initiating salesperson's approach. This type of high-involvement shopper conduct and subsequent verbal approach from a salesperson occurs in sequence 2 (Extract 7.2 and Figure 7.2).

Extract 7.2 (corresponding to Figure 7.2) ['S' = salesperson, 'Sh' = shopper]

```
1   S:    Can I help you at all?
2         (0.4)
3   Sh:   Oh, (0.3) I want a new (battery) fitting.
4         (1.0)
5   Sh:   (For that please.)
```

The arrowed shopper has been standing in the same position, at the same sales counter, looking at the same product(s) for over ten seconds.

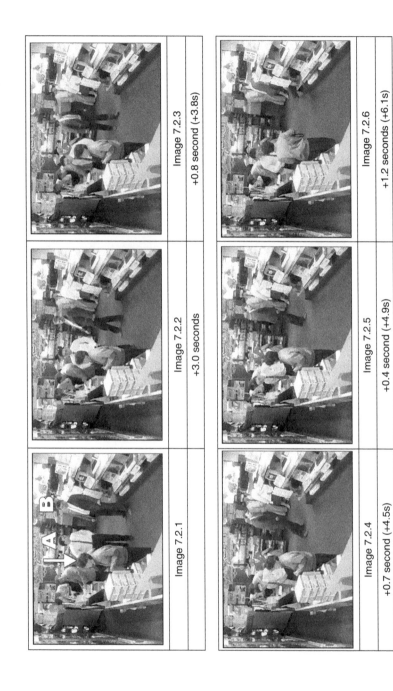

| Image 7.2.1 | Image 7.2.2 | Image 7.2.3 |
| | +3.0 seconds | +0.8 second (+3.8s) |

| Image 7.2.4 | Image 7.2.5 | Image 7.2.6 |
| +0.7 second (+4.5s) | +0.4 second (+4.9s) | +1.2 seconds (+6.1s) |

Figure 7.2. Sequence 2: salesperson initiating a verbal encounter with a shopper displaying high-involvement body conduct

In Image 7.2.1 salesperson A, who has already noticed this shopper (and appeared to be about to initiate contact with her before being sidetracked by salesperson B), is talking with salesperson B and another salesperson who is out of camera shot beyond the bottom right-hand corner of the images. In Image 7.2.2, salesperson A has now finished talking with the other salespeople and is approaching this shopper. Images 7.2.3 and 7.2.4 were taken, respectively, at the start and completion of sales-person A's contact-initiating utterance 'Can I help you at all?' Prior to and during this utterance the shopper has not moved from the position first shown in Image 7.2.1. It is only at Image 7.2.5, after the start of the shopper's contact-accepting response 'Oh ...', that the salesperson and shopper first establish mutual eye contact. Thus, in this verbal encounter, mutual eye contact occurs *after* verbal contact.

However, we can also see that this shopper, prior to and while being contacted, is displaying almost the same high-involvement bodily con-duct relative to the product(s) she is looking at that was (1) eventually displayed by the shopper in sequence 1 (Figure 7.1) relative to the salesperson with whom he established a verbal encounter (see Image 7.1.7) and, indeed, that (2) she also displays to salesperson A just after her verbal encounter has commenced (Image 7.2.6). The shopper in sequence 2 (Figure 7.2) is standing close to a sales counter; her head, torso and legs are all in alignment, and she is positioned square on to that sales counter and the product(s) she is looking at. This type of high-involvement bodily conduct with respect to merchandise, store furni-ture (display cabinets, sales counters and the like) and/or a salesperson was the most common way in which open-to-contact SUs made them-selves 'seeable' as being open to and available for a verbal encounter with a salesperson and, on this basis, appeared to have occasioned a verbal approach from a salesperson. Figure 7.3 shows four other similar examples of the typical bodily configurations adopted by individual open-to-contact shoppers ($n = 39$) when stationary and looking at dis-play goods.[8] The timings under each picture indicate the duration each arrowed shopper's featured stationary position was held. In each case a verbal encounter was initiated by a salesperson (and accepted by the shopper) shortly after the featured bodily configuration and before any major changes in that bodily configuration.

Open-to-contact shoppers often displayed other forms of even higher-involvement bodily conduct. For example, the arrowed shoppers in Images 7.3.1, 7.3.3 and 7.3.4 are standing much closer to the product(s) they are looking at, and the shoppers in Images 7.3.2 and 7.3.3 are,

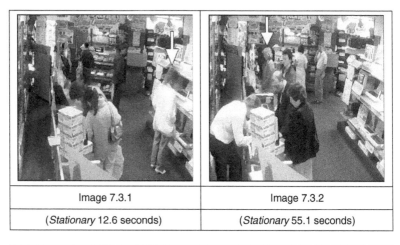

Image 7.3.1	Image 7.3.2
(*Stationary* 12.6 seconds)	(*Stationary* 55.1 seconds)

Image 7.3.3	Image 7.3.4
(*Stationary* 10.7 seconds)	(*Stationary* 54.1 seconds)

Figure 7.3. Characteristic body configurations of open-to-contact shoppers when stationary and looking at display goods

respectively, touching and leaning over the sales counter at which they are standing. The shopper in Image 7.3.4 is not only touching but also using the product he is looking at. In other sales settings such high-involvement conduct relative to merchandise and sales-related furniture is often treated, by salespeople and shoppers alike, as conveying a high level of interest in the product(s) being looked at and aligned to and comprises accountable and obligating actions that regularly precede (and sometimes are invoked by salespeople to constrain) not only verbal encounters but also a purchase (C. Clark and Pinch 1988, 1992, 1995a; B. Brown 2004; C. Clark 2004).

Browsing shoppers

In contrast, browsing shoppers tended to display systematically different and relatively lower-involvement bodily conduct; by doing so, they identified themselves as shoppers who were not inviting and were not open to a verbal encounter with a salesperson. This can be seen in Figure 7.4 which shows four examples of the bodily configurations typically adopted by individual browsing SUs ($n = 31$) while stationary and looking at display goods.

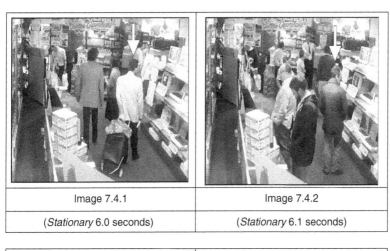

Image 7.4.1	Image 7.4.2
(*Stationary* 6.0 seconds)	(*Stationary* 6.1 seconds)

Image 7.4.3	Image 7.4.4
(*Stationary* 9.6 seconds)	(*Stationary* 5.3 seconds)

Figure 7.4. Characteristic body configurations of browsing shoppers when stationary and looking at display goods

In these cases, as was typical, each arrowed shopper is standing further away from the product(s) they are looking at and the sales counter/product display at which they are standing. Furthermore, only their head is oriented to what they are looking at – their torso and at least one of their legs/feet are directed elsewhere. This type of torqued, non-aligned head–torso/legs configuration (Schegloff 1998a), by virtue of the vast majority of the body being directed away from what the shopper is looking at, projects that the shopper's current involvement (looking at display goods) is likely to be only a passing, 'side-' and low-involvement level of interest (Goffman 1963; Schegloff 1998a) that, at least at that juncture, neither requires nor warrants a verbal approach from a salesperson. More generally, browsing shoppers tended to avoid looking towards or making their eyes available to be caught by a salesperson (thereby avoiding encounter-obligating mutual eye contact) and walked around the store in a furtive manner that reduced the likelihood of drawing attention to themselves.

Open-to-contact and browsing MPSUs

Multi-person shopping units bring into play the added dimension of how the relative bodily conduct of each shopper within an MPSU could reinforce or dilute the level of involvement collectively displayed by their MPSU and their identity as shoppers who were open or not open to a verbal encounter with a salesperson. Figure 7.5 presents four examples of the bodily configurations typically adopted by open-to-contact MPSUs ($n = 22$) when stationary and looking at display goods. Again, in each case a verbal encounter was initiated by a salesperson (in Images 7.5.1–7.5.3 by the marked salesperson) and accepted by the shopper shortly after the featured bodily conduct and before any major changes in that bodily conduct.

In these examples, as was typical, each shopper in an MPSU tended to display a high level of involvement relative to the product(s) they were looking at *and* spend most of their time looking at the same product(s) – characteristics that synergistically amplified their identity as an SU that collectively was open to a verbal encounter with a salesperson. In contrast, members of browsing MPSUs ($n = 7$) usually adopted the same type of low-involvement bodily configurations as individual browsers (see Figure 7.4) but also diluted the low level of involvement and product interest collectively displayed by their SU by tending not to look at the same product(s) as the other member(s) of their MPSU. This can be seen in Figure 7.6 which features two browsing MPSUs. Each

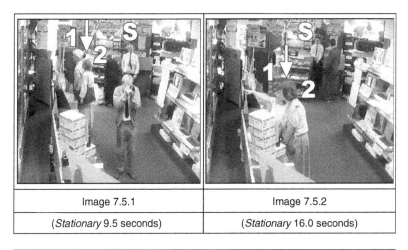

Image 7.5.1	Image 7.5.2
(*Stationary* 9.5 seconds)	(*Stationary* 16.0 seconds)

Image 7.5.3	Image 7.5.4
(*Stationary* 18.0 seconds)	(*Stationary* 33.4 seconds)

Figure 7.5. Characteristic body configurations of open-to-contact MPSUs when stationary and looking at display goods

shopper in each MPSU (and in each picture) displays, and most often displayed, separate and low product involvements.

There were two other aspects of browsing shoppers' bodily conduct that regularly served to dilute even further their characteristically low level of displayed involvement with and interest in the goods they were looking at, thereby reinforcing their identity as shoppers who were neither seeking nor open to a verbal encounter with a salesperson. First, they tended to have their hands placed fixedly in 'closed' positions. In Image 7.4.2, the shopper has his hands in his pockets, in Image 7.4.3 the shopper's thumbs are hooked in his pockets and in Image 7.4.4

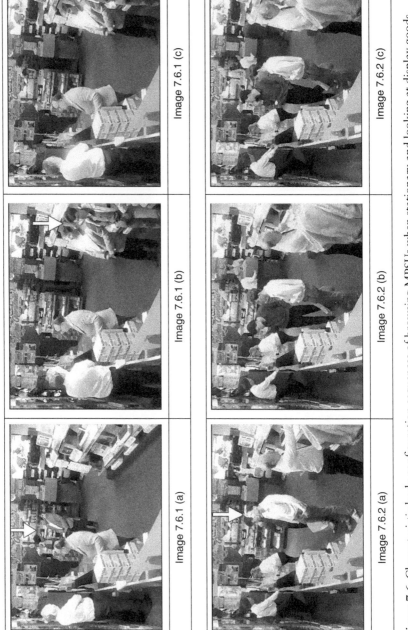

Figure 7.6. Characteristic body configuration sequences of browsing MPSUs when stationary and looking at display goods

the shopper's hands are clasped behind his back. In these ways the shoppers displayed it was unlikely that they would, at least imminently, engage in the particularly high-involvement, buying-implicative and encounter-warranting conduct of touching (let alone using) any merchandise in the store (C. Clark and Pinch 1988, 1992, 1995a; C. Clark 2004).

Secondly, browsing shoppers also tended to move around the store more, look at a higher number of different products (both within and between different product categories) and spend less time than open-to-contact shoppers looking at each of the products they did look at. For instance, one browser – who was by no means unusual – adopted eight separate low-involvement stationary browsing configurations, all at different product displays, and looked at a minimum of forty-six different products during his 94-second visit to the store. In contrast, the shopper in Figure 7.2, after briefly walking around the section of the store we studied, stayed at the same sales counter and looked at only three different products (while remaining in the same stationary position) during the seventy-six seconds that elapsed before she was contacted by salesperson A. We can get a further sense of this difference by comparing the timings of the stationary positions adopted by the open-to-contact shoppers in Figures 7.3 and 7.5 with those for the browsers in Figure 7.4. In Figures 7.3 and 7.5 all of the shoppers, aside from the shoppers in Image 7.5.1, remained in their featured stationary position for a longer period of time.

Actively seeking and avoiding verbal encounters with salespeople

On many occasions the open-to-contact shoppers' high level of involvement in the product(s) they were looking at seemed enough to prompt a verbal approach from a salesperson, as happened in Figures 7.2, 7.3 and 7.5. On other occasions, though, such shoppers more actively sought a verbal encounter with a salesperson.

Actively seeking a verbal encounter with a salesperson

Most of the SUs that actively sought a verbal encounter with a salesperson did so by modifying their high-involvement bodily conduct after hearing sounds or seeing activities in the store that had potentially imminent contact relevance for shoppers, like themselves, who were not already engaged in such a verbal encounter. The most common

contact-implicative sounds/activities immediately preceding the changes
that took place in these shoppers' bodily conduct were: (1) the cash register
being opened, closed or ringing up a sales transaction; (2) a verbal
encounter or phone call involving a salesperson reaching a conclusion;
(3) a salesperson who was alone but ending a preoccupation; (4) the
stockroom door opening, thereby heralding a salesperson's entrance into
the main showroom of the store; or (5) a salesperson who was approaching or passing nearby. One of the most common ways these shoppers
actively sought and regularly occasioned a verbal encounter with a salesperson at these contact-implicative junctures was by heightening their
already high level of involvement in the product(s) they were looking
at – for example, by moving even closer to the product(s) they were
looking at and/or starting to touch or use the product(s), particularly
when a salesperson was looking in or heading towards their direction.
In this way they more explicitly drew attention to themselves as shoppers
who were seeking a verbal encounter and warranted an approach.
Another way these shoppers regularly occasioned such a verbal encounter
was by managing to 'catch the eye' of (thereby establishing encounter-
obligating mutual eye contact with) a salesperson who was passing nearby
or had just finished, or was just about to finish, a verbal encounter with
someone else. Shopper 2 does this with salesperson A in sequence 3
(Figure 7.7 and Extract 7.7).

Extract 7.7   (corresponding to Figure 7.7)

```
1  Sh1:   Anyway, (0.5) thanks for your help.
2  SA:    Okay [Mister Sm[ith,
3  Sh1:        [Great.   [Right, chee[rio.
4  SA:                           [See you. Bye.
5          (1.0)
6  Sh2:   [Makes a loud throat clearing noise.]
7          (1.0)
8  SA:    [Addressing shopper 2:] Hello.
```

At image 7.7.1, taken at the start of shopper 1's 'Anyway, (0.5)
thanks for your help', salesperson A and shopper 1 are ending their
verbal encounter. Shopper 2 is waiting to be served by salesperson B
who is at the cash register processing shopper 3's purchase. Shopper 2
is stationary and displaying high-involvement, open-to-contact bodily
conduct by standing close to a sales counter and, judging by the position
of his head, also looking at salesperson B. His head, torso, legs and

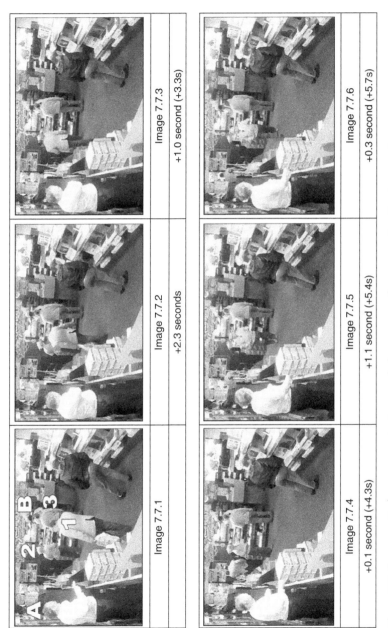

Figure 7.7. Sequence 3: shopper occasioning a verbal encounter after contact-implicative sounds

feet, which are all in frontal alignment with and oriented towards
salesperson B, display, like the shopper in Figure 7.1, the potential object
of his next involvement – in this case, salesperson B. Shopper 2 is also
displaying his buyer status and thus his high worthiness of being contacted: he is holding the product he will purchase in one hand and the
money to pay for it in his other hand. Image 7.7.2 is the end of the
salesperson A's '... Smith' and the start of shopper 1's 'Right'. By the end
of salesperson A's 'Bye' (Image 7.7.3), shopper 2 has already started to
turn towards salesperson A – a move he commenced just before salesperson A's 'See you'. By Image 7.7.4, taken at the end of the ensuing 1.0-
second silence, shopper 2 is now looking at salesperson A and can see that
he is not looking at him. Indeed, salesperson A appears to be starting a
new involvement – he has begun to look at something on the sales counter
in front of him. Shopper 2 then makes a loud and somewhat theatrical
throat-clearing noise and, as salesperson A turns to look at him, has
already started to turn the rest of his body and take his first step towards
salesperson A. In Image 7.7.5, taken 0.7 second into the subsequent
1.0-second silence, this salesperson and shopper appear to establish
mutual eye contact. Approximately 0.3 second afterwards (Image 7.7.6)
the salesperson commences their verbal encounter by saying 'Hello'. Thus,
in sequence 3, shopper 2 appears to have occasioned a verbal encounter
with salesperson A by virtue of having recognised the verbal exchanges
between salesperson A and shopper 1 as being encounter-terminating
exchanges (Schegloff and Sacks 1973) and then, as a result of turning
towards salesperson A and ostentatiously clearing his throat, attracting the
visual attention of that newly non-engaged salesperson. Furthermore, by
starting to walk towards the salesperson as encounter-obligating mutual
eye contact is established, shopper 2 makes it more difficult for the salesperson to decline a verbal encounter with him.

    Other ways shoppers actively sought a verbal encounter included
searching for a salesperson, looking at and orienting their body towards
a passing salesperson, visually tracking the movements of a nearby or
passing salesperson at head height, and doing quick 'double-take'
glances between two or more (usually preoccupied) salespeople or two
or more places in the store from where a salesperson may emerge. In
most of these cases the shoppers were not only offering their eyes to be
caught by a salesperson but also, via their head and/or bodily orientation, their potential next involvement. Sometimes these shoppers would
also occasion a verbal encounter with a salesperson after displaying

their dissatisfaction or impatience with the length of time they had been waiting for a verbal encounter by, for example, ostentatiously playing with money or a shopping list, emitting a deep sigh, studiously looking at their watch or, more ominously, the store exit, slowly and resignedly shaking their head, tapping a foot, drumming their fingers on a sales counter, switching their body weight from one leg to the other, or restlessly pacing back and forth about where they were standing.

Actively avoiding verbal contact with a salesperson

The aforementioned contact-implicative sounds/activities, particularly those projecting or occurring at encounter-ending junctures, also comprised the most common resource browsing shoppers relied on when actively attempting to avoid verbal contact with a salesperson. What distinguished these shoppers from those who actively sought contact with a salesperson was the nature of their apparent reactions to these sounds/activities and, in particular, their general aversion to looking towards the likely source of these sounds/activities. By doing so they reduced the chance of their eye ever being caught by a salesperson thereby rendering themselves under an obligation to accept a verbal encounter. One common reaction was for such shoppers to lower their involvement in the goods they were looking at just before a salesperson was able to (or was more likely to) witness their bodily conduct, the net result of which made it more apparent that an approach from a salesperson was neither warranted nor likely to be accepted. Shopper 2 does this in Figure 7.8.

In Image 7.8.1 the salesperson, who is serving shopper 1, is searching for something behind the top sales counter that shopper 1 had asked for on a previous visit and has returned to the store to collect. Shopper 2 is browsing the computers. In Image 7.8.2 the salesperson (now arrowed) has found what he was looking for and is moving behind the sales counter, en route to handing this item to shopper 1 (see Images 7.8.5–7.8.6). Shopper 2 has already started to stand up straight, thereby abandoning his more involved, closer inspection of the product(s) he continues to look at. By Image 7.8.3 shopper 2 has finished this move and is now sidling slowly (and somewhat furtively) to his right, further away from the approaching salesperson – a move that ends at Image 7.8.5. Thus shopper 2 lowers his displayed involvement in the product(s) he is looking at, apparently after hearing the salesperson ending his own involvement. (Shopper 2 never looks at the salesperson, even

Figure 7.8. Sequence 4: browsing shopper lowering his displayed involvement with store merchandise

peripherally.) He also completes the bulk of his standing up straight and his move away from the salesperson while the latter is preoccupied and his view of the shopper is still largely obscured by the left-hand side of the wall on which the computers are displayed. From Image 7.8.3 onwards shopper 2 presents himself as someone who is less involved or interested in the goods he is looking at and therefore is less likely to accept a verbal encounter with a salesperson, doing so prior to the point at which the approaching salesperson could more readily witness his bodily conduct and be more likely to consider whether he was a shopper who warranted contact. Like non-engaged shoppers more generally, this shopper *aurally* monitors for contact-implicative sounds/changes in the store.[9]

Shoppers being served by a currently absent salesperson

Another form of bodily conduct, which both affirms and relies on the previously described bodily configurations via which shoppers regularly occasioned or avoided verbal encounters with salespeople, tended to be adopted by those shoppers already in a verbal encounter with a salesperson whilst the latter had temporarily left their encounter and was elsewhere in the store (e.g. in the stockroom). These shoppers, upon being left by their serving salesperson, would usually be exhibiting (at least initially) high-involvement, open-to-contact bodily configurations similar to those of open-to-contact shoppers (e.g. in Figures 7.1, 7.2 and 7.3). One ever-present consequence of such shoppers maintaining their high-involvement conduct was their increased vulnerability to receiving an approach from another salesperson who may not have been aware they were already being served. On the fifty-two occasions where SUs were left on their own in this way, forty-one (78.9 per cent) quickly modified their conduct after their serving salesperson had left them and adopted a particular high- *and* low-involvement bodily configuration that further demonstrates just how subtle and interrelated the type of interactional organisation we have described actually is. Figure 7.9 shows two examples of this bodily configuration – the first involving an individual shopper, the second an MPSU. In each case the serving salesperson was visiting the stockroom (situated just past the bottom right-hand corner of the pictures).

Here, as was typical, the arrowed shoppers display a combination of high-involvement conduct (by standing very close to and, in many cases, touching a sales counter) and low-involvement conduct (by facing away

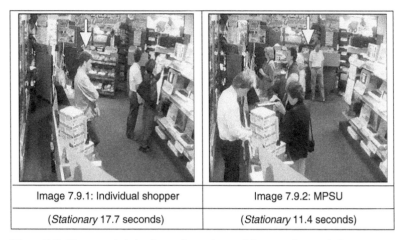

Image 7.9.1: Individual shopper	Image 7.9.2: MPSU
(*Stationary* 17.7 seconds)	(*Stationary* 11.4 seconds)

Figure 7.9. Characteristic body configurations of shoppers in a verbal encounter while their serving salesperson is currently absent

from the sales counter at which they are standing, adopting closed body/ hand positions, and looking at goods from an even greater distance than that typically adopted by browsing shoppers). This very specific high–low-involvement configuration served as a way in which the SUs (1) distinguished themselves as shoppers who should not be approached by a salesperson because they were already being served by someone else, and (2) could make themselves seeable as such by virtue of this particular bodily configuration being a distinct but also visually related element of the wider bodily involvement organisation we have described earlier in this chapter.

Discussion

The bodily conduct we have documented forms the principal components of an integrated communicative organisation that provided the shoppers and salespeople with the fundamental 'tool-kit' of resources (Schegloff 1999) to accomplish establishing and avoiding verbal encounters with one another in an orderly and characteristically unproblematic fashion.[10] As we have seen, this conduct and the organising principles that underpinned it is not exclusive to the particular shoppers or retail setting we studied but, rather, forms part of a wider, conventionalised 'body idiom' (Goffman 1963: 33–4). Mutual eye contact regularly precedes and occasions verbal contact in other face-to-face encounter-initiating situations, and eye contact avoidance is a common means of circumventing verbal encounters (e.g. Goffman 1963: 90; Kendon 1990; in sales and service encounters see B. Brown 2004: 6).[11] Similarly, visual displays of a person's involvement with something or someone manifest themselves and are acted on by others in quite standardised ways in many diverse interpersonal situations (e.g. Goffman 1959, 1963; C. Goodwin 1981; Heath 1986; Kendon 1990; Schegloff 1998a; Robinson 1998; Heath and Hindmarsh 2002; in sales encounters, see C. Clark and Pinch 1995a; B. Brown 2004; C. Clark 2004). Researchers have also highlighted the importance of people's bodily involvements with regard to the material features of an interactional setting – for example, furniture as well as other objects and artefacts – as a means by which they can reliably understand one another's conduct and accomplish many kinds of social actions (Heath 1986; C. Clark and Pinch 1995a; Robinson 1998; Heath and Luff 2000; Heath and Hindmarsh 2002; B. Brown 2004; C. Clark 2004). In this respect the communicative organisation, processes and actions we have described are both generic and context-free (Sacks, Schegloff and Jefferson 1974). But, in our data, there were a number of ways these actions and processes also, and simultaneously, displayed the shoppers taking into account and being influenced by the local, store-wide 'context' within which their conduct was produced.

The local, situational basis of the shoppers' conduct

By 'context-free' we do not mean to suggest of course that the shoppers' bodily conduct was oblivious to or produced independently of local, encounter-related contingencies occurring within the section of the store we studied. In fact, our data strongly indicate that, prior to a verbal encounter with a salesperson, wherever shoppers walked and dwelled in the store and whatever products they looked at and how they did so (and for how long they did so) were regularly, if not predominantly and principally, influenced by such considerations. To demonstrate this we now provide six examples that embellish the communicative organisation we have reported and highlight the characteristically encounter-related, salesperson-oriented basis of much of the shoppers' pre-verbal encounter conduct work.

First, at least 40 per cent of the 156 SUs who established a verbal encounter with a salesperson had, prior to their encounter, looked only at products that had nothing to do with the subsequently expressed purpose of their store visit. The products these shoppers did look at seemed primarily to derive from the encounter-related consideration of being in a place or position where they could more easily (1) monitor and be available for a particular, already engaged or preoccupied sales-person (as happens in Figure 7.1, particularly at Image 7.1.3) and/or (2) be seen by any salesperson as being open to or seeking contact (as appears to happen in Figure 7.2).

Secondly, in most of the cases involving open-to-contact and actively-seeking-contact shoppers, verbal encounters were ratified and established by the shopper looking away from the product(s) they were involved with and offering their eyes to an approaching or passing salesperson. The readiness with which these shoppers abandoned what they were looking at and, routinely, had exquisitely synchronised the onset of their gaze on the salesperson to coincide with the point at which the latter was looking at them or had reached the distance – usually around two metres – where mutual eye contact ordinarily would be (and usually was) first established suggests two things: (1) that these shoppers had been aurally or periph-erally monitoring that salesperson (or the salespeople) while looking at product(s); and (2) that their prior, characteristically high level of product engrossment had also been, to some significant extent, affected for the salespersons to witness and act on the contact-inviting shopper identity it embodied.

Thirdly, although browsing shoppers' bodily configurations were almost identical to that displayed by the open-to-contact shopper in Figure 7.1 (in Images 7.1.1–7.1.3), there was one regular and important difference: browsing shoppers' projected potential next/main involve-ment (embodied in the orientation of their torso, legs and usually one of their feet) was almost without exception *not* directed at a salesperson, particularly a salesperson not already in a verbal encounter with another shopper. (See the shoppers in Figure 7.4.) Whenever a sales-person stood in the projected line of a browsing shopper's main, poten-tial next involvement the latter usually quickly modified the orientation of these elements of their body or moved elsewhere in the store. The systematic absence of such a bodily orientation is consistent with these shoppers attempting to reduce the chance that their conduct could appropriately be viewed by a salesperson as inviting or warranting a verbal encounter.

Fourthly, another type of absent-salesperson, high–low-involvement bodily configuration – adopted by sixteen (72.7%) of twenty-two SUs while their serving salesperson was elsewhere but, on these occasions, still visibly present in the same section of the store – was that the shoppers' gaze, torso and legs/feet (i.e. the means by which they displayed the object(s) of their current *and* their main, potential next involvement) had been re-oriented not in the direction of some distant product but, instead, to the salesperson that was still serving them. (Shopper 1 is doing this in Figure 7.8.) This alteration of bodily conduct seemed consistent with these shoppers, faced with this particular and temporary situation, actively discouraging approaches from other salespeople by making the object with whom they are still involved (their salesperson) more apparent.

Fifthly, Figure 7.5 shows examples of the typical differences in the relative level of displayed product involvements between the 'principal shopper' in an MPSU (marked as 1) – who talked most with the salesperson that served them and usually announced the purchase/non-purchase decision during their subsequent encounter – and their companion shopper(s) (marked as 2). The latter routinely adopted a slightly lower level of involvement, or lowered their involvement just before or during a salesperson's approach, seemingly to encourage that salesperson to contact the principal shopper. By so doing, these shoppers revealed their fine-grained sensitivity to the non-equivalent potential impact on the salespeople of displaying even minor differences in their level of bodily involvement (see also B. Brown 2004: 6–7).

Sixthly, almost all (>96 per cent) of the contact-seeking and shopper-impatience displaying actions the SUs (n=>1,325) engaged in occurred only when one or more salespeople were present in the section of the store we studied and were able – at least potentially – to hear or see their conduct. When there were no salespeople in this showroom such shoppers consistently did not engage in such conduct. This strongly suggests that these actions had been produced with at least one eye (and not just a metaphorical eye) on them being witnessed and acted on by at least one of the salespeople.

Although the bodily conduct the shoppers adopted and engaged in provided the salespeople with the means to recognise and appropriately act on their displayed encounter-related identity, it by no means guaranteed such treatment.[12] The type of data base and research approach we have employed provides an accurate way of discovering the extent to which the salespeople did or did not recognise and appropriately act on the shoppers' encounter-related conduct. It also enables researchers to determine the impact and consequences of two other types of context-related situational factors that, in our data, also evidently influenced the shoppers' conduct: (1) their reactions to the anticipated or actual treatment of their bodily conduct by the sales staff; and (2) the impact of factors deriving from decisions made by the retail company's senior management.[13]

Implications of the research findings

The shoppers we examined systematically displayed and regularly altered their bodily conduct to take account of the presence and preoccupations of the sales staff and to deal with encounter-related changes and contingencies in the store. This conduct and the identity it embodied and projected were not simply, solely or even primarily a manifestation of the shoppers' inner, 'psychological' or 'emotional' state(s) that stemmed from anything like their consumption-related motivations or from what they 'really' thought about the products they looked at, enquired about or purchased. Nor were the shoppers passively playing out some abstract, pre-constituted consumer role or revelling anarchically in their newly ascribed status of 'customer is king' (cf. the type of consumer commonly portrayed in the organisation studies literature, e.g. du Gay and Salaman 1992; Sturdy 1998; Rosenthal and Peccei 2007). By actively and most often delicately working, first and foremost, to manage the manner in which they attempted to occasion or avoid verbal encounters with salespeople, and by regularly and subtly modifying their shopper identity in the light of local situational contingencies within the store, the shoppers were also displaying the fundamentally social, interactional and accountable nature of their conduct and actions. In this respect our study highlights the existence and the importance of a more fundamental and primordial dimension of marketing and consumer behaviour that, because of the general reluctance or antipathy of researchers and practitioners to examine recordings of actual, real-life occurrences of, say, retailing activity, consumer product involvement and service quality evaluation – and to do so from the perspective of the participants' own *evident* practices – has been all but neglected or ignored. We hope to have shown that the type of data base and research approach we have adopted is not only a viable method of inquiry but can also yield original, important and eminently practicable insights about the actual, real-life nature of marketing, retailing and consumer conduct.[14]

Another issue that arises from our findings, which also merits further study, is how the assumptions held and decisions made by senior members of organisations (particularly executive-level managers) may not only negatively influence the type of training that employees (e.g. salespeople) receive but also the latter's subsequent ability to recognise and appropriately act on the displayed conduct and 'needs' of those outside their organisation (e.g. shoppers) with whom they routinely interact. Our study suggests that such factors can compromise the ability of an organisation to achieve its principal objectives (e.g. product sales and positive customer service quality evaluations). For example, fulfilling a directive to 'contact all shoppers' would be likely to place the salespeople in a situation where they alienated browsing shoppers by not having treated them in an appropriate manner.[15] The pre-verbal encounter conduct we have documented is one of the first junctures at which shoppers systematically displayed what type of (encounter-related) shopper they were, and the subsequent treatment of their conduct by salespeople constitutes a central basis upon which the shoppers were liable to form (or re-evaluate) first impression service quality evaluations of the store and the staff employed within it and act on these evaluations in consequential ways. This shopper conduct, and the social and interactional organising principles, expectations and obligations that underpinned, informed and influenced it, comprised a vitally important resource in which the retailing company and their salespeople could recognise and, in our data, could certainly have better understood and more effectively served both the evident economic, encounter- and sales-related 'needs' of the shoppers we studied and the organisational objectives they were employed to achieve.

Notes

1. For a review and examples of these kinds of methods in business research see Aaker, Kumar and Day 2004.
2. There is almost no academic literature on this subject. Nevertheless, this assumption is often made, or implied, in the research into service encounters/ quality (e.g. Solomon *et al.* 1985), and this prescriptive advice is often reproduced in the trade literature (e.g. Bolen 1970) and student textbooks on retailing (e.g. McGoldrick 1990; Levy and Weitz 1998).
3. For other examples of similar misunderstandings and their negative impact in selling and retailing situations see C. Clark, Drew and Pinch 1994; Underhill 1999. The extent to which these types of misunderstandings

stem from an overreliance on intuition, personal experience or the more traditional, predominantly hypothesis-driven, research methodologies being deemed to be an adequate or more accurate substitute for the analysis of shoppers' and salespeople's own real-life conduct is beyond the scope of this chapter, but it is probable that this is the case.

4. This store offers the public a range of electrical goods (cameras, computers, TVs, hi-fis, etc.) and the consumables and peripherals associated with these products. The recordings were made with a small video camcorder which provided the authors with a near-full view of the store's main showroom. This section of the store included the only cash register, sales floor telephone, entrance and exit to/from the store, and door to the stockroom. The camera was positioned on top of a high display cabinet, out of the normal viewing range of the salespeople and shoppers, and was set to record automatically using the available light in the store. Only those shoppers that remained in this showroom for their entire visit to the store were analysed.

5. To give readers a sense of the pace and flow of these sequences we have provided timings under each picture indicating the number of seconds that elapsed (to the nearest 0.1 second) between each successive picture and, in parentheses, a running total of the elapsed time since the first picture in each sequence.

6. These cases involved SUs that (1) had no verbal contact with a salesperson and where there was no indication that the shoppers had attempted to establish verbal contact with a salesperson ($n = 81$) or (2) had attempted unsuccessfully to establish verbal contact with one or more salespeople and then left the store ($n = 6$).

7. The other six encounters, verbally initiated by shoppers, were all problematic from the start. In each case eye contact seemed to have been withheld by the contacting shopper and its absence appeared to serve to herald 'a problem' to the contacted salesperson by virtue of breaking the organising principle that mutual eye contact should precede verbal contact.

8. By 'stationary' we do not mean statuesque. On most occasions the shoppers made small movements while in their stationary positions – usually of their head/eyes (e.g. the minor shift in the shopper's gaze/head between Images 7.2.2 and 7.2.3 in Figure 7.2) and, to a lesser extent, their legs and feet. But these movements did not undermine the bodily configurations the shoppers characteristically held and we, consequently, have featured.

9. One common occurrence, which adds much credence to the shoppers' modifications of their bodily conduct at contact-implicative junctures as not being coincidental, was that more than one SU tended to react, independently, and at the same time, to the same contact-implicative sounds/ activities in the store. For example, in Figure 7.8, as shopper 2 lowers his

displayed involvement in the product(s) he is looking at, shoppers 3 and 4 (who are not together) modify their conduct in a way that is consistent with them seeking contact with this salesperson. In Images 7.8.3 and 7.8.4 shopper 4 is skewing her head round to look at the returning salesperson. In not catching his eyes she then turns her head the other way to look at the salesperson and offer her eyes to him as he ends his encounter with shopper 1 (Image 7.8.6). Between Images 7.8.4 and 7.8.6, shopper 3, without ever looking towards the salesperson, heightens his displayed involvement in the product(s) he is looking at by aligning himself more squarely and more closely to the sales counter at which he is standing, and touching this counter with both of his hands. Conversely, it was not unusual to see two or more browsing SUs lowering their involvement or starting to head out of the store just as a salesperson was reaching the end of an encounter with another shopper.

10. For a detailed example of one type of communicative organisation see Sacks, Schegloff and Jefferson 1974. For a more general account of various types of communicative organisation see Schegloff 1999.

11. Indeed, in our study, eye contact avoidance was the most common way the sales staff managed to avoid verbal encounters with shoppers.

12. By 'appropriate' we mean treatment by the salespeople that was consistent with the encounter-related identity displayed or projected by the shopper(s)' bodily conduct.

13. A research report containing findings on these two topics is available from the authors.

14. Reviews and examples of this research, which almost exclusively relies on data obtained via more traditional research methodologies, can be found in Bitner, Bernard and Tetrault 1990; Hess, Ganesan and Klein 2007.

15. This directive was in effect during the period when we collected the data for this chapter.

8 | The work of the work order: document practice in face-to-face service encounters

ROBERT J. MOORE, JACK WHALEN AND
E. CABELL HANKINSON GATHMAN

Introduction

A critical feature – and resource – of many face-to-face service encounters is a ubiquitous bureaucratic document, the 'standard form' (see
especially Suchman and Whalen 1994). But despite Max Weber's
classic observations of the crucial role played by written documents
('the files') and the work of those who generate and administer them
('subaltern officials and scribes of all sorts') in all matters of organisational business (Weber 1978: vol. II, 957), study of the functions
and uses of documents in modern organisations, whether paper or
electronic, has been largely neglected by the human sciences.
Strangely, this has even been the case for studies of formal organisations and bureaucracies, which rarely make more than a passing
reference to any actual documenting, reading or filing activities. And
this is despite the fact that from the invention of the first writing
systems in the late fourth millennium BCE, and especially from the
printing revolution that began in early modern Europe (Eisenstein
1983) and continues to this day, written documents were absolutely
crucial to the co-ordination of many people across time and space by
rendering information concrete and readily distributable (see especially Giddens 1979, 1987).

In this chapter, we undertake a detailed empirical examination of
how documents enter into the concerting and co-ordinating of organisational activity and, in doing so, how this opens up and ties locally
achieved co-ordinative practices into courses of action beyond a
particular interaction. We thus consider the problem of how documents, by enabling 'action at a distance' (D. E. Smith and Whalen
1997; see also D. E. Smith 1990), play a constitutional role in entire

activity systems – systems that may not be organised around physically and temporally co-present actors, where documents can then serve to co-ordinate the action at one point in time with sequences of action at other points in time, perhaps involving a different set of actors. To do this, we will examine the use of a standard form, in a particular work site: the walk-up service counter at a reprographics business, Eastside Reprographics (the name, like all others in this chapter, is a pseudonym). Our focus is on the practical reasoning involved in the situated use of these standard forms.

One of the few fields in the human sciences that has examined document use in organisations, especially the practical reasoning involved therein, is ethnomethodology. For example, in their study of psychiatric files, Harold Garfinkel and Egon Bittner (1967) show that the sense of any organisational record is found only in the context of the ordinary accounting practices (e.g. professional, legal) in which such records are used. Similarly, Albert Meehan (1986) analyses how the police use patrol logs and incident cards in everyday practice; Jack Whalen (1995) examines how the call-record form for a police and fire emergency communications system is assembled and used to relay descriptions of situations from callers to call-takers to radio dispatchers; Graham Button and Wes Sharrock (1997) report how the work-ticket and other artefacts are used in a xerographic print shop to make the state of production visible; and Paul Drew (2006) shows how documents can serve as interactional resources in educational and medical settings. Other ethnomethodologically informed studies, including Paul Luff, Christian Heath and David Greatbatch (1992), Richard Harper and Abigail Sellen (2002) and Jack Whalen, Marilyn Whalen and Kathryn Henderson (2002) have examined the distinct affordances of the most common document medium, paper, for practical action and reasoning in a variety of workplaces. For instance, these studies show how paper allows for easy writing and annotation, can be laid out in useful arrangements around a work space and can readily make information available 'at a glance' through postings on the walls of a cubicle or insertion in flip files that are immediately to hand. This ethnomethodological attention to practical reasoning and action with documents for organisational purposes serves as the footing for our own investigation of the copy shop we call Eastside Reprographics.

At Eastside Reprographics, writing on the paper work order enables the co-ordination of multiple employees across multiple work shifts. Orders may be 'taken' over the front counter during one shift by one employee produced on a second shift by a second employee, and returned to the customer during a third shift by a third employee. This kind of rationalised division of labour allows for flexibility in the scheduling of jobs, but also requires a specialised kind of document literacy. Each employee must be competent in reading and writing on this form in order to achieve an unbroken chain of communication across customer and employees. In this chain of communication, customers first describe what they want in person, using talk and gesturing around and with the originals (see Moore 2008). These vernacular, embodied descriptions are then translated by the employee into institutional, documentary ones by filling out a work order form. And finally the paper work order is passed back to machine operators who interpret it and translate it into a series of embodied actions. In other words, the work order is the most basic communication medium for managing orders and thus for doing business at Eastside.

This co-ordination is facilitated by the fact that Eastside's work order is a standard form, that is, one that communicates standardised descriptions of job requirements. While 'standardisation' is a methodological issue in sociology, in ethnomethodology it is treated as a topic for research – a phenomenon in its own right. Prior work by Jack Whalen (1997), Douglas Maynard and Nora Cate Schaeffer (2002) and Robert J. Moore and Maynard (2002) shows how standardisation is an achieved result rather than one that is prescribed by organisational policy or rules, for example, in survey research and public safety communications. In the context of the copy shop, the work order both enables and enforces a standardised method for describing a target output document. The objective of this standardisation is to produce descriptions that any employee can understand, not just the one who spoke to the customer directly. One employee called it 'drop-dead order taking': if the person who spoke with the customer were to drop dead, any other employee should be able to pick up the work order and understand the job. In the words of Garfinkel and Harvey Sacks (1970), the purpose of the work order is to attempt to replace indexical expressions for characterising job requirements with objective ones.

In our analysis of the Eastside work order, we extend prior studies on customer service, document use and standardisation by analysing how acts of writing on and reading work orders are embedded within particular situations of institutional interaction and practice and are thereby shaped by the distinctive demands of that work setting. We will thus show how both writing and reading are oriented to the task of enumerating an objective list of instructions for producing the customer's desired document, which *any* competent employee can execute. This 'work of the work order' is a response to the institution's demand for a rationalised division of labour in which jobs can be produced by any available employee (compare Wray-Bliss 2001 on the 'availability' of call centre clerks). The standard form is thus a vestige of the trend towards the increasing rationalisation of production and customer service.

Methods

The data for this study were collected in the context of a broad ethnographic study of Eastside Reprographics' operations. A team of five researchers carried out the study over a three-year period at four different locations in northern California (Eastside is a local chain). The team conducted hundreds of hours of direct observation and collected approximately 400 hours of video of naturally occurring work and interactions with customers. Each hour of video recording was logged, and collections of key events, such as 'order placements', 'order production' and 'order pick-ups', were assembled and transcribed using conversation analytic conventions.

In addition, three members of the team also conducted three months of participant observation during which they worked as employees, serving customers and producing jobs. The researchers took real orders and served real customers, who did not know that the researchers were anything but ordinary (if somewhat inexperienced) employees. The tacit knowledge gained by this direct participation in Eastside's operations enabled the researchers to see more of the orderliness and skill that are exhibited by employees in the hours of video recording collected for the study. For example, where we first saw employees rushing through interactions with particular customers, we later saw employees competently managing the load of customers at the counter when it was heavy.

Eastside Reprographics and its work order

Unlike the verbal and embodied description that occurs between customer and employee order taker, descriptions on the work order take a standard graphical form (see Figure 8.1).

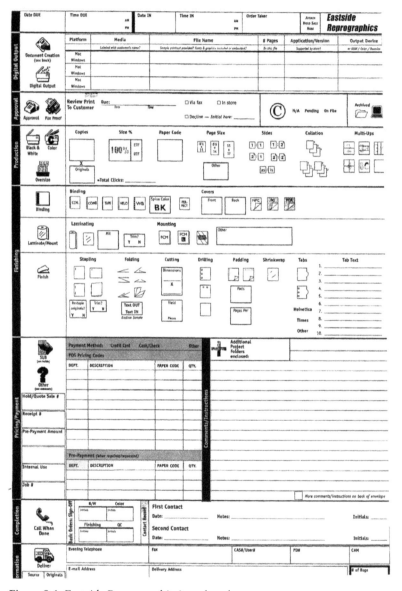

Figure 8.1. Eastside Reprographics' work order

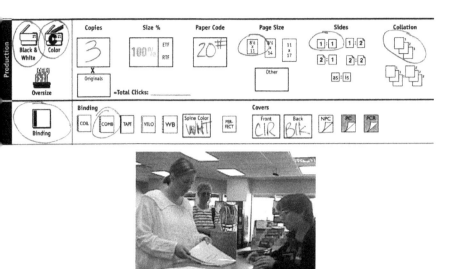

Figure 8.2. 'I need three copies of *this* please'

Specifications for the desired output, or target document, consist primarily of numbers or codes in boxes and circled icons. Yet, this kind of formal description could apply to any number of documents. It does not tell the employee, for example, how long the document is, what proportion is colour vs black and white, if there are text and/or graphics or even what type of document it is (manual, programme, reader and so forth). Therefore, the definite sense of the completed form presupposes knowledge of the originals. And so print shop workers must always read the form in conjunction with a close inspection of those originals. For example, Figure 8.2 shows an extract from an Eastside order form and an image of the customer presenting her originals.

The standardised description embodied in the standard form can then be decoded by any competent employee as more or less the following (the order of the description corresponds to the order of items on the form as read from left to right, starting with the top row):

The document to be copied contains both black and white *and* colour printed pages. Make 3 copies. Use 20 pound, 8.5x11-inch white paper. The copies should be single-sided and collated. Bind each copy with a white comb binding, with a clear cover and black back.

However, the customer does not actually produce this detailed description. Instead she simply says, 'I need three copies of this please' (line 2) as she presents the original document to the employee. It is the employee who produces the technical description by examining the document and asking the customer a long series of questions, the first of which is presented below (lines 7–end).

Extract 8.1

```
 1  Emp:   [Okay, you need-]
 2  Cust:  [I need three cop] ies of this please.=
 3  Emp:   =Okay. .hh
 4              (2.9)
 5  Cust:  They're uh-
 6              (1.0)
 7  Emp:   This ↑ colour?
 8              (1.3)
 9  Cust:  Uh, >colour doesn't matter.<
10              (0.8)
11  Emp:   I'm sorry?
12              (0.2)
13  Cust:  Colour doesn't matter.
14              (0.4)
15  Emp:   Okay. ↑ Well uh do you- but do you want the copies in:
16              (0.7) ((Emp points to a colour page))
17  Emp:   For that page do you wan' 'em in colour or ↑ no.
18          Black an' white?
19              (1.1)
20  Emp:   [Or do you wan'       'em-]
21  Cust:  [What's the difference] in co:st.
22              (0.1)
23  Cust:  [(                )]
24  Emp:   [Colour: are nine] ty nine cents.
25              (0.4)
26  Cust:  Versus black an' white is how much.
27  Emp:   Uh:: single sided seven cents.
28              (0.7)
29  Cust:  Oh:. We'll jus' do regular then. Black an' white
30          for e[veryth] ing.
31  Emp:        [Oka:y?]
32              (4.0) ((Cust flips through booklet))
```

```
33  Cust:    Actually I take it backh.
34           (0.2)
35  Cust:    I'm sorry.
36           (0.2)
37  Emp:     D[o-
38  Cust:    [Colour for everything.
39           (0.3)
40  Emp:     I- are you sure?=
41           (.)
42  Cust:    Yeah.
43           (0.9)
44  Emp:     F:er everything that's colour right?
45           (.)
46  Cust:    Ye[ah.
47  Emp:       [Or is it all colour.
48           (1.5)
49  Emp:     °Okay.°
50           (1.4)
51  Emp:     So colour an' black n' [whi:te?]
52  Cust:                           [Certain] things.
53           (0.8)
54  Emp:     hhh Three copie:s. um n we're gonna do it (.)
55           double sided? Or single.
56           (.)
57  Emp:     single now.
58  Cust:    uh: I think (.) s::ingle?
59           (.)
60  Emp:     kay.
61           (0.2)
62  Emp:     You want regular white paper? Or do you want the
63           laser paper.=the colour's gonna be run on la:ser.
64           (.)
65  Cust:    Okay then regular white paper. [I don't really need]
66  Emp:                                    [      okay.      ]
67  Cust:    Yeah. Right.
```

The employee thus begins to deconstruct the presented object into a set of specifications in interaction with the customer. Juxtaposing the marked-up order form with the transcript of the interaction reveals that each mark on the form is the product of a collaboration between employee and customer. For example, the employee begins by probing the customer about the kind of printing that should be used (i.e., colour printing or black and white). She says simply, 'This colour?' (line 7), as she begins to inspect the inside pages of the booklet, thus prompting the customer to confirm her characterisation of the document. However, instead of confirming it, the customer indicates that reproducing the colour pages is not important (lines 9 and 13), thus refining her implicit request to reproduce the document as is (line 2). Rather than accepting this specification of 'black and white', the employee probes further. She flips through the pages of the document (line 16), finds a page with colour and asks the customer specifically if she wants that colour page printed in colour or black and white (lines 17–18). In response, the customer inquires about the 'difference in cost' between colour and black and white (lines 21 and 26), which the employee tells her (lines 24 and 27). Based on this discussion of price, the customer reconfirms that she wants black-and-white printing (lines 29–30), but then a moment later, after flipping through the booklet (line 32), she changes her mind and indicates 'colour for everything' (lines 33 and 38). The employee then confirms this specification with the customer (lines 40–2).

Yet still the employee hesitates in recording the specification. She proposes a further refinement to it by suggesting that the customer wants colour printing *only for the colour pages* (line 44), thus introducing the possibility of a mixed specification. The employee then sums up the specification as 'colour and black and white' (line 51), which the customer confirms (line 52), and records it by circling both icons on the form (Figure 8.2, upper-left). We see then that a great deal of collaboration and interactional work went into producing those two circled icons on the form. Furthermore, the employee probes the customer's articulation of the specification at several points and leads her towards the final one, which is nonetheless a collaborative achievement. In this context, leading the customer in this way is not necessarily a bad thing. In fact, it is a way that the employee brings her experience to bear on this particular order.

Not only does the employee lead the customer in her choice of alternatives, but the order form itself also influences (or is used to influence) the structure of the interaction. The ordering of items on the form influences the order in which the employee asks particular questions. The employee begins by asking about 'colour' printing (line 7), the first item on the specifications section of the work order (Figure 8.2, 'colour' icon in upper-left corner). She then confirms the number of copies the customer mentioned earlier (line 54), asks about the sidedness of the pages (lines 54–5) and asks about the type of paper (lines 62–3). The employee's ordering of the questions she asks follows closely, although not exactly, the order of items of the form (see Figure 8.2): toner type > number of copies > paper type > sidedness (the employee reverses the order of the last two). This rough correspondence between the interaction and the standard form was a general pattern we observed.

Situated writing: form filling as a collaborative achievement

As we saw above, deciding on the specifications for the order is a collaborative achievement between customer and employee. Yet the collaboration goes beyond this. Even the actual marking-up of the paper form can at times become collaborative. Since the work order and the employee's writing upon it are visually available to the customer, customers sometimes monitor what is being written. They of course have an interest in ensuring that the recorded account of what they said adequately captures what they said or meant to say. This is especially important when the specifications in question are complicated, as in the case of 'mixed' specifications. The following case involves such an order. In it we can see how customers can monitor what employees record on the order form.

In this case, the order includes two specifications for 'sidedness' – 1:1 (or single-sided to single-sided) and 1:2 (or single-sided to double-sided), as indicated on the work order by the two circled icons under 'Sides' (Figure 8.3). The challenge then for both customer and employee is to clearly indicate which parts of the original document should be printed 1:1 and which 1:2. But we see that the customer has already devised a solution for this, prior to the interaction, using a system of blue tags.

Extract 8.2

8   Cust: And I'll explain >this to you that.< (.) some of it
9   is double sided some of it's stapled.

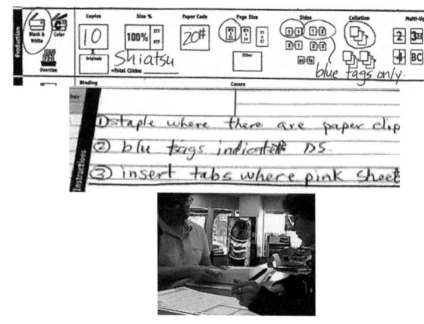

Figure 8.3. Blue tags indicate double-sided

```
30                    (1.1)
31  Emp:     Okay?
32                    (0.4)
             ((Sequence omitted))
53  Emp:     Okay, uh:m how are we gonna know what's single sided
54                    (0.3) ((Cust grips blue tag))
55  Cust:    >I wz js gonna tell you [that (right now)<]
56  Emp:                             [ O k a y ? ]
57  Cust:    This where it's uhm
58                    (0.4) ((Cust shakes blue-tagged pages))
59  Emp:     Blue stickies?=
60  Cust:    =Ye:ah.
61                    (0.2)
62  Cust:    That means you do double sided.
63           (3.9) ((Emp circles '1:1' and '1:2' icons))
64  Cust:    Only where its- *only this:. ((*Cust shakes blue t
65                    (0.1)
66  Cust:    The rest is single. Most of it's single.
```

```
67              (8.4) ((Emp writes in Comments box))
68  Emp:    Is it double sided already? or [no.
69  Cust:                                 [No it's not.
70  Emp:    °Okay.°
71              (4.0) ((Emp continues writing in Comments box))
72  Emp:    °°No(h) t(h)abs°°
73              (0.2)
74  Cust:   °Mka:y?°
75              (0.8) ((Emp lifts pen))
76  Emp:    RR ((frustration))
77              (0.2)
78  Emp:    Blue tags indica:ted,
79              (0.9)
80  Emp:    No indicate [(0.2) double sided. ((Emp writes comment))
81                      [((Cust returns gaze to Emp's pen))
82              (0.4) ((Emp lifts pen))
83  Emp:    Okay.
84              (0.4)
85  Emp:    So most of it's r- single sided you said right?=
86  Cust:   =Yeah most of it is single sided.
87              (4.8) ((Emp writes annotation under Sides icons))
88  Cust:   The [blue tags] only thank you:.
89  Emp:        [O k a y ?]
```

Up front in her description of the job, the customer announces that 'some of it is double sided' (lines 28–9) and thus implies that other parts of the job are single-sided. After some discussion of stapling (omitted), the employee returns to the topic of sidedness. Specifically, she asks, 'how are we gonna know what's single sided' (line 53). In response, the customer grips and shakes a set of pages in the booklet that are tagged with a blue sticky note (line 54; Figure 8.3, bottom) and proposes that the employee is getting ahead of her (line 55). The customer then begins to describe her system of tagging both verbally and through an embodied demonstration. She verbally and visually refers to the blue-tagged set of pages (lines 57–8), and the employee displays recognition by saying, 'Blue stickies?' (line 59). The customer continues by formulating what the blue stickies are intended to indicate: 'That means you do double sided' (line 62). In response, the employee visibly moves her pen from the Comments box up to the

'Sides' icons, circles 1:1 and 1:2, and returns her pen to the Comments box where she hesitates for a moment (line 63). The customer follows the employee's pen with her eye gaze. While looking at the employee's pen at the Comments box, the customer expands her specification (lines 64–6).

At this point, the employee begins to write a special instruction in the Comments box (line 67; Figure 8.3). But before completing it, she asks the customer if these pages are 'double sided already' (line 68), which has ramifications regarding whether 1:2 or 2:2 is the correct specification. This diverts the customer's gaze back to the originals as she indicates that it is not (line 69). The employee continues to look down at the Comments box and to write in it (line 71). She says very quietly as if to herself, 'no tabs' (line 72) and lifts her pen and stops writing (line 75) just before uttering a 'frustrated' uvular trill (line 76). Then she reads what she has written aloud, 'blue tags indicated' (line 78) and, after nearly a one-second hesitation (line 79), she verbally self-corrects the tense of the verb, 'no indicate' (line 80). Through these vocalisations, the employee thus provides feedback to the customer regarding her progress in filling out the form, publicly exhibiting cognitive difficulty in formulating the particular instruction. When the employee utters the verbal correction, she visibly catches the customer's attention who returns her gaze to the employee's pen. The employee completes the instruction in the Comments box both verbally and in writing (line 80) and lifts her pen (line 82). However, the employee does not stop here. She confirms with the customer that 'most of it's r- single sided' (lines 85–6) and then writes a short annotation to the circled 1:2 icon itself (line 87; Figure 8.3, top right). To further combat possible ambiguity regarding which parts should be double-sided and which single-sided, she draws a short curvy line from the 1:2 icon and writes 'blue tags only' (line 87). The customer, who is still watching the employee's pen, reads the annotation aloud, 'The blue tags only' (line 88), displaying that she was in fact monitoring what the employee was writing and thanks her (line 88).

In this example, we see then that the filling out of the record itself can be a collaborative achievement. Not only does the customer provide instructions that the employee translates and records, but customers also sometimes check what the employee writes. Here the customer displays that she is monitoring what the employee writes by following the pen with her gaze and by reading portions of what was just written. By acknowledging what the employee wrote and thanking her for it, the customer interactionally ratifies the written instruction.

The chronic insufficiency of standard forms

Although the standard icons and boxes on Eastside's work order enable employees to produce sets of specifications that any employee can decode, they are nonetheless routinely insufficient for producing a usable description, as we saw in Extract 8.2. By 'usable' we mean one that will enable a machine operator to produce the desired output or target document. Order taking at copy shops is more complex than that at a restaurant, where customers choose from a menu, because every order is a custom order. Customers bring in unique originals and request unique combinations of services. As a result, taking orders using a standard form can require some creative fitting.

Eastside's order-takers encounter at least two kinds of routine troubles in trying to fit the particulars of a given order to the standard items on the form (compare Whalen 1995). First, although there are boxes and icons for most quick-print services, there is not an item for everything (e.g. binding on the top). Secondly and more commonly, when an order is 'mixed' in some respect (i.e. some single-sided, some double-sided, as we have seen), the logic of the form often does not accommodate this complexity. Two icons can be circled, but this does not specify to which pages of the originals each circle refers. So the order-taker faces a problem in indicating the physical referent of each form item, a problem of documentary reference.

But, in addition to these routine troubles, the order form also provides two resources for repairing its own inadequacies. First, the rather large Comments box enables the writing of rich free-text notes since the form is on paper. So for example, when there is no standard item for a service, it can be written or drawn in the Comments box (e.g. binding on the top; see Figure 8.4). Secondly, when a job is mixed, as in Extract 8.2, particular items on the form can be annotated directly. The order-taker can write an explanatory free-text note and 'anchor' it to a particular form item (see Figure 8.5).

Figure 8.4. Adding icons to the form

Thus, order-takers routinely accommodate the insufficiencies of the standard form with these practices.

Other practical solutions to the problem of documentary reference with mixed jobs are pointing and tagging. In a face-to-face encounter, when customers have a hard copy of their originals, they can refer to parts of the originals simply by pointing to them with their hands. This of course cannot be repeated on the order form, but it can be simulated by tagging the originals, e.g. with Post-it notes, as we saw in Extract 8.2. These then are all ad hoc, creative methods of reference and description that enable employees to make the standard form work in practice; they are part of work order literacy skills.

Situated reading: re-introducing non-standard features

We turn now from the collaborative production of a completed work order to the other end of the chain of communication: de-coding the markings on the form by a second employee. Again the virtue of the

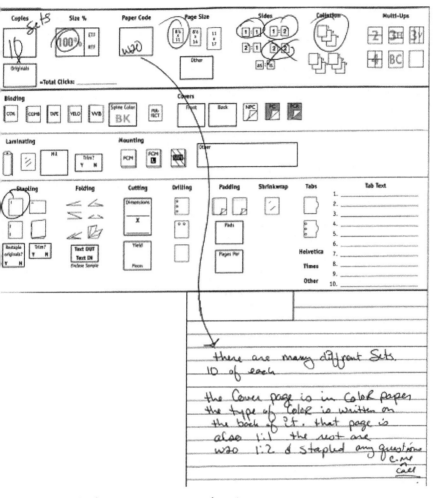

Figure 8.5. Anchoring a comment to a form item

standard form is that it helps enforce a standard method of description which any other employee is supposed to be able to understand. But although annotated notes, such as those in the preceding case, are often effective as a practical solution to the chronic insufficiency of the form, they reproduce the very thing that the form is intended to eliminate, namely non-standard methods of description or indexical expressions (Garfinkel and Sacks 1970). As a result, annotations can themselves become a source of troubles in interpretation.

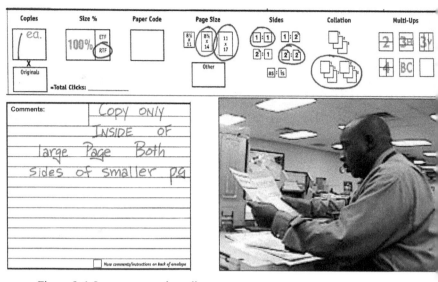

Figure 8.6. Large page and smaller page

In Extracts 8.3a–8.3e, we see what can happen when a production employee, known as a Key Operator (or 'Key Op' for short), receives a completed work order and a set of originals. This particular case involves another example of mixed specifications (see Figure 8.6) (although it is not the same order as in Extract 8.2). In this case, two Page Sizes and two Sides icons are circled. As with any mixed job, there is the problem of repairing the form such that the physical referent for each item is clear to the reader. No tags are used here, but there is a free-text note in the Comments box. The note uses the terms 'large page' and 'smaller pg' and determining the physical referent of both is crucial for understanding the description.

The originals for this order consist of two standard booklets of sheet music (Figure 8.7). One booklet consists of a single folded sheet, the other of a folded sheet and an insert page. In the following transcript, we can see that the Key Operator who receives this job encounters some trouble in interpreting what the work order suggests he should do with these music sheets (the Key Op is externalising his reasoning for the ethnographer who is shadowing him).

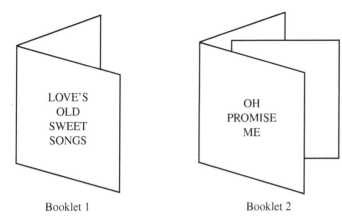

Figure 8.7. Music sheets

Extract 8.3a

```
1              (3.5) ((Key Op picks up order folder
2                    and inspects the form))
3  Key Op:  A:h:
4              (6.0) ((Key Op continues to inspect form))
5              (4.3) ((Still holding the folder in one hand
6                    he begins to inspect next folder in job))
7  Key Op:  Huhhhh (0.5) .tch .tch .tch .tch .tch
8              (0.3) ((Looks back at previous folder))
9  Key Op:  .tch .tch .tch (0.3) .tch .tch .tch .tch .tch .tch
10           .tch .tch .tch .tch .tch .tch .tch .tch .tch
11             (7.4) ((He opens folder and inspects originals))
12 Key Op:  Copy only inside of the pa- la:rge pa:ge:.*
13             (0.5) ((* He holds booklets up next to each
14                   other, one in each hand, and compares
15                   their relative lengths))
16 Key Op:  They're both large:. We:ll *this is larger.
17             ((* Holds up Booklet 1))
18             (5.6) ((He puts down Booklet 2 and opens up
19                   Booklet 1 and looks back at work order))
20 Key Op:  Both si:des
21             (3.8)
```

While inspecting the work order (lines 1–4), the Key Operator begins to do his thinking publicly for the observing ethnographer by producing a series of alveolar clicks, ".tch" (lines 7, 9–10). A moment later he reads the instructions from the Comments box on the work order aloud (lines 12 and 20). As he reads the instructions, he holds the music booklets up side by side (along their longest edge) thus visibly comparing their relative sizes. He proposes that one of the booklets is slightly larger than the other (lines 16–17) and thus must be the referent of 'large page'.

However, the Key Operator hesitates in running the job. He continues to study the order form and the originals. After a few more minutes he elaborates his interpretation of the instructions to the ethnographer.

Extract 8.3b

```
38  Key Op:   I get it now.
39            (0.6)
40  Ethnog:   S'[what
41  Key Op:    [They just want *this one (1.3) this is- cuz
42            **one t' one?
43            ((* He points to Booklet 1;
44            ** He points to icon on order form))
45            (0.2)
46  Ethnog:   Mh[m
47  Key Op:      [That they just want (0.9) this copy (.)
48            the insi:de (0.6) then the smalla one's (0.8) were I
49            guess wi' be *this .hhh an' it'll be two t' two.
50            ((* He points to Booklet 2))
51            (1.1) ((He flips through pages of Booklet 2))
52  Key Op:   So I'll copy everything.
53            (3.4)
54  Key Op:   That's wha' I'm getting from it.
55            (3.6)
56  Key Op:   *>Dis one i' larger one, they just wa'< (0.3)
57            the (.) one copy then **these ones they want one (0.4)
58            of both si:des:.
59            ((* He holds up Booklet 1;
60            ** He points to Booklet 2))
```

The Key Op reiterates his interpretation that 'large page' refers to Booklet 1 and 'smaller pages' refers to Booklet 2. He thus plans to copy the former single-sided and the latter double-sided.

Nonetheless, on this occasion the instructions prove to be ambiguous, as the ethnographer proposes an alternative reasonable interpretation to the Key Op.

Extract 8.3c

```
119  Eth:    Maybe *that's a larger page too.
120          ((* He points to Booklet 1))
121          (0.8)
122  K. Op:  Pro:[bly:
123  Eth:        [There's two larger pages an' one (0.3)
124          *smaller page.
125          ((* He picks up insert to Booklet 2))
126          (.)
127  K. Op:  Ye:ah:.
```

The ethnographer thus suggests that 'large page' refers to the folded pages of each booklet, while the 'smaller page' refers only to the insert page of Booklet 2. According to this interpretation, the resulting job would reproduce the music contents of both booklets, but not their front and back covers.

In the face of this ambiguity, the Key Op comes up with the following resolution. Rather than running the job, he 'puts it on hold' (lines 133–4) by leaving it for the employee who spoke with the customer directly to run the job in the morning before it is due. The standardised description and the chain of communication thus break down.

Extract 8.3d

```
133  K. Op:  I know what to do! (0.2) Jus' put it on
134          ho:ld
135          (0.6)
136  K. Op:  'Cuz it's not due 'til ni:ne an' the person
137          that did it will be here befo:re the:n.
138          (0.7)
139          [so:
140  Eth:    [Nine in uh morning?=
141  K. Op:  =Ye:ah:.
142          (0.6)
143  K. Op:  So [they c'n (0.1) figure it out. They took=
144  Eth:       [( )
145  K. Op:  =the order.
```

The next day, the ethnographer spoke with the employee who took the order. This employee confirmed that the 'large page' indeed referred to the large folded page of each booklet, and 'smaller page' to the insert page of the second booklet. The two large pages should be single-sided and the single insert page double-sided.

What leads the machine operator down the wrong path? A few idiosyncratic details of the form appear consequential. First, the order-taker used non-standard terms of reference – 'large page' and 'smaller page' – in her instructions. As we saw, these originals can be 'larger' or 'smaller' in different ways. Terms such as 'covers' and 'inserts' are more technical and thus somewhat less vulnerable to ambiguity. Although the type of document involved in this job is common, the print shops we observed lacked a particular term for it. This document type consists of a folded 'tabloid' or 11x17-inch sheet of paper which is then printed such that it creates an 8.5x11-inch booklet with four pages. And in this case a technical term, such as 'tabloid booklet', could perhaps have helped the order-taker refer more clearly to the pages in question. Secondly, the order-taker confirmed for the ethnographer that there was in fact an error in the way she filled out the form. She circled the 8.5x14 and 11x17 paper-size icons instead of *8.5x11* and 11x17 icons. Thus the fact that the output was supposed to be a 'tabloid booklet' may have been obscured for the machine operator by this error. Thirdly, the order-taker uses a particular abbreviation at the end of her instruction (see Figure 8.6), no doubt because she ran out of room in the box to write. But the handwritten abbreviation appears somewhat ambiguous as to whether it is 'pg' or 'ps': the former would be read as 'page' while the latter as 'pages'. This proves consequential as there is only one 'smaller page' according to the order-taker's intended meaning. Yet 'smaller pages' is consistent with the machine operator's interpretation according to which there are two 'smaller pages', that is, the folded 11x17 and the insert pages of the second booklet. In fact, when the machine operator reads that part of the instructions aloud, he reads it as 'pages' (line 8):

Extract 8.3e

```
6   K. Op:   ((Reading)) .h Copy only insi:de o:f first
7            (1.2) mm: the: la:rge pa:ge:, (0.5) both sides of smaller
```

```
8              pages:.
9              (7.0) ((Key Op picks up and inspects originals))
10             (8.6) ((Key Op looks back at instructions))
11  K. Op:    Hmm
12             (2.4) ((Key Op inspects another page of original))
13  K. Op:    Okay.
14             (8.2) ((Looks back at instructions))
15  Eth:      What's the large p(h)age
16             (0.4)
17  K. Op:    I d' kno:w. They're both pretty large aren't they.
18  Eth:      Y(h)eah huh huh
19             (1.3) ((He lines up Booklet 1 on top of 2))
20  K. Op:    Pro'a'ly *this one.
21             ((* He holds up Booklet 1))
```

The handwritten abbreviation thus may have thrown the machine operator off as he is looking to identify multiple 'smaller pages' in the originals. Ironically, then, we see that the free-form 'comments', while necessary for fitting the standard form to the particular job, also introduce the very types of idiosyncratic features into the description that the standard form was intended to eliminate. Non-standard methods of description can indeed create troubles in understanding, although at other times they are just the thing needed to make the work order intelligible to the reader. As Garfinkel and Sacks (1970) insist, non-standard or indexical features of description are unavoidable, and therefore managing them on any particular occasion is a key feature of document use.

Discussion

We saw that situated writing on a standard form is a key feature of front counter employees' work in serving customers; however, it is a feature of service work that is rapidly disappearing. While we conducted our observations at Eastside Reprographics, we witnessed some interesting transformations in customer service, transformations that George Ritzer and Todd Stillman (2001) might call shifts from 'McDonaldised' service to 'systemised' service. As noted above, at Eastside the work of 'customer service' is separated from that of 'production'. That is, the role of the 'front counter worker' is to serve customers, primarily by taking their orders and accepting their payment, and it is separated from the role of 'production worker', which is to run the printers and fill the orders. The front counter worker role is treated by Eastside management as a relatively 'de-skilled' role in that they start novice employees in it, with whom they see high turnover. The more 'skilled' roles are considered that of 'machine operator', who runs the printers, and 'digital specialist', who uses desktop publishing software. Ritzer (1998: 59–70) would no doubt call front counter work at Eastside a 'McJob'.

However, during our observations, we witnessed two transformations of front counter work, both of which consisted of what Ritzer and Stillman (2001) would call 'systemized service'. First, an automated credit card payment system was introduced in the do-it-yourself area of the shop (see Vinkhuyzen and Szymanski 2004 for more detail). Prior to this, a significant amount of the front counter workers' time was spent 'ringing up' customers for small transactions, sometimes for as little as six cents. So the new 'pay-at-the-pump' transactions, as one employee called them, relieved a great deal of pressure on the front counter in terms of customer load, and freed up counter employees to devote more time to serving customers in less mechanical ways, such as consulting with them on orders.

Secondly, an electronic web submission system was introduced across all of Eastside's copy shops. This enabled customers to submit electronic orders from their homes and offices. While customers had been submitting orders by e-mail for some time, there was no standardised process for doing this. Customers simply wrote a free-text note and attached their files. The new web submission system required customers to fill out a standard form, and it automatically converted their files to a standard format, .pdf. Thus the use of work orders underwent a significant transformation when order submission was moved to the web: they were now being filled out by customers rather than employees. The customers now had to confront the standard form alone. This is potentially problematic because, as Moore (2008) shows, customers often demonstrate troubles in understanding Eastside's document services and its official vocabulary for referring to them. Customers thus rely on employees' expertise in translating vernacular and embodied descriptions into standardised, documentary and actionable ones. However, we also observed that, when production workers encountered troubles in interpreting work orders submitted by the web, they routinely attempted to compensate for this by calling customers back. In other words, when the document-mediated chain of communication broke down, workers attempted to repair it by establishing a real-time, telephone-mediated interaction with the customer. This appeared to be somewhat effective, although the new challenge was reaching the customer by telephone quickly enough to meet the job's deadline. Thus, while the automated payment system clearly seemed to improve the level of service for customers, the benefits of the web submission system for customers seem more mixed.

Conclusion

Having examined in detail the use of a particular standard form in practice, and finding that the coding scheme embodied in the form is chronically insufficient for usable description, we nevertheless also demonstrated that the order form as an active document is routinely adequate for accomplishing organisational business. We then specified some of the literacy practices – free-text notes, annotations on paper and tagging – that practitioners use to make the form work. Ironically, though, we found that these remedial practices re-introduce the very non-standard features that the form was designed to eliminate. Yet the form could not be used effectively for co-ordinating action without them. This tension makes the use of documents for the co-ordination of action challenging and always requires some degree of improvisation.

Making the work order work as a reliable document in and through such practices concomitantly makes Eastside Reprographics work as an organisation by enabling the concerting and co-ordinating of action at a distance. That is to say, if we understand (formal) organisations to be something like 'systems of coordinated and controlled activities that arise when work is embedded in complex networks of technical relations and boundary-spanning exchanges across time and space' – as John Meyer and Brian Rowan (1977; see also Scott 1981) describe one fairly standard view – then we must demonstrate precisely how this co-ordinating and controlling take place over temporal and spatial expanses so that such activities achieve social facticity as a 'system', an identifiable organisation or corporate firm. By 'precisely', we mean empirically, in the action itself and in all its detail; conceptual stipulation of the sort that glosses the concrete particulars of mundane organisational life and its incarnate practices, such as taking a customer order or trying to make sense of the documentary representation of that order as a prerequisite for fulfilling it, will not do. Similarly, we need to closely observe and carefully record mundane actions such as these if we are to understand how organisations can be 'collective actors' (see Coleman 1974 for a useful historical account of the concept of a collective or juristic person). Crucial empirical evidence of such collective concerting can be found in the details of the most ordinary document practices.

While one may be tempted to contest that the temporal and spatial distance required for such co-ordination at Eastside seems rather small to provide sufficient support for our intentionally far-reaching analysis – a day or two and some ten to twenty metres between the front counter where orders are taken and the document machines where the jobs are 'run' to fulfil them – the simple fact remains that any activity system, no matter how small or large, that is organised around actors that are not physically and temporally co-present will depend heavily on documents such as Eastside's standard form to both enable and enforce standardised methods for describing things in order to reliably co-ordinate the action. In this crucial respect, order taking and fulfilment at Eastside can stand for comparable work activities anywhere. Moreover, the artful interpretive work required of Eastside's employees to try and remedy the insufficiency of their form relies on very general human solutions to a chronic and inveterate rather than idiosyncratic problem.

In this chapter, as in prior ethnomethodological and conversation analytic studies (Suchman and Jordan 1990; Suchman and J. Whalen 1994; Whalen 1995; Moore and Maynard 2002), we have also examined the theme of 'standardisation as collaborative achievement'. Standardisation is a pervasive and growing feature of modern organisations (see Ritzer and Stillman 2001); however, it is not a static feature, but a practical, situated accomplishment of members working to co-ordinate their actions. Across the varied sites of standardisation, we see similarities in practice, as in the case of emergency call-takers (J. Whalen 1995) and copy shop order-takers creatively fitting particular cases into standard forms, or survey interviewers (Moore and

Maynard 2002) and copy shop order-takers using the order of items on a standard form to structure their interactions with respondents or customers (although this structuring is certainly much more rigid in the case of the former). Such forms of institutional standardisation are many and varied and in need of explication in future studies.

We hope our analysis can serve as an exemplar, then, suggesting how studying the situated use of documents such as the Eastside Reprographics work order (and its innumerable standard form relatives) provides us with a window – unfortunately all too rarely opened by researchers – on 'how it really works' (D. E. Smith 1990), on how documents are actually taken up in the course of everyday activities to organise the provision of services and the production and distribution of goods in both the private and public spheres of activity. And, in this way, our description and analysis of the practical use of the work order, much like Dorothy Smith and Jack Whalen (1997), also open up the possibility of re-specifying traditional concepts of bureaucracy, formal organisation and the like.

9 The interactional accomplishment of a strategic plan

DALVIR SAMRA-FREDERICKS

Introduction

This chapter draws on a study of organisational members doing their everyday work in a large UK private sector company. It forms part of a programme of work inspired by ethnomethodology (EM) seeking to examine the ways particular members constitute 'strategy' and facets of 'organisation' alongside a situated identity we know as either 'senior manager' or 'strategist' (Samra-Fredericks, 2003a, 2003b, 2004a, 2004b, 2005a, 2007). From having audio/video recorded organisational members' naturally occurring interpersonal routines over time and space, in this chapter, I focus on the behind-the-scenes efforts of two senior members refining for the nth time a written draft of their strategy document into a polished version for consumption both internally (employees, executive and the board of a public limited company (PLC)) and externally (City analysts, investment companies, media and the like). This chapter touches on how an annual strategy document was interactionally assembled and, as part of this, how members built elusive and spectacular objects and phenomena such as 'markets' and 'environment' as well as consolidated claims to knowing. Given that the strategic story is arguably the most costly story to be told in organisations (D. Barry and Elmes 1997; Samra-Fredericks 2003b), real-time studies of the 'work' of strategic story writing form an important field of study within organisation studies. However, fine-grained studies of everyday strategic management practice-as-interactionally-done as proposed here remain rare.

Undertaking EM informed research into members' naturally occurring talk-based interactional routines – i.e. 'the work' – brings to the fore the issue of members' background expectancies, reasoning procedures or 'methods'. In this empirical case these are deployed to produce a plausible document which makes visible epiphenomena such as the 'market'/'environment' (and elsewhere the 'future': Samra-Fredericks

2005a). Like Harold Garfinkel's (1967) jurors, the senior members are preoccupied with and settle upon what is an 'adequate account, adequate description and adequate evidence'. By doing so, we begin to answer the question posed by Garfinkel (1967, reproduced in 1974: 15) in his jurors' study regarding 'what makes them jurors?' – only here, it is 'what makes them strategists?'. This is one analytical theme in this chapter which, in terms of Charles Goodwin's (1994) ethnomethodological notion of 'professional vision', integrally builds 'objects of knowledge'. The acquisition of 'professional vision' by one organisational member is another element touched upon, albeit briefly, in this chapter. Inevitably, given space issues, just one moment from the everyday ebb and flow of talk/work-in-interaction is reproduced and discussed. The encounter transcribed and reproduced in this chapter was where the 'market' as the strategists' core object of knowledge and a pivotal element of the 'environment' was initially 'seen' and textualised as 'consolidating'. Through forms of talk, use of classification schemes, embodied gaze and the like – all finely and sequentially co-ordinated – together with putting-to-work their assumptions about the audience and the particular use to which the document will be put, the organisational members accomplish this work.

The chapter is structured as follows: the next section briefly outlines a broad and orthodox understanding of strategy work as well as mentioning relevant recent developments within organisation studies. Next, particular features of EM are briefly summarised together with Charles Goodwin's (1994) notion of 'professional vision'. This is followed by an outline of the research approach and then reproduction and discussion of one brief illustrative extract. The conclusion includes a summary of the range of contributions these kinds of studies make to organisation studies.

Strategy work and practice

Within the broad field of organisation studies, one sub-field termed 'strategic management' centrally promulgates the idea that developing strategic direction is an important but also complex and risky venture since ascertaining opportunities and threats given notions such as high environmental uncertainty, information ambiguity, bounded rationality and so on are not easily resolved. Practitioners face a mosaic of dilemmas, contradictions and paradoxes as they invest effort to determine a realistic (realisable) future. Consequently they use an array of tools and techniques (for example, SWOT-type of analysis)[1] to assist and organise a mass of information, opinion, values/beliefs and feelings and to facilitate some grasp of 'approximations' to manage their 'world' (environment). Studies of this process continue to attract attention from organisation studies scholars (for an overview see Johnson, Scholes and Whittington 2005; Mintzberg, Ahlstrand and Lampel 2002). Traditionally, this sub-field was dominated by disciplines such as economics or functional specialisms such as marketing; hence notions of market development and securing competitive advantage characterised the field. This also resulted in a situation in which the everyday work that constitutes 'strategy' or strategising, and the use of tools and technologies in this work, remained 'black-boxed' until very recently (Johnson, Melin and Whittington 2003; Samra-Fredericks 1996, 2003a, 2003b, 2004a, 2004b, 2005a, 2005b).

Focusing on just one component of strategy work – especially in large companies – we will see two organisational members developing and writing a strategy document. This document has also been variously conceptualised: for example as a rational-functionalist 'item' enabling senior managers to both take and communicate their decisions and/or intentions; or as performing symbolic-legitimating functions which are, of course, historically and culturally established and bearing particular political and ideological elements (Knights and Morgan 1991; Lilley 2001; see also Alvesson and Willmott 1996). Today, especially in large listed PLCs in the UK such as the one from which Extract 9.1 is reproduced, executive teams, PLC boards, City analysts, institutional investors and so forth all expect some sort of (annual) assessment and update on strategic matters. Given this, as expected in the company from which Extract 9.1 is reproduced, a formalised strategic planning cycle (a routine) was in place, and one important and concrete outcome was the annual strategic plan or document (these terms were used interchangeably by the members themselves). My interest has been in how they actually do this strategy work, turn by turn, simultaneously invoking and reproducing phenomena deemed to be 'macro' – that is, 'organisation', 'markets', 'the City' and so forth. It necessitated getting close to practitioners and seeing such work being done in 'real time', there-and-then, in the course of collaborative work as far back as 1991.

Other streams of research which have also sought to get close to practitioners at work in light of both the 'linguistic turn' and the 'practice turn' in social theory (Schatzki 2005; Schatzki, Knorr Cetina and von Savigny 2001) include studies of situated learning or 'communities of practice' (Lave and Wenger 1991; Wenger 1998), learning-in-practice (Nicolini, Gherardi and Yanow 2003; Gherardi 2000) and activity systems (Blackler, Crump and McDonald 2003; Engestrom 1987). As part of their work, they too aim to examine the tools and technologies members use and remain sensitive to the language and knowledges deployed. In addition, and given this chapter's substantive topic, we also find that the emerging strategy-as-practice sub-field aims to examine the praxis, practice and (strategic) practitioner trinity close up (Whittington 2006; see also Johnson, Melin and Whittington 2003; Jarzabkowski, Balogun and Seidl 2007). However, fine-grained study of practitioners' *talk*-based *inter*actional routines as displayed in this chapter has yet to gather momentum even though referrals to ethnomethodology's potential contribution within organisation studies and the strategy-as-practice sub-field are evident (Clegg, Carter and Kornberger 2004; C. Clark 2004; for a fuller review, see Samra-Fredericks and Bargiela-Chiappini 2008; Samra-Fredericks 2005b).

However, 'workplace studies' (Hindmarsh and Heath 2000; Hughes, Randall and Shapiro 1992; Luff, Hindmarsh and Heath 2000) do consider the finely tuned embodied co-ordination of talk, activities and the ways that objects, technologies and artefacts are mutually constituted. Moreover, given their attention to talk-in-interaction as envisaged within ethnomethodological and conversation analytic (CA) traditions, these studies undertake video and audio recordings of members-at-work, enabling researchers to explicate the delicate and intricate array of skills or competencies in terms of practical reasoning 'methods' necessary to do the work. By doing so, they promise to extend our understandings of organising, managing and strategising beyond that currently found within organisation studies.

Ethnomethodology and strategic 'vision' at work

Seminal studies of practical reasoning in organisational settings (Bittner 1974; Cicourel 1968; Garfinkel 1967; Silverman and Jones 1973; Wieder 1974b; Zimmerman 1971b) and studies of institutional talk emerging from the conversation analytic tradition (e.g., Drew and Heritage 1992b; Heritage 1997; Silverman 1997b) indicate the ways in which we can advance our understanding of the delicate, skilled, contingent nature of what organisational members do to accomplish work tasks. Having already inspired workplace studies and allied approaches, Garfinkel's (1967, 2006; Rawls 2008) ethnomethodology paves the way to explicate organisational members' – here, those deemed to be doing strategy work – taken-for-granted *methods* or their practical reasoning procedures for producing order that constitutes sense (see also Heritage 1984; Turner 1974a). It is shared 'methods' that provide for social 'things' to be seen in common and yield a situated order. Further, properties of sequential and contingent detail are crucial. In addition, from Anne Rawls' (2008) consultation of Garfinkel's unpublished manuscripts, the 'identified actor' or situated identity is also shown to be a delicate sequential achievement.

The indexical nature of words as well as an acknowledgement that members exploit this feature in order to be able to 'go on' means that preservation of the sequential and contingent detail is paramount for understanding how members do what they do. In Garfinkel's (1974: 17) EM, talk is not only a 'resource' but also 'something that while using and counting on he [the member] also glosses'. In glossing, the member

ignores certain features; he does not want to make a lot of it. He wants, in fact, to remove himself from that so as to recommend in the report on a world not of his doings that which for him is now available as the thing he could put together in his account of ordinary affairs. (Garfinkel 1974: 17)

One pervasive way this 'removing' is undertaken is through deployment of one of three methods foregrounded in Goodwin's (1994) research – the method of 'classifications'. Goodwin's three broad methods offer one route for the close analysis of members' collaborative efforts constituting 'professional vision': the latter 'consists of socially organised ways of seeing and understanding events that are answerable to the distinctive interests of a particular social group' (C. Goodwin, 1994: 606) – which, in this research setting, makes them 'strategists'. Lodged within 'endogenous communities of practice' professional vision is, of course, continually enacted and finetuned against an evolving sense of contingencies *including* members' observed relational webs, as we shall see shortly. The focal method evidenced across Extract 9.1 is use of 'classification schemes' in terms of the words, jargon or language used, with the second method of 'highlighting' only briefly mentioned here. The third method is not discussed due to space issues and deals with the production and use of 'material representations' such as graphs and, for us, even the strategy document itself. Clearly, each of the three methods is underpinned by a complex array of reasoning procedures and inferential practices, also discernable in Extract 9.1. Additionally, what this chapter also touches upon is the *acquisition* of professional vision as a subtle and intricate everyday interactional achievement. In other words, we glimpse forms of everyday learning-on-the-job.

It is through use of such methods, inferential practices, sequential sensitivity and so on that the strategists come to construct their core 'object of knowledge' as well as consolidate their professional vision. For the archaeologists in Goodwin's study, their collaboratively constituted 'object' was a map of a field site where 'ancient remains' were plotted. This was their 'built material cognitive artefact' (C. Goodwin 1994: 626) arising from engagement with a material entity, the soil. For our organisational members, though, there is an added complexity. While on the one hand they too build a 'material cognitive artefact' which animates their field and discourse of 'strategic management' in the form of a strategic document, on the other hand, they must also integrally create layerings of 'objects of knowledge' which remain elusive conceptual phenomena. There is no material entity to which, for example, the 'market' or the 'environment' neatly or even tenuously corresponds. They remain in the cognitive-conceptual realm but our organisational members talk *as if* they can see and touch them. It is here that talk as a 'resource' to 'gloss' is shown to deliver a distancing and objectivity which exude that 'world not of his doings' (Garfinkel 1967, 1974).

To pave the way for the empirical illustration, the next section begins with a very brief overview of the research approach and some contextual information.

An empirical illustration of members interactionally accomplishing the strategy plan

The study involved the observation and recording of groups of senior managers in various locations (e.g. private offices, public meeting rooms or other collectively realised spaces such as corridors, taxis and lifts). Data were collected over significant periods of time – from five- to twelve-month periods – and usually for one to three days per week. This chapter specifically focuses on the real-time interactional accomplishment of one aspect of their practice, namely, the strategy plan/document. The tape recordings, the generated transcripts, the documents collected and the field notes provide the basis for scrutiny of this work.[2] Additional details surrounding the methodology and the practical issues that arise from undertaking this research are available elsewhere (Samra-Fredericks 2004a, 2004b); this includes debates around remaining 'transcript-intrinsic' data and the relevance and place for 'transcript-extrinsic' data arising from the ethnographic component.

In one chapter-length offering it is inevitable that only a fraction of the analysis is touched upon and that ethnographic detailing is kept to a minimum. Briefly, the company from which Extract 9.1 is reproduced is a large PLC (listed in the FTSE 100) employing tens of thousands of employees with a turnover of thousands of millions of pounds sterling. On the particular day from which the reproduced extract is drawn, Peter (a pseudonym – formally titled the director of strategy) had scheduled a series of meetings in his office to refine for the *n*th time the (draft) strategy plan/document. The particular colleague present in the extract is a senior manager from finance, Colin (a pseudonym) who was integrally involved in writing the document. Peter and Colin are both white, in their mid-forties and seated at a small table in a room in a high-rise office block in a large city. They are labelled 'strategists' hereafter but it must be emphasised that this is a situated and intersubjective accomplishment.

In terms of a broad description of the encounter, Peter read or glanced at portions of the draft; then he and Colin talked about it alongside various other pieces of information and expressions of opinions and feelings that had arisen from prior streams of interactions; Peter then wrote 'in' or scribbled 'out' portions of text in the draft document. In this way, reading and writing were reflexively tied to talk. Physical proximity to another colleague was critical too for effective co-ordination and object construction. Notably, on entering the office and by selecting a seat to sit next to Peter, Colin was able to closely track Peter's 'gaze' on the pages of the draft document and correspondingly orchestrate his own page turns in a seamless, split-second fashion. As for Jon Hindmarsh and Christian Heath's (2000: 537) workers, gaze is, then, conceptualised as an 'additional embodied resource' for effective task completion. Indeed, on other occasions when particular members sat apart – deliberately as it transpired – they caused an interpersonal disruption (ineffectiveness) as they asked for 'specifics' in terms of page numbers or what the paragraph referred to began with and so on. Others then waited for the pages to be turned and the text to be located which, altogether, made the proceedings more formal. Without doubt, it is in the trivial or the minutiae that formality and notions such as politics and interests are often done and made consequential.

Extract 9.1

```
 1  Peter:    so we really need to make this (.)
 2            ((pen points to location)) something like
 3            that one needs to be about the economic downturn
 4            and impact on market structure
 5  Colin:    um ((brief silence as both read))
 6  Peter:    what did you say on that (.) you said (.) when
 7            you say (name of division) do you
 8            mean (group name)?
 9  Colin:    er yeah (name of company) and the organisation,
10            the external market
11  Peter:    I'd think I'd call that recent trends
12            ((quietly speaks as reads)) 'survival' ((brief
13            pause as reads)) it's another bit that goes in
14            there, I think you've got it somewhere
15            else but the urm the dirt cheap asset prices
16            need to go in there
17  Colin:    yeah I've got that in the main body of the
18            report and the competition but yeah we
19            can out that in there as well
20  Peter:    I think it's part of the (.) if you made that
21            into market structure=
22  Colin:    =yes=
23  Peter:    =what that says is (.) here's a big
24            consolidation piece ((inaudible three
25            words)) its (.) consolidation
26            ((spoken as he writes))
27            ((and less than a minute later))
28  Peter:    so some of that um (.) er I would call that
29            (brief pause) mobilising our strategy
30  Colin:    um um right=
31  Peter:    =I'd call that ((as he writes he says))
32            'mo ::bili:sing ' (.) and I'd make that the
33            last one
34  Colin:    sure
```

```
35  Peter:   in the hope that they'd got bored by then and
36           won't read it properly (.) I'd call that
37           mobilising our strategy or a sub-heading
38           (inaudible word) 'business
39           transformation' ((writes as says this))
```

As briefly noted above, through tracking Peter's gaze and orches-
trating his own page turns together with orientating to Peter's pen-
pointing on his page – an embodied referential practice – Colin was
able to swiftly 'find' the particular item being indexed when Peter said,
for example, 'this' or 'that' (lines 1–2). Here, 'that one' at line 2
indexed a chart representing financial data and the instruction was
that 'we' need to make 'this' – the information on the 'economic
downturn and impact on market structure' – like *'that'* chart (itself
one of Goodwin's material representations). The indexical properties
of 'this' (L1), 'that one' or 'that' (lines 2–3, 6, 11, 17, 19, 20, 23,
28, 31), 'there' (lines 14, 16, 19), or 'here's' (line 23) were found to be
swiftly resolved given this proximity but, more than this, meaningful-
ness and object construction hinged on the sequential unravelling of
particular 'thises' and 'thats' as well as the use of particular words or
classifications which specifically framed and guided Colin to 'see' it
too (discussed shortly). Here, each subsequent 'that' indexed: at line 6,
a particular division; at line 11 it was a table and summary text to be
marked as 'recent trends'; Colin's two 'thats' (lines 17, 19) referred to
the phenomena captured under the Peter's phrase 'dirt cheap asset
prices'; and notably, only at line 21 did all these prior 'thats' – a split
second earlier organised as 'recent trends' – come to be organised by
Peter under 'market structure'. Not only was this re-labelling one
important textual form of *highlighting*, there-and-then, the sequentially arrived-at judgement was one that now 'says ... consolidation'
(line 24). Further, while it is unsurprising that careful positioning of
portions of text 'there' (lines 14, 16, 19 – a location in the document)
was evident, judging positioning also arose from forms of sequential
reasoning-out-loud (lines 11–16) which invited specific next turns (e.g.
lines 17–19) and subsequently, here, brought forth a 'thought' or
'idea' (lines 20–1).

What Peter comes to see from this sequencing is 'consolidation'
(line 24) and he alludes to an assumption – shared knowledge or
idea – that others will see it that way too. He makes aspects of his

reasoning available to Colin, and yet Colin's responses were also crucial for arriving at this point where they settled on what 'it' all meant. Given the prior turns and, hence, the sequential order properties, the *inference* was that when 'dirt cheap asset prices ... go in there' 'it's part of the ... market structure', which – *if done* – 'says ... big consolidation'. This also displaces the earlier suggested 'recent trends'. The conditional qualifier 'if' momentarily suggests the presence of other possibilities or scenarios, and it could even be describable as a moment of uncertainty or not-knowing, or a form of 'testing out' that came to be swiftly 'fixed' (lines 23–4). In this mundane, taken-for-granted fashion members 'work' to stabilise the lived flow and render particular phenomena amenable to 'knowingness' and 'control' (Samra-Fredericks 2005a). Here, across just three turns-at-talk (Colin's 'yes', line 22) latching on to Peter's prior turn, to which Peter's next turn does the same) they swiftly moved from 'if' and possibilities to 'say[ing]' we have 'big consolidation'. On hearing this, there was a form of rehearsal underway, too, in the sense of evaluating if 'it' all sounds plausible. Overall, object construction was underway while, of course, subsequent turns-at-talk may re-cast prior turns into meaning something different; in this light, each next turn constantly and relentlessly made clear the prior. This is what sensemaking entails, taking us beyond Karl Weick's (1979) more general notion.

On this occasion, in talking and referring to the range of 'thats', Peter reasoned out loud and came to 'see' *this* 'pattern'. He drew upon and met background expectancies (the logic-in-use, historically and culturally established) that when 'economic downturns' 'impact on market structure' (lines 3–4) and are *coded* ('I'd call that ...?') under 'recent trends' (line 11), and linked to *classifications* such as 'dirt cheap asset prices' (line 15) and information on 'competition' (line 18), it not only *highlights* or generates a particular reality in terms of a 'market' but one further finetuned into 'consolidation' (line 24). Clearly, specific forms of language use, words or classifications are vital for such social 'things' to be seen in common.

Words, words and more words

Forms of classificatory language (and the coding schemes into which they are often arranged; see conclusion, pp. 213–16) furnish particular distinctions that characterise and constitute a profession or field of activity (archaeology, law and, here, strategic management) (C. Goodwin 1994; Samra-Fredericks 2003b, 2005b). In Extract 9.1, a cursory glance beginning at line 3 yields two major phenomena – also constituting the field of activity known as strategic management – that is, 'economic downturn' and 'market structure'. Subsequently, we journey through a vocabulary pointing to/constituting the institutional relevancies and character of this encounter as well as furnishing 'what makes them strategists'. So we have 'external markets' (line 10), 'recent trends' (line 11), 'survival' (line 12), 'dirt cheap asset prices' (line 15), 'competition' (line 18), 'market structure' (line 21), 'consolidation' (lines 24, 26), 'mobilising our strategy' (lines 29, 37) and 'business transformation' (lines 38–9). However, it is not just these words/classifications alone but also the allied inferential practices and indexing of specific 'thises' and 'thats' which *sequentially* and all together, evoked their core object of knowledge.

Following Garfinkel's stance, this is also an occasion where information – just like objects, like words, like identities (see Rawls 2008) – is constituted as a recognisable and intelligible object through just these sequence orders and ways of 'making sense of a world in common'. As Rawls contends, it is the relationship between the items that constitutes the information for those competent enough to read it (like Heath and Luff's (2000) doctors). So when 'recent trends' and 'cheap assets' and so forth are sequentially ordered in *this* way (and textualised), then the relationship between the items delivers a recognisable, plausible or mutually intelligible object of a 'market' consolidating. In other words, in talking as they do and given *this* sequenced 'social organisation of referring' to the range of 'thats' noted above, allied with *this* use of particular words or classification, it all becomes clear in terms of meaning *this* and not that. Since no word is clear on its own – indeed what does 'dirt cheap assets' mean? – words have particular meaning because of where/when they were spoken – that is, the sequential order properties – and give rise to particular inferences as we begin to discern in this instance. Further, it is in this mundane, taken-for-granted way that they render the 'object as independent of the experience or perception of any one individual' (D. E. Smith 1996: 187, cited in Hindmarsh and Heath 2000: 529). In other words, as Garfinkel (1967) observes, talk as a 'resource' to 'gloss' delivers a distancing and objectivity which exude a 'world not of his doings'. Here, it is the apparent concretisation of the epiphenomena – a 'market' – in a particular way and as the strategists' core object of knowledge, that is made mutually intelligible or 'good enough' (Rawls 2008) for present purposes.

Knowledge or *a* piece of information is a sequentially derived and co-produced accomplishment, and what is often glossed as *judgement* – in this light, the 'fact' of a market consolidating – is also a sequential 'accomplishment of details' (Rawls 2008: 706). Further, as each minor move laminates (Boden 1994) onto the next, this becomes even more 'fixed' and 'real' as I discuss further elsewhere (Samra-Fredericks 2005a, 2003a). Recalling more formally the character of reflexivity where what is said is always taken in relation to the last – that is, it reflects back on the last – as a reflexive sequential chain, Peter and Colin then constitute the basic order of sensemaking here (Rawls 2008). In doing their work, they inevitably trade on a common stock of shared knowledge, whereby Peter presumes that Colin will 'get' the inferences he is making in terms of the market consolidating. He does not need to explain his moves, but also, as we see in the next section, he simultaneously instructs Colin how and what to see too.

Doing instruction and acquiring 'vision'

In a business studies classroom, students on receipt of Extract 9.1, were able to identify the more knowledgeable organisational member. So, what did they notice or cue into? One opening feature may be that it was Peter who asked Colin a question (lines 6–8) setting up the sequential context obliging another to provide an answer. Who selects the 'topic' is another obvious analytical route: here it is Peter who 'pulls' out portions of the text to comment upon, giving rise to subtle asymmetries of participation (Heritage 1997: 175–8). Something the students did not have easy access to, though, was the observation that Peter wrote on his copy of the draft *first* and turned his pages *first* and Colin followed a split second later. However, this could be presumed to be occurring given *what* is *said* and *when* it is *said* and what follows. The earlier mentioned observation of taking the lead with 'this' (line 1) and 'that' (line 6) is also relevant. In many respects, we have one member 'marking' (appraising) another's written work with the latter confirming or consolidating this description given his next utterances and embodied actions/orientations.

Another key noticeable element were utterances such as those at lines 11–16, where Peter suggested how to group 'items' together and what to 'call' particular pieces of information. It was this language use that initially marked out for me that here is the everyday and *momentary* constitution of the relational pairing of expert and novice. In other words, the analysis of this meeting (and others) suggested that the use of 'I'd think I'd call that' (line 11) and, shortly after, 'I would call that ...' (line 28), 'I'd call that ...' and 'I'd make that ...' (lines 31, 32) – and given *where* they were located and *what* the talk dealt with (content or topic) – occasioned 'learning-on-the-job'. Hence, Peter is engaged in verbal (and textual, when written down) *highlighting* akin to Goodwin's archaeologist enabling a junior/less knowledgeable colleague to 'see'. The CA notion of turn-design also brings to the fore the ways such turns taken by Peter were designed to select particular next actions – that is, agreement or clarification on what to 'call' items. At the same time, we can also glimpse a particular interactional contingency being managed when one member amends or appraises another's work. It invites 'caution' (Silverman 2001), which then necessitates mitigation, which is accomplished through these language forms while simultaneously being publicly hearable as an instruction. This is confirmed in light of Colin's responses (lines 5, 10–19, 30, 34). Such turns inevitably render Peter and Colin as particular identified actors; these identities are sequentially achieved (Garfinkel 2006; Rawls 2008). Here not only are they 'strategists', but *momentarily* ones blended with less or more knowledge; and thus, teacher and novice. The emphasis on 'momentarily' is an important aspect too since at another point in this same meeting Colin's understanding of 'finance' meant that the teacher–novice relational pairing was also swiftly switched around.

On this occasion, though, through the use of *these* linguistic forms in *these* locations, Peter did instruction and guided Colin on what to 'call' something and where to place it and, hence, how to *highlight* it. As also noted earlier, Peter makes visible his reasoning and inferential practices – his professional vision – and he *leads* Colin to 'see' in these terms too. Peter also exudes an 'air' of certainty through the assertive 'I' but even this notion of certainty remains a joint accomplishment, since without Colin's responses in *those* locations Peter may not have quite 'seen' 'consolidation' just then or re-labelled text as 'recent trends'. This prefacing ('I'd call that' and so forth) invites particular responses (agreement, checking out and the like) which are then also a method for Colin (lines 10–19, 22, 30, 34) to publicly and progressively display that he has seen and appreciates the nature of the object that Peter 'sees' (a market consolidating). But can we go further and claim that shared seeing/understanding is *really* gained? What *is* gained is an 'intersubjective alignment' (Hindmarsh and Heath 2000: 557) but one which constantly shifts and is worked on. So, for example, Colin could still be waiting to 'see' what it all meant at a later point in interactional time. This retrospective-prospective nature of talk also takes us back to Garfinkel's (1967: 41) more fundamental notion of trust:

> The anticipation that persons *will* understand, the occasionality of expressions, the specific vagueness of references, the retrospective-prospective sense of a present occurrence, waiting for something later in order to see what was meant before, are sanctioned properties of common discourse. (Garfinkel 1967: 41)

In this light, Colin's minimal turns (lines 5, 22, 30, 34) were occasions where the 'continuers' or 'response tokens' (Silverman 2001: 135) may have *meant* agreement and shared 'seeing' or actually provided a 'breathing space' as he waited for Peter's subsequent talk in order to 'see what was meant' or being done. It is the next turns that guide our interpretation: so while Colin's 'ums' at line 30, for example, could be potentially heard in a number of ways, given the prior *and* subsequent more assertive turn by Peter it was *heard* as hesitation by Peter (and there is acknowledgement here that this is one occasion where the tone of voice assists interpretative possibilities). Given Peter's response, then, he has interpreted that Colin is uncertain that the text be re-labelled as proposed. He latches on and repeats more assertively (lines 31–3) what he 'would call that', which indicates this and marks his efforts to secure intersubjective alignment.

When turning to the utterance at lines 31–3 and 35–6, we can also begin to discern the complex ways that prior experiences – when recalled (occasioned; Sacks 1992) and elusively put-to-work – generate consequences as well as *r*eproduce here what is often termed a politicised/blame culture.

Strategists' stratagem for mitigating the 'effects' of strategy work

When Peter adds that 'I'd make that the last one' 'in the hope that they'd got bored by then and won't read it properly' (lines 31–3, 35–6), one question raised is: why does he hope that? Equally, was this a serious or genuine 'hope' or a flippant, amusing remark? Peter has also assumed that, given the task underway, Colin knows who is indexed by this referral to 'they'. On one level the action of placing this portion of text 'last' suggests a general characterisation of this as a political 'move'. The 'item' they seek to place 'last' deals with 'mobilising our strategy' – in other words an update on 'implementing decisions' to bring about the strategic changes envisaged – hence, the sub-heading 'business transformation'. Yet, mobilising the 'strategy' (in terms of the specified strategic changes) was proving difficult so if this section were to be read first – i.e., when the reader is alert (near the beginning of the document) – it could be highly problematic.

Other known-in-common 'formal' but backgrounded knowledge is that Peter is accountable for recording progress around 'mobilising strategy' – he is director of strategy, after all – but he and a small team of colleagues (including Colin) were not responsible for *managing* progress. This important detail had been overlooked on previous occasions, which had led to members being blamed for 'outcomes' that they were not responsible for. Hence, this task needs to be set against an institutional 'know-how' (Heritage 1997: 176) in terms of particular organisational contingencies being a source of difficulty and needing to be handled. First, then, in general terms, for 'organisation' to take shape or form, a complex mesh of historically and culturally finetuned role-based rights and obligations need to be observed. Here, in terms of the 'they' being the chief executive officer, executive and PLC boards, one right or expectation is to receive timely and relevant information on 'mobilising'/implementing the strategy. However, the corresponding 'obligation' on the part of Peter and his colleagues to supply that information could detrimentally affect them as it had in the past. In other words their 'rights' to be treated fairly (through recognition of the fact that the implementation issue was beyond their remit) had been breached before. Thus, we can start to see how actions in the past are recalled and subtly put-to-work disrupting the formal organisational forms of rights and obligations and how those rights and obligations are subtly re-calibrated during everyday conduct. Indeed, without this practical understanding of their relational webs being woven into the document in this way, they would *not* be effective practitioners in a volatile and politicised environment – of course, in observing it in such a subtle and mundane form, they continue to reproduce elements of it.

Given this stratagem, then, there is a double meaning to the word 'strategic', since our senior managers are also being strategic in an everyday and practical sense when they attend to the sequential placing of portions of text and what to 'place last' so that it is more likely to be hidden or lost. *It is their 'stratagem' to do strategy work and to mitigate the 'power effects' of what they themselves produce* (Knights and Morgan 1991; Samra-Fredericks 2005b). Very much like Goodwin's notion of expert testimony, they too are 'metapragmatically aware' of the communication practices which organise their work and to which they will be held accountable. Inevitably they write thinking forwards and, hence, assumptions of how the document will be read are being utilised as a means to effectively accomplish – strategically design – the strategy document. The point here is that prior 'lived' experience or a shared biography is also invoked, and sequentially and interactionally – but also diffusely – evoked, spoken, textualised and made consequential. Such stocks of knowledge remain crucial 'resources' shaping or guiding their practical reasoning whilst also, in this case, delivering a subtle and elusive form of critique of their localised social structure while still meeting basic rights and obligations. From a critical (Foucauldian) perspective, subtle forms of self-discipline are underway, while, in Garfinkel's ethnomethodology, account-making and accounting practices glimpsed here are indeed 'one way that institutional conduct, power and inequality manifest in interaction' (Rawls 2008: 718). Peter's utterance, then, evokes a context of accountability and can be seen as akin to Wieder's (1974b) 'Telling the Code' study, since he too is 'refusing to comply with formal institutional expectations' (Rawls 2008: 715). No other explanation was necessary: Colin knew the code while, importantly, for me to access it and draw the correct inferences necessitated fieldwork over time.

Conclusion

Being unremittingly pulled back to situated actions to see what people actually do, we begin to open up what has remained 'black-boxed' in strategic management (Samra-Fredericks 1996, 2003a). For example, a claim that practitioners face a mosaic of dilemmas, contradictions and paradoxes as they invest effort to determine a realistic (realisable) future led to the crucial 'how question': how do they deal with such phenomena and do the work? The challenges around accessing organisational members doing their everyday work, analysing their work and then reproducing empirical illustrations and allied detailed descriptions are immense. Beginning in the mid-1980s – and having been exposed to the intellectual infrastructure of ethnomethodology (Garfinkel 1967) and conversation analysis (Sacks 1992; Sacks, Schegloff and Jefferson 1974) – I wanted to see and to record organisational members' talk-in-interaction in order to 'understand our world as it happens' (Boden 1990). This would also provide the basis from which to substantiate the claim that EM and CA have much to offer organisation studies (Samra-Fredericks and Bargiela-Chiappini 2008). Through recording and tran-scribing members' talk-in-interactional-organising efforts, we preserve members' sequential, contingent accomplishments – that is, the interac-tional complexity – beyond what we have routinely seen in the field of organisation studies. Furthermore, explicating the *in situ* contingent accomplishment of phenomena and hence 'the work' and 'the methods' is also easily stretched to embrace critical forms of scholarship where we can open up for empirical study how power is exercised and asymmetric relations accomplished (Samra-Fredericks 2003a, 2005b).

The approach also advances scholarship in *process* which currently animates various quarters of the organisation studies field as well as broadening conceptions of effectiveness (Samra-Fredericks 2003b) – not only as an interactional accomplishment, but also in terms of detailing the mosaic of knowledge and skills or competencies that encompasses minutiae, easily overlooked or deemed too trivial for scholarly attention. These are the 'gaps-in-between' reported by Iain Mangham and Annie Pye's (1991) executives, which will continue to elude researchers doing 'interviews' as opposed to fine-grained studies as indicated here.

Although Extract 9.1 remains just one fleeting behind-the-scenes moment, it does, however, begin to enable us to glimpse a practical and contingent form of reasoning when these members first voiced/ 'saw' and textualised 'the market' as 'consolidating'. Some of the dis-tinctive features of (strategy) work and 'what makes them strategists' are also available. Through attending closely to the observable turns-at-talk taken, at particular points (lines 11–16, 23–26, 28–9 and 31–3) we do see, for example, Peter explicitly engage in making *the* distinctions that characterised their field and discourse, constituting 'professional vision'. In the process of reasoning out loud, and through marked forms such as 'I'd call that …', which enabled Colin to acquire 'competence', sense was constituted and the contours of the object known as the 'market' were discerned and 'fixed'. Simultaneously, Peter realised a situated identity as strategist and, momentarily here, as one who was more knowledgeable. He subsequently continued to display and consolidate 'what it means to see the world' as this-or-that kind of individual – in other words, what it is that makes him a strategist. In this light, then, the research reported here is also a form of study that potentially contributes to studies of identity work, another growing field within organisation studies. In addition, and given the delicacy of appraising another's efforts as well as practically instructing another on the required changes to the document, it is also an approach that contributes to studies of learning-in-practice as a dynamic, intricate and wholly interactional affair. In many ways, it offers a contrast to the pervasive idea and (I assume) practice of an annual or periodic workplace appraisal. Instead, we find that everyday forms of appraising another's competence proliferate in these nuanced ways. Significantly, too, local, experientially derived forms of knowledge are also invoked and made consequential – rendering a practical, political-cultural and morally imbued effectiveness that cannot be easily taught.

At this particular point in interactional time, for these particular members, a market consolidating could have been either a good thing or not (an opportunity or a threat). Only as each next minor move laminated onto the next minor move did the participants interactionally make visible their *reasoned* production of particular 'facts' or 'truths' (Samra-Fredericks 2003b) as well as – inadvertently – constituting an array of power 'effects' (Samra-Fredericks 2005b). They did, then, come to answer the question: will we be able to reap advantage and thus 'survive' the 'economic downturn' or not? Explicating their arrival at a 'good-enough' answer could not be taken up here but what can be noted is that later, during this same meeting, they assembled a 'judgement' that their current depiction of the market offered an 'O' (opportunity) for the 'organisation' as it was currently 'fixed'. To those versed in strategic management as a field of study and activity, mention of 'opportunity' in *this* realised setting for *these* members orientating to accomplishing *this* task evokes the SWOT schema or 'tool' which is one dominant coding device (C. Goodwin 1994) – with the other categories being 'threats', 'strengths' and 'weaknesses'. Particular words or specialist forms of classifications are often arranged into coding schemes and SWOT is one such device – a tool or technique of the trade (Samra-Fredericks 2005a). Such tools structure and 'transform the world into the categories and events' (C. Goodwin 1994: 608) that are relevant for these organisational members' work. Extract 9.1, then, is where these speakers began to lay the foundations for populating this SWOT device – that is, a market consolidating being 'entered' into the 'O' quadrant.

In sum, their moment-by-moment interactional management of contingent detail meant that they produced a 'mutually recognisable' order and, like Garfinkel's (1967) jurors, settled on what was an 'adequate account, adequate description, adequate evidence' (Garfinkel 1974: 16). Crucially, this account and descriptive work are what we know as the strategic story, and it is a costly story told in and by 'organisations' given the resources they consume and the consequences that follow (D. Barry and Elmes 1997; Samra-Fredericks 2003b). It is then even more important that the real-time 'work' involved in strategic story writing is scrutinised – and in the ways proposed here. More generally, too, leading organisation studies scholars such as Stephen Barley and Gideon Kunda (2001) have called for researchers to get close to organisational members doing their work if we are to avoid impoverishing theoretical developments. Yet, the challenge is: can the field abandon conventional theorising and embrace 'the details' as proposed by Rawls (2008)? Furthermore, if

[e]ach and every time we encourage a colleague to look at an object with us and establish some shared sense of that object, we once again affirm our existence in a common workplace (and world) with others. It is moments and practices such as these that underpin the organisation of collaborative work. (Hindmarsh and Heath 2000: 559)

Then, should not *our* 'moments and practices' be scrutinised and, by doing so, conventional theorising further challenged and 'the details' embraced? A fleeting glimpse of two organisational members' affirming the existence of their core object of knowledge – the market – and, thus, themselves as strategists was offered and similarly, in so many ways, doing this chapter affirms my existence as a researcher and student of organisation studies.

Notes

1. SWOT analysis involves the identification of an organisation's strengths and weaknesses as well as the opportunities and threats offered by the environment in which the organisation operates.

2. The need for confidentiality and anonymity also means that no one else listens to the tapes; hence, all transcription has been undertaken by the author. Further, all references to members' names, the products, services, financial details, technology and so forth are excluded from the transcripts. Instead, a broad description of the omitted term is included in parentheses in the transcript.

10 Peripherality, participation and communities of practice: examining the patient in dental training

JON HINDMARSH

Introduction

The concept of 'communities of practice' (CoP) has gained significant purchase in the study of learning within and between organisations since it was originally introduced by Jean Lave and Etienne Wenger (1991) and subsequently elaborated by Wenger (1998). The concept is bound up with a thoroughly social theory of learning that emphasises the inherently collective and participative character of becoming skilled in an occupation, a profession or indeed any activity in everyday life. A CoP involves members engaging in joint enterprise who inevitably develop a shared repertoire of skills, norms and competencies. Learning is then seen in terms of centripetal movement and shifting identity from peripheral (novice) to central participation (expert) within a particular community of practice.

The development of the concept was grounded in a series of ethnographic studies of apprenticeship, but as Ash Amin and Joanne Roberts (2008) and others (e.g. Cox 2005) argue, it is increasingly engaging a more formal, indeed managerialist, agenda:

As CoPs thinking proliferates, the original emphasis on context, process, social interaction, material practices, ambiguity, disagreement – in short the frequently idiosyncratic and always performative nature of learning – is being

I am deeply indebted to the students and staff of the dental clinic for allowing me to record and report their daily work. I am further particularly grateful to Patricia Reynolds and Stephen Dunne for their academic and practical contributions to this project. I would also like to thank Nick Llewellyn, Davide Nicolini and Gerry Hanlon for their comments on aspects of the work presented here. This research has been funded by King's College London and by the Economic and Social Research Council/Engineering and Physical Sciences Research Council 'HapTEL' project (RES-139-25-0387).

lost to formulaic distillations of the workings of CoPs and instrumentalist applications seeking to maximise learning and knowing through CoPs. (Amin and Roberts 2008: 353–4)

Indeed CoPs are now often positioned as knowledge management 'tools' (Roberts 2006) which draws debate and discussion to consider the character of 'communities' and how they can be fostered. This is at the expense of more detailed accounts of the 'practices' that sustain, reproduce and indeed define those communities (see Gherardi 2006). In response to concerns that 'practice' is lost in contemporary literature on CoPs, this chapter attempts to return to studying apprenticeship learning in order to consider the distinctive value in investigating some of the 'real-time' interactional practices in a CoP.

The chapter considers the case of clinical dental training. It treats this as an instance of apprenticeship learning (although admittedly a relatively formal one) in order to explore potential contributions of ethnomethodologically informed studies of interaction to the emerging literature on CoPs. In doing so it considers aspects of the real-time organisation of the dental apprenticeship and delineates some of the embodied practices in and through which the dental CoP reproduces itself.

The chapter focuses on the moments when supervisors (known as 'demonstrators') arrive chairside to assess the progress of the student and to discuss a patient's case. Routinely these discussions draw the demonstrator to inspect the mouth of the patient during which time the demonstrators discuss aspects of what can be seen in the context of the work being presented by the student. In these short episodes the students are exploring how to see and inspect the mouth of the patient and how to develop appropriate treatment plans. However, they are not divorced from the participation of the patient. It is here that the chapter attempts to contribute to extant literatures. The chapter considers how the co-participation of the patient is organised as peripheral and yet is fundamentally central to the production of these episodes and of the dental CoP more generally. In doing so it explores an often ignored aspect of the CoP literatures – that there are numerous individuals engaged in practice who are not following centripetal trajectories to becoming expert practitioners. Thus one aim of the chapter is to demonstrate the value of taking 'peripherality' seriously in studies of practice in communities of practice.

Analysing a dental community of practice

The trajectory of the apprentice outlined by Lave and Wenger (1991) from peripheral and limited participation to increasing access to new modes of behaviour and responsibility is clear in the apprenticeship of UK dental students. They participate in clinical settings from an early stage of their studies. In the first year they assist more experienced fellow students, by the end of the second year they start to treat a small number of regular patients and by the fourth and fifth years they may be acting as the regular 'dentist' for up to twenty-five patients. While the forms of apprenticeship that Lave and Wenger considered tend to be informal, the dental apprenticeship is formally organised and involves clear examination and assessment prior to students being allowed to move on to the next level of development. Nevertheless, as they progress through their undergraduate degree they take on more responsibility in dealing with more complex cases and more complex procedures.

The clinical environments in which the dental students operate are intriguing domains as the activities of formal education exist alongside and intertwined with the delivery of dental care. All students are developing their skills in history-taking, case presentation, diagnosis and restorative techniques, and they are also tending to real patients with real dental problems – they are, for all intents and purposes, their dentist. However, the dental students are in training, so they are supervised by demonstrators who regularly assess their progress and discuss next steps. Indeed an issue that cuts through this chapter concerns the ways in which matters of discussing professional knowledge and practice intersect with matters of managing patient care.

The chapter is organised around the analysis of audio/video recordings of naturally occurring dental training episodes within one clinical unit in a major UK dental school. These are not contrived situations, so the data were collected after ethical and research clearance had been given by the local National Health Service (NHS) trust. In collecting the materials, written consent was sought from the patients involved, the dental students in the room (whether or not they were to be filmed), the dental nurses and the demonstrators. The presentation will be structured around the detailed analysis of a series of data extracts drawn from the wider corpus of recordings.

As with the other studies in this volume, the analytic gaze is drawn primarily from ethnomethodology and conversation analysis. Essentially the concern of these video-based studies is to explicate the range of resources that participants have to hand in co-ordinating and co-organising conduct with one another in real time. These are brought to the very heart of the analysis of social interaction. In this regard video-based studies play into some of the central concerns of contemporary practice-based studies more generally in organisational analysis – namely concerns with 'situation', 'embodiment' and 'materiality'. The distinctive angle that video-based studies bring to these matters is the concern with the real-time organisation of action and interaction: the moment-to-moment order and organisation of practice.

Professional vision in apprenticeship training

Lave and Wenger's (1991) argument that learning can be seen in terms of increasing participation in a CoP is elaborated through the consideration of series of ethnographic accounts of apprenticeships involving tailors, midwives, meat-cutters and the like. However, given the conceptual thrust of the work, the accounts of apprenticeships rather gloss the action and interaction involved in real-time situations. Indeed, while numerous studies of professional socialisation and apprenticeship have adopted an ethnographic approach, few consider the real-time organisation of apprenticeship, that is, the ways in which 'expert' and 'apprentice' interactionally organise training on a moment-by-moment basis. One influential exception can be found in the studies of 'professional vision' by Charles Goodwin, and especially his research on the archaeological apprenticeship (C. Goodwin 1994).

His notion of professional vision refers to the 'socially organised ways of seeing and understanding events that are answerable to the distinctive interests of a particular social group' (C. Goodwin 1994: 606). Goodwin argues that there is an interdependence between a profession's discourse and the material artefacts around which the profession concerns itself; thus the features of a setting are tied to the activities of the profession in that setting. Pursuing this theme, Goodwin suggests that 'the ability to see relevant entities is lodged not in the individual mind but instead within a community of competent practitioners' (C. Goodwin 1994: 626). So in his studies he discusses how, in the course of *in situ* training, learning to be a competent practitioner involves linking professional categories to specific visible phenomena and explores three practices in and through which such professional vision is articulated: through the creation and application of coding schemes; through the embodied practices of highlighting salient features; and through the production and use of graphical representations or inscriptions. He argues that:

a relevant *object of knowledge* emerges through the interplay between a *domain of scrutiny* ... and a set of *discursive practices* (dividing the domain of scrutiny by highlighting a figure against a ground, applying specific coding schemes for the constitution and interpretation of relevant events, etc.) being deployed with a *specific activity*. (C. Goodwin 1994: 606)

Most relevant to this chapter are the practices of highlighting where, for Goodwin, the patch of dirt that his archaeologists view becomes a locus for embodied work practice rather than a site of contemplation. It is in and around this patch of dirt that 'expert' and 'apprentice' practice their craft in collaboration and in doing so work through the situated (re-)production of routines, knowledge, problems and the rest. This resonates with a range of studies that highlight the ways in which modelling, observation, imitation and learning-in-practice are extremely important parts of learning processes (e.g. Sheets-Johnstone 2000; D. E. Smith 1996; Gherardi and Nicolini 2002a). Indeed as Silvia Gherardi and Davide Nicolini suggest:

Novices learn first by watching, looking, seeing and listening to others while carrying out meaningful activities. Language plays a fundamental role both by providing a 'scaffold' for the unfolding activities and by furnishing the elements that allow the novice to make sense of situations and contexts. Linguistic productions, such as linguistic acts and narratives, enable the novice to learn how to see, listen and feel. (Gherardi and Nicolini 2002a: 216)

In our case, interactions between demonstrators and dental students are often organised around a collaborative viewing and discussion of the (work in the) patient's mouth, similar to the training episodes that underpin Goodwin's discussion of archaeological apprenticeships.

When demonstrators are requested to come chairside, they are routinely asked to assess work, whether that work is a case presentation, charting of the teeth and fillings, removal of decay or old fillings, a restoration or whatever. In these moments the demonstrators often examine the work for themselves. This not only involves visual inspection, which might be possible simply by looking over the student's shoulder, but also involves a tactile inspection with fingers and probe – for example, to feel decay in a tooth, to feel the mobility of a tooth, to feel the solidity of a filling and so forth.

These inspections are not organised in isolation from the student. Not only do students frame the inspection by introducing the progress that they have made but they also routinely bend down to *look with* the demonstrator into the mouth. These episodes partly involve a 'modelling' approach to teaching, in which the student watches whilst the demonstrator silently examines the mouth. That said, at certain moments, the demonstrators provide an account of what they can see or feel in the mouth of the patient, what has been termed elsewhere (and in a very different context) an 'online commentary' (Heritage and Stivers 1999).

Consider a simple example, Extract 10.1, in which the demonstrator (D) is undertaking an oral examination to assess the state of a tooth being worked on by the student (S). The letters in bold in the transcript highlight the temporal location of the associated images.

Extract 10.1

```
 1       (3.2) [A]
 2   D:  it loo^ks like there's a cra:ck there,=
 3   S:  =yeah:.= [B]
 4   D:  =(going) all the way across. [C]
 5   S:  mmhm
 6       (2.5)
 7   D:  there's err::
 8       (0.5) couple of options^
 9       there. one is to put G I C
10       core: in there,=
11   S:  =yep.
12       (0.7)
13   D:  just to see how that responds.
14       (3.2)
15   D:  there is: a crack there.
16       (0.5)
17   S:  yeah:.
```

Extract 10.1 begins with the demonstrator examining the tooth with a dental mirror. During this examination the demonstrator provides a series of comments on what can be seen and felt (starting with 'it loo^ks like there's a cra:ck there', line 2). These comments 'highlight' aspects of the phenomenal field for the student. This one is coupled with a subtle

Figure 10.1. From left to right, Images A, B and C. The demonstrator and the student examine a crack in the patient's tooth

re-orientation by the demonstrator of his body and of the dental mirror. These delicate shifts in orientation of tool and body encourage the student to move from her general over-the-shoulder observation to lean in further to view the visual trace of this possible crack (see Figure 10.1, Images A and B). Once the student re-aligns and produces an appropriate response token ('yeah:') the demonstrator then progresses the examination further by revealing the shape of the crack '(going) all the way across' the tooth (see Figure 10.1, Image C). So the talk of the demonstrator shapes and is organised in relation to the emerging participation of the student (see also Hindmarsh, Reynolds and Dunne forthcoming).

However, these inspections are not always purely visual. Indeed, as the examination progresses the demonstrator reaches for an oral probe which marks a shift from a visual inspection using the mirror to a visual–tactile exploration of the tooth and the potential crack. Following this switch the demonstrator announces much more definitively 'there is: a crack there' (line 15). The visual features have been shown already and the tactile sensations, the *feel* of the crack, are not available for collaborative viewing. Nevertheless he continues the probe work which may make the resistance of the probe in the crack available to the student. Indeed the student moves very slightly to look more closely following the comment.

As the inspection progresses, the assessment and the potential treatment plan move from being rather tentative or ambivalent to more assured and definitive; there is a move from 'it might be a crack' to a later discussion of the type of filling material to use. So the examination is wrapped up with the discussion of further treatment;

indeed, the visual evidence under discussion forms the basis on which to build the discussion of the treatment plan. Thus the student is not only given direction but is shown how that direction is reached as the demonstrator provides access to aspects of his visual inspection and tactile exploration.

The patient in training

These training conversations involve reports and assessments of symptoms as well as evaluations of students' work and discussions of potential treatment plans. While the focus for the above description rests purely with the demonstrator and student, learning to become a dentist very much involves the patient. However, in the main patients have a peripheral position during the training conversations.

Partly of course, the patients are peripherally positioned, prone and facing away from the demonstrator and student, making it more difficult to engage in conversation. Also, the examination is in the mouth, which severely restricts the patient's opportunities to speak and makes it impossible for the patient to view the features under discussion. Furthermore, some of the technical details of the diagnostic discussion are out of the realm of everyday language and knowledge, and therefore make it more difficult for patients to contribute. So while the diagnostic reasoning and treatment alternatives are explicitly discussed by demonstrators and students, these are only partly available to the patients due to their inability to see the problem or understand some of the more technical terminologies.

Either the demonstrator or the student routinely provides some account of action following the training conversation. However, the accounts presented to patients tend to be of a procedural rather than a diagnostic character. For example, see Extracts 10.2 to 10.5, which focus on a series of accounts presented to patients following these training episodes (for the implications of these accounts being presented by demonstrators as opposed to students, see Hindmarsh, Reynolds and Dunne 2008).

Extract 10.2

S: okay^ I'm just going to go grab the filling material, and we'll (solve) that problem for you

Extract 10.3

D: we're just going to note down all the fillings and things
    in your mouth and then I'll come and have another look,
    alri:ght?

Extract 10.4

S: okay, so we're going to fill it err. just before I do that …

Extract 10.5

D: so what we're going to do: (.) is we're just going to co-
    do a couple of little tests on this tooth here. (.) to: see:
    whether it's ali:ve. (.) alright? we think it is^ (.) but we just
    want to see how: alive it is. (.) alright? (.) okay?

Each of these includes mention of what will happen next, but does not
comment on or explicitly link to the discussion between student and
demonstrator. Furthermore it is unusual even at this point for the
patient to raise questions about what they have previously heard.
Although the discussions have been clearly audible to the patient, it
would be unusual for the patient to say 'I heard that earlier.' Rather they
take it as news and are complicit in the interactional separation of
training and health care delivery.

However, there are some occasions in which they are explicitly drawn
in to the discussion. Consider for example Extract 10.6. The student has
just presented the patient's case – running through the dental and
medical history, symptoms and the like, and now the demonstrator is
undertaking an initial examination of the teeth and gums. We join the
action towards the end of this examination.

Extract 10.6

```
 1  D:  Now push your tongue ri:ght out for me and over
 2      to one si::de^ (1.3) and now: the other way. (0.7) pop your
 3      tongue over this way^ (.) tha:t's lovely. (1.0) that's all
 4      fi: ne isn't it.
 5  S:  mmhm.
 6  D:  good.
 7      (.)
 8  D:  and yes: these these gingivi down here: do look ni:ce.
 9      you've got (stiv) [there.
10  S:                    [yeah.
```

```
11      (2.3)
12  D:  'nd no si:gns of inflamm[ation there:^
13  S:                        [mmhm.
14      (2.0)
15  D:  a little bit of recession.
16      (0.5)
17  S:  mmhm.
18      (0.7)
19  D:  mmhm.
20      (1.0)
21  D:  .tch [    and   it's a:        ] class:ic denture
22  S:       [(and it's the outside as)]
23  D:  stermatitis cos it's just in the are[as where
24  S:                                       [yeah.
25  D:  the: (1.5) plas:tic [is, isn't it? it's not even
26  S:                      [mmhm:
27  D:  where the metal is.
28  S:  mmhm.
29      (1.3)
30  D:  so we'll nee:d to have a look at tha:t.
31      (3.0)
32  S:  tch [wha-
33  D:      ['ts not sore: up there, is it?
34      (0.5)
35  P:  no::
36  D:  no. off- often it's rea:lly really bright red and
37      they don't get any soreness at all:.
38  S:  'kay.
39  D:  but we could give her something to pop on that
```

First, it is clear that one way in which patients are drawn in to training conversations is when they are given instruction. So at the start of Extract 10.6, the demonstrator encourages the patient to move her tongue in particular ways in order to improve visual purchase on the phenomena of interest (lines 1–3). At these moments the patient is active even though she remains silent. However, the patient is cast as an object for inspection in that what can be seen is framed for the viewing student rather than 'translated' for the patient. The comments on what can be seen ('tha:t's lovely. (1.0) that's all fi:ne isn't it') are designed for and directed towards the student and treated as such by the student ('mmhm'). The patient, who remains silent, similarly treats the comments as designed primarily for the student in that she does not acknowledge these comments in any way.

Indeed the demonstrator continues by highlighting the 'gingivi' (gingivitis), the inflammation of the gums, around the roots of one tooth in particular. This 'case' is framed as 'nice' and later 'classic'. It stands as a textbook example of the symptoms of 'denture stermatitis'. They are clearly not 'nice' or 'classic' for the patient, but rather for the matters of training and indeed for appreciating actual instances of dental phenomena (or textbook categories). Subsequently a series of visible 'symptoms' are introduced one by one ('you've got (stiv) there', 'no signs of inflammation', 'a little bit of recession', 'in the areas where the plastic is'). There is a delicacy to this work because the very fact that the demonstrator renders them visible means that, if the student has not in fact previously noticed them, then they can now find them.

This sequence from lines 8 to 32 involves no verbal contribution designed explicitly for the patient or produced by the patient. However, in line 33, a question is asked directly of the patient, ''ts not sore: up there, is it?'. The tone of the question is markedly distinct from the previous sequence which helps to highlight the change in recipient, as does the physical movement of the demonstrator to lean in towards the patient. The question itself projects a negative answer and indeed gets one. Then the response is again used to stand as a further typical feature of denture stermatitis – the answer is trans- formed to present the patient at hand and her experiences as repre- sentative of the typical manifestations of the problem ('often it's rea:lly really bright red and they don't get any soreness at all:', lines 36–7). So the inclusion of talk from the patient in these moments is used to help the student to recognise this as one of a class of real cases of denture stermatitis.

Within the course of these episodes the visual and verbal conduct of the patient is routinely put to the service of the activities of training. However, it is not that the demonstrator and student 'marginalise' the patient; indeed the patient shows no expectation that she might be included more within these discussions. The patient, just as much as the students and demonstrators, orients to these principally as training episodes and not overly bound up with the matters of a standard dental consultation. Of course the patients recognise that there are other occasions in the consultation when they will be informed by the student what is happening and what might happen next. Nevertheless all parties contribute to the production of these episodes as training conversations.

Managing knowledge 'front-stage'

The previous sequence also reveals how the triad of demonstrator–student–patient is in some ways sustained as two dyads (demonstrator–student, demonstrator–patient). When the demonstrator is chairside, it is very rare in these moments for the student to talk directly to the patient. In part this character of the interaction is founded on and sustained by the spatial organisation of the triad, with the student behind the patient and the demonstrator to the side and enabling mutual gaze with the patient. However, on occasion the distinctive knowledge and experience of the patient become highly relevant to the shape of the training encounter and the talk of the student. Take, for example, Extract 10.7 in which the fourth-year student (S) is processing a new patient. Each time a new patient begins with a student, the student must take the medical, personal and dental history as well as undertaking an initial examination and developing a treatment plan. They must then present this work to their demonstrator.

Extract 10.7 begins as the student is re-presenting the history he has taken. In many ways he is summarising or recounting part of a discussion he has had with the patient some twenty minutes previously. The patient can hear the discussion, and so her presence can enable the demonstrator to check information provided by the student. In this portion of the presentation the student is introducing the range of medications currently being taken by the patient. Of course the presentation of this information is not only relevant for assessing the quality of the work of the student, but also has implications for the course of treatment that might be decided upon.

Extract 10.7

```
1  S:   her: medication, she has arthritis, so she's taking
2       arthritis- arthitic fifty?
3  D:   mm-hmm.
4  S:   er:m tramadol for the pain. err codemerol. (.) I'm
5       not sure what co- is [it a pain killer?
6  P:                         [°cocodamol°
7  D:   cocodamol?
```

```
 8  P:  yeah.
 9  D:  yes. they're pain killers.
10  S:  co- [yeah. okay.
11  D:      [that's paracetamol and codeine.
12  S:  yeah(.) °I thought she said° codemerol. huh.
13      (.)
14  D:  coco:::damol.
15      (1.0)
16  S:  okay.
17  D:  mm-hmm.
18  S:  erm quinine erm [because she gets cramps [err.
19  D:                  [yes.                    [right.
20  S:  ranitidine for lining the stomach. [and,
21  D:                                     [mm-hmm.
22  S:  stomatidol? stom-?
23  P:  stemitol.
24  D:  stomita. stomi- [stemital. stemital.
25  P:                  [stemitol.
26  P:  hmmm.
27      (0.5)
28  S:  stemi-
29      (0.3)
30  P:  ss:[:
31  D:     [that's:
32      (1.2)
33  S:  stemitol?
34  D:  ss- (.) that's for [indigestion?
35  P:                     [for the the the the dizzy spells.
36  D:  for the dizzy sp[ells.
37  S:                  [dizzy spells.
38  D:  right. okay. you ought to look that up then if you
39      don't know
```

There are two moments of particular interest here – around the patient's contributions in lines 6 and 23.

There is an explicit intervention from the patient following a problem in the case presentation around line 6. The student announces the next medication as 'codemerol' (line 4) and when the demonstrator nods in acknowledgement (in the micro-pause in line 4), the student takes this as ratifying the drug name so asks not whether he has the right drug name, but rather what it is: 'I'm not sure what co- is it a pain killer?' (lines 4–5). As soon as troubles are marked by the student, the patient quietly re-formulates the drug name to 'cocodamol' and the demonstrator immediately turns to her and asks 'cocodamol?'. The patient confirms and the demonstrator then elaborates on the nature of the medication ('they're pain killers', 'that's paracetamol and codeine') and re-utters the name to help the student to spell it as he enters it into the patient record.

Two further drugs (quinine and ranitidine) are announced along with the reasons the patient is taking them. Each is acknowledged and accepted by the demonstrator ('yes', 'right', line 19; 'mm-hmm', line 21). Then the student in his very announcement of the next drug (line 22) indicates troubles, as he adds a questioning intonation on his first version of the name and even begins to present a second version within this turn ('sto-matidol? stom-?', line 22). The question is not directed at the patient, but rather at the demonstrator – it is a question about what this candidate drug name might actually be. The patient then – much more clearly and loudly than in the last instance – reformulates the name ('stemitol.'). The question is not designed for her, but the patient takes the opportunity to interject and the demonstrator turns to her. After continued confusion over the name of the drug (covering some ten lines of the transcript), the demonstrator then checks why the patient is taking the medication ('that's for indigestion?', line 34). The patient replies that it is to treat dizzy spells and this leads the demonstrator to turn back to the student to say 'right. okay. you ought to look that up then if you don't know' (line 38).

So presenting a case history in the presence of the patient raises some intriguing opportunities and challenges for demonstrator and student alike. The fact that the patient is present means that the accounts of the medical and dental history (as well as the symptoms) presented by the student are open to assessment by them. Thus the demonstrator has an additional resource to assess the quality of the case presentations. Pamela Hobbs argues that student case presentations in medical training are fundamentally bound up with abilities to 'bridge the gap between the clearly formulated lists of symptoms and the confusion of incomplete or misleading information extracted from the history and examination' (Hobbs 2004: 1603). In these cases the demonstrator has present the very source of some of the patient information that the student is attending to.

On the other hand, much of the 'back-stage' (Goffman 1959) work implicit in making assessments and diagnoses is pushed 'front-stage' (i.e. before the audience of the patient) in these training situations. In ordinary health and dental care consultations, questions and uncertainties about the nature of one drug or another may be straightforwardly masked or concealed by the practitioner – and then 'looked up' offline. However the real-time demands of training render these uncertainties hearable and available to the patient. Thus the demonstrator, the supervisor, is faced with additional burdens in managing uncertainty before not only the student but also, more importantly in some ways, the patient. The uncertainty in this case is re-cast as an issue for the student to pursue ('you ought to look that up then if you don't know'), almost as a matter related to training, rather than by topicalising, or continuing to attend to, the uncertainty itself (e.g. 'I don't know what that is'). So the presence of the patient seems to impact on the shape and character of the discussions between demonstrator and student. Furthermore we have strong evidence that, far from being straightforwardly passive and peripheral, the patient is intimately attentive to the details of the training conversations.

Other forms of patient participation: vision of a different kind

Thus far the primary focus for the analysis has been the verbal contributions of patients and how they are attended to. However, there are also more subtle and delicate ways in which the patients participate in these training episodes. Consider Extract 10.8 for example. During the student's description of the case (lines 1–5), the demonstrator is putting on a pair of protective latex gloves and just after he does this he turns to pick up a probe and mirror from the table to the side of the dental chair. The student continues with his description of the case as the demonstrator grasps these tools and begins to inspect the patient's teeth.

Extract 10.8

```
 1  S:  and there was staining around
 2      the sides. and I put my probe
 3      in (.) and there were slightly
 4      sticky [A] areas. (.) [B] so:
 5      on the treatment plan we devised
 6      when she first came in [C] one
 7      of the things was to remove
 8      (.) the old amalgam restoration
 9      [and clear the (caries).
10  D:  [°kay°
11      (7.0)
12  D:  °I can't see any more or feel
13      any more decay.°
```

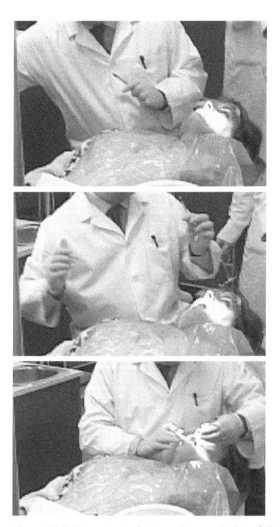

Figure 10.2. From top to bottom, Images A, B and C. The patient readies her mouth for inspection

What is significant is that the student's account is not interrupted. This is significant because while the student was talking, the demonstrator sat down beside the patient, put on his gloves, picked up the mirror and probe and began an inspection in the patient's mouth – without any need for a verbal request for the patient to 'open wide'. This reveals how the patient is intimately aware of the emerging trajectory of the activity. In Figure 10.2, notice how in the first image the mouth is closed as the demonstrator reaches over to grasp the instruments. However in the second image her mouth is open wide. Indeed just at the point that the demonstrator begins to turn his torso back towards her and retract his arms towards her head, she opens her mouth ready for inspection. This allows him seamlessly to begin the oral examination while the student can continue to describe the previously agreed treatment plan.

There follows a sustained period in which the demonstrator continues to inspect the work undertaken by the student. He is able to conduct the examination in the light of the planned work that the student has described. Therefore the patient's attentiveness and active, although non-vocal, participation supports the on-going training activities of the demonstrator and student.

Similarly, consider again Extract 10.1.1, previously presented purely in terms of the interaction between demonstrator and student. In the earlier account the patient was rendered passive, and yet it turns out that she plays a delicate but active role in supporting the work of the others. There is a moment in the extract when the demonstrator, having visually examined the mouth using a dental mirror, reaches over to retrieve an oral probe to continue the inspection. This involves taking his hands out of the patient's mouth.

Extract 10.1.1 (segment)

```
 7  D:  [A] there's err::
 8      (0.5) couple [B] of options^
 9      there. one is to put G I C
10      core: in [C] there,=
11  S:  =yep.
12      (0.7)
13  D:  just to see how [D] that responds
```

While the demonstrator stretches his right hand over to the tray of instruments at chairside (during 'there's err::'), he keeps his left hand hovering above the patient's face holding the mirror, not in the mouth but a few centimetres above it (see images A and B in Figure 10.3). As the demonstrator's hands leave her mouth, the patient relaxes her jaw but does not close her mouth. It remains readied for further inspection. As the mirror is lowered again, towards the very end of the pause in line 9, the patient immediately widens her mouth to enable the examination to continue without any direct request required. So, when the

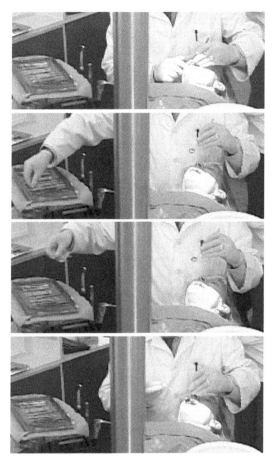

Figure 10.3. From top to bottom, Images A, B, C and D. Managing a momentary break in the oral examination

demonstrator initially lifts his hands out of the patient's mouth this can be seen, and is treated by the patient, as a temporary halt to the examination. This enables the discussion of the treatment plan to continue seamlessly.

In studies of general dental practitioners, Timothy Anderson (1989) found that dentists recurrently had to call on patients to open their mouth. Here, in these student dental clinics, it is rather rare to hear a phrase such as 'open for me, please'. In these data, patients present themselves for inspection, such that there is rarely need for a call to

'open wide'. These are extraordinarily typical features of the training
episodes in these data. So, in rather subtle ways, patients actively support, indeed underpin, these training episodes through a very simple
activity – readying the mouth for inspection. The work of the patients
enables the training conversations to progress as they *actively* present
themselves as *passive* objects for inspection.

Discussion: considering participation and peripherality

These encounters involve students learning to see, learning to feel,
learning to structure oral examinations, learning to link evidence to
treatment plans and the like. In these moments, then, we are considering
in fine-grained detail the embodied practices that underpin the reproduction of a community of practitioners through joint attention and
highly situated learning. Interestingly, while Wenger (1998: 47) notes
that practice 'includes all the implicit relations, tacit conventions, subtle
cues, untold rules of thumb, recognizable intuitions, specific perceptions, well-tuned sensitivities, embodied understandings' and that these
are critical to success in CoPs, it is very rare for studies in this field to
consider such real-time details of practice. They reveal features of the
community's work and character that would otherwise remain hidden –
for example, with regard to identity, participation and even how specialist knowledge is managed and displayed.

   However, the episodes discussed in this paper do not just feature
'expert' and 'novice' working on inanimate materials, but also the
patient impacts on the organisation and even the content of the training
conversations. Interestingly we have seen that all parties work to com-
partmentalise these training conversations within the wider organisation of dental care in the clinic. In general, the patients do not join in
with diagnostic discussions and do not tend to pursue 'translation' or
explanation during the course of these conversations. Such co-
orientation to the character of the conversations as 'training' enables
them to proceed without regular interruption and delay – otherwise
each step of the diagnostic discussion would have to be re-formulated
for the patient. Even though patient participation is compartmentalised
in some ways, it is not that the patients are ignored. Demonstrators
often greet the patient and, more importantly, discussions about the
broader treatment plans take place regularly at other moments during
the consultations. So all parties, the patient included, are complicit in

organising the patient's position as peripheral when the demonstrator comes chairside.

However, while patients are organised as peripheral, they are also simultaneously central to the seamless organisation of these episodes. They are, in various ways, highly attentive to the practices of teaching and learning, and thus they are ready to contribute where relevant. We have considered, for example, how the patient responds to instruction and questioning that is routinely re-formulated by the demonstrators for the purposes of discussing dental phenomena with students. We have also seen how the patient can interject in minimal but significant ways to the training conversations in order to clarify symptoms, medications and the like. These interjections, whilst minimal, are significant for the matters of training and provide both a resource and a challenge for students and demonstrators alike.

We have also seen how the patient physically participates in these episodes. While patients cannot see the phenomena under discussion (which are of course in the mouth), they do have some access to the activities that constitute inspection. Indeed we have revealed the abilities of patients to anticipate trajectories of inspection activity such that they can contribute in minimal ways (e.g. readying their mouth). Goodwin argues that 'members of a profession hold each other accountable for – and contest – the proper perception and constitution of the objects of knowledge around which their discourse is organised' (C. Goodwin 1994: 628). Within these training episodes demonstrators explicitly hold students accountable for their constitution of objects as an indicator of professional competence. Interestingly, however, demonstrators can also be seen to implicitly expect a certain level of patient attentiveness and competence in being able to see and anticipate when to ready the mouth for inspection.

These variable forms of participation that place the patient as peripheral to and yet central for the training conversations suggest potential implications for CoP studies and literature more generally. Highly relevant here is an extract from the foreword to *Situated Learning* by William Hanks in which he calls on readers to:

Think of all the everyday situations in which people coparticipate to a limited extent, thereby gaining access to modes of behaviour not otherwise available to them, eventually developing skills to certain kinds of performance. Participating members of religious congregations, athletes training together

... patients being seen by doctors – all of these interactions initially involve limited, highly asymmetric forms of coparticipation. All seem to have the potential to transform the participants, even if their trajectories and thresholds of change differ widely. (Hanks in Lave and Wenger 1991: 18)

The potential of this call seems to have been lost in the contemporary CoP literature and the ways in which they consider 'peripherality' (e.g. Wenger 1998: 167). At various points in the CoP literature the peripheral character of some participants is acknowledged. For instance Wenger (1998: 154) discusses 'peripheral trajectories' and Karen Handley *et al.* (2006: 644) note that 'not everyone aspires to (or can achieve) full participation'. However, the explanations for this tend to be bound up with choice or power: that some people choose not to identify with the community or that some are denied the rights to progress. These discussions reside with a single CoP and are preoccupied with those who could be on centripetal trajectories. By focusing on interactional practices we are forced to consider the variable forms of participation and types of participant that resist these accounts. Doing this encourages us to take more seriously overlapping 'communities' and forms of membership.

There is some interesting recent work engaging with these very issues. For instance, in studying how members learn practices of safety in the Italian building trades, Gherardi and Nicolini (2002b) were drawn to explore the 'constellation of interconnected communities of practices' that sustain and mediate diverse and concurrent cultures of safety. Furthermore Dawn Goodwin *et al.* (2005) demonstrate the ways in which operating theatre practitioners (e.g. anaesthetists, auxiliaries and so forth) have intertwined occupational trajectories, where they each exhibit centripetal tendencies but on different trajectories within the community. They engage in practice but they identify with distinct yet overlapping communities.

Here, we are pushing this issue a little further. The patient has a peripheral and highly limited trajectory within the dental 'community of practice'. They are not in a separate CoP. They may become increasingly attuned to the working practices of dentists, but they cannot be classed as a dental 'practitioner' of any kind.

The patients who attend the student dental clinic are regular patients; they come often and for long consultations. For this they get free treatment and the knowledge that they are helping to train the next generation of dental practitioners. Through this participation they become skilled in what is required of them – most notably opening and closing the mouth at appropriate moments, which rests on a knowledge of the embodied work of demonstrators and their students (what I have termed elsewhere 'intercorporeal knowing'; see Hindmarsh and Pilnick 2007). Of course there are always new skills to learn, and some of these may be learnt within the course of a consultation or maybe in a few moments of being asked to perform some task a few times. It could then be said that they have a limited centripetal trajectory as 'patients' in becoming 'good' or even 'expert' patients, and in doing so they can support the other participants.

Patients' abilities to anticipate trajectories of embodied conduct are such that they can contribute, in subtle ways, to the seamless progression and organisation of training discussions. Thus, while patients are clearly peripheral to the dental community of practice, they are also central to the practices of the community. In this way patients do not have a fixed 'role', but as we have seen, through their verbal and visual conduct, they variously support, mediate and at times shape the character of the training discussions.

So while most analyses of CoPs have considered the central figures, the 'experts' and the 'novices' moving with centripetal tendencies, the focus on the study of interactional practices reveals the complexity in the organisation of CoPs. In doing so, analyses of this kind highlight the variable forms of participation engaged in by members to the encounter. It reveals how more peripheral figures in a CoP can be critical to the practices in and through which CoPs reproduce and sustain themselves. In the case at hand, the reproduction of the dental CoP in these moments rests on the patient orienting to the 'trainingness' of the encounter and participating in ways that support its progression. Furthermore it reveals how the discussion of knowledge and procedure can be affected by the presence and participation of peripheral members in the encounter between expert and novice.

Given the increasingly managerialist agenda in the CoP literature, there is a danger that glossing 'practice' may mean that the critical contributions of 'peripheral' participants are overlooked. In turn, developing strategies for sustaining communities may well be impoverished by a lack of understanding of these very contributions. Peripheral participants are not unique to dental CoPs, but have equivalents in numerous settings of health care apprenticeship and similarly in CoPs in which customers, clients and the like are variably involved. I would argue that to understand 'practice' in these CoPs requires careful consideration of the ways in which such 'peripheral' members variably, and sometimes quite subtly, participate in the activities of the CoP. This demands an attention to the interactional production of practice in the community of practice.

References

Aaker, D. A., V. Kumar and G. S. Day (2004). *Marketing Research*, 8th edn. New York: John Wiley and Sons.

Abolafia, M. Y. (1988). Markets as Cultures: An Ethnographic Approach. *Sociological Review* reprinted in Callon 1998, pp. 69–85.

— (1996). *Making Markets: Opportunism and Restraint on Wall Street.* Cambridge, MA: Harvard University Press.

Adler, P. and B. Borys (1993). Materialism and Idealism in Organizational Research. *Organization Studies*, 14 (5): 657–79.

Alby, F. and C. Zucchermaglio (2006). Afterwards We Can Understand What Went Wrong, But Now Let's Fix It: How Situated Work Practices Shape Group Decision Making. *Organization Studies*, 27: 943–66.

Alvesson, M. and H. Willmott (eds.) (1996). *Making Sense of Management: A Critical Introduction.* London: Sage.

Amin, A. and J. Roberts (2008). Knowing in Action: Beyond Communities of Practice. *Research Policy*, 37 (2): 353–69.

Anderson, W. T. (1989). Dentistry as an Activity System: Sequential Properties of the Dentist–Patient Encounter. In D. T. Helm, W. T. Anderson, A. J. Meehan and A. W. Rawls (eds.), *The Interactional Order: New Directions in the Study of Social Order.* New York: Irvington, pp. 81–97.

Arminen, I. (2005). *Institutional Interaction: Studies of Talk at Work.* Aldershot, UK: Ashgate.

Ashenfelter, O. (1989). How Auctions Work for Wine and Art. *Journal of Economic Perspectives*, 3: 23–36.

Ashenfelter, O. and K. Graddy (2002). *Art Auctions: A Survey of Empirical Studies*, NBER Working Paper No. 8997. Cambridge, MA: National Bureau of Economic Research.

Atkinson, J. M. (1978). *Discovering Suicide: Studies in the Social Organisation of Sudden Deaths.* Pittsburgh: University of Pittsburgh Press.

— (1982). Understanding Formality: The Categorization and Production of 'Formal' Interaction. *British Journal of Sociology*, 33: 86–117.

Atkinson, J. M. and P. Drew (1979). *Order in Court: The Organisation of Verbal Interaction in Judicial Settings.* London: Macmillan.

Atkinson, J. M. and J. Heritage (eds.) (1984). *Structures of Social Action: Studies in Conversation Analysis*. Cambridge: Cambridge University Press.

Atkinson, M. A., E. C. Cuff and J. R. E. Lee (1978). The Recommencement of a Meeting as a Member's Accomplishment. In J. N. Schenkein (ed.), *Studies in the Organisation of Conversational Interaction*. New York: Academic Press, pp. 133–53.

Baker, C. (1997). Ticketing Rules: Categorization and Moral Ordering in a School Staff Meeting. In S. Hester and P. Eglin (eds.), *Culture in Action: Studies in Membership Categorization Analysis*. Washington, DC: University Press of America, pp. 77–98.

Baker, W. E., R. R. Faulkner and G. Fisher (1998). Hazards of the Market: The Continuity and Dissolution of Interorganizational Market Relationships. *American Sociological Review*, 63: 147–77.

Balogun, J. and G. Johnson (2005). From Intended Strategies to Unintended Outcomes: The Impact of Change Recipient Sensemaking. *Organization Studies*, 26: 1573–1601.

Barley, S. and G. Kunda (2001). Bringing Work Back In. *Organization Science*, 12 (1): 76–95.

Barry, A. and D. Slater (2002). Introduction: The Technological Economy. *Economy and Society*, 31 (2): 175–95.

Barry, D. and M. Elmes (1997). Strategy Retold: Towards a Narrative View of Strategic Discourse. *Academy of Management Review*, 22 (2): 429–52.

Beckert, J. (2007). *The Social Order of Markets*. MPifG Discussion Paper 07/15. Cologne: Max-Planck-Institut fur Gesellschaftsforschung.

Bergström, O. and D. Knights (2006). Organisational Discourse and Subjectivity: Subjectification During Processes of Recruitment. *Human Relations*, 59 (3): 351–77.

Biggart, N. and R. Delbridge (2004). Systems of Exchange. *Academy of Management Review*, 29 (1): 28–49.

Billig, M. (1978). *Fascists: A Social Psychological View of the National Front*. London: Academic Press.

(1999). Whose Terms? Whose Ordinariness? Rhetoric and Ideology in Conversation Analysis. *Discourse and Society*, 10: 543–58.

Billig, M., S. Condor, D. Edwards, M. Gane, D. Middleton and A. R. Radley (1988). *Ideological Dilemmas*. London: Sage.

Bitner, M. J., H. B. Bernard and S. M. Tetrault (1990). The Service Encounter: Diagnosing Favorable and Unfavorable Incidents. *Journal of Marketing*, 54 (January): 71–84.

Bittner, E. (1967). Police Discretion in Emergency Apprehension of Mentally Ill Persons. *Social Problems*, 14: 278–92.

(1974). The Concept of Organisation. In Turner 1974a, pp. 69–81.

Blackler, F., N. Crump and S. McDonald (2003). Organising Process in Complex Activity Networks. In Nicolini, Gherardi and Yanow (eds.) 2003, pp. 126–50.

Blau, P. (1956). *Bureaucracy in Modern Society*. New York: Random House.

Boczkowski, P. J. and W. J. Orlikowski (2004). Organisational Discourse and New Media: A Practice Perspective. In Grant *et al.* (eds.) 2004, pp. 359–78.

Boden, D. (1990). The World as It Happens: Ethnomethodology and Conversation Analysis. In G. Ritzer (ed.), *Frontiers of Social Theory*. New York: Columbia University Press, pp. 185–213.

(1994). *The Business of Talk*. Cambridge: Polity.

(1995). Agendas and Arrangements: Everyday Negotiations in Meetings. In A. Firth (ed.), *The Discourse of Negotiation: Studies of Language in the Workplace*. Oxford: Pergamon, pp. 83–100.

Boden, D. and D. Zimmerman (1991a). Structure-in-Action: An Introduction. In Boden and Zimmerman 1991b, pp. 3–21.

(eds.) (1991b). *Talk and Social Structure: Studies in Ethnomethodology and Conversation Analysis*. Cambridge: Polity.

Bodle, Y. G. and J. A. Corey (1977). *Retail Selling*, 2nd edn. New York: McGraw-Hill.

Bogen, D. (1999). *Order Without Rules: Critical Theory and the Logic of Conversation*. New York: SUNY Press.

Boje, D. (1991). The Storytelling Organisation: A Study of Story Performance in an Office-Supply Firm. *Administrative Science Quarterly*, 36: 106–26.

(1995). Stories of the Storytelling Organisation: A Postmodern Analysis of Disney as 'Tamara-land'. *Academy of Management Journal*, 38 (4): 997–1035.

(2001). *Narrative Methods for Organisational and Communication Research*. London: Sage.

Bolen, W. H. (1970). Customer Contact: Those First Important Words. *Department Store Management*, 33 (3): 25–6.

Bolton, S. and M. Houlihan (2005). (Mis)Representations of Customer Service. *Work, Employment and Society*, 19 (4): 685–703.

Boyce, M. E. (1995). Collective Centring and Collective Sense-Making in the Stories and Storytelling of One Organisation. *Organization Studies*, 16 (1): 107–37.

Brown, A. D. and C. Coupland (2005). Sounds of Silence: Graduate Trainees, Hegemony and Resistance. *Organization Studies*, 26 (7): 1049–69.

Brown, B. (2004). The Order of Service: The Practical Management of Customer Interaction. *Sociological Research Online*, (9) 4, www.socresonline.org.uk/9/4/brown.html.

Brown, M. and T. Tilling (1997). *So You Want to Own the Store: Secrets to Running a Successful Retail Operation.* Lincolnwood (Chicago): Contemporary Books.

Burawoy, M. (1979). *Manufacturing Consent: Changes in the Labour Process Under Capitalism.* Chicago: University of Chicago Press.

Burrell, G. and G. Morgan (1979). *Sociological Paradigms and Organisational Analysis.* London: Heinemann.

Button, G. (1987). Answers as Interactional Products: Two Sequential Practices Used in Job Interviews. *Social Psychology Quarterly,* 50: 160–71.

(ed.) (1991). *Ethnomethodology and the Human Sciences.* Cambridge: Cambridge University Press.

(1992). Answers as Interactional Products: Two Sequential Practices Used in Job Interviews. In Drew and Heritage 1992b, pp. 212–31.

(ed.) (1993). *Technology in Working Order: Studies of Work, Interaction, and Technology.* New York: Routledge.

Button, G. and W. Sharrock (1997). The Production of Order and the Order of Production: Possibilities for Distributed Organisations, Work and Technology in the Print Industry. In *Proceedings of the Fifth European Conference on Computer Supported Cooperative Work.* Dordrecht: Kluwer Academic Publishers, pp. 1–16.

(2002). Operating the Production Calculus: Ordering a Production System in the Print Industry. *British Journal of Sociology,* 53 (2): 275–89.

Callon, M. (ed.) (1998). *The Laws of the Markets.* Oxford, UK: Blackwell.

(2005). Why Virtualism Paves the Way to Political Impotence: A Reply to Daniel Miller's Critique of *The Laws of the Markets.* In O. Velthius (ed.), *Economic Sociology European Electronic NewsLetter,* 6 (2): 3–39.

Casey, C. (1995). *Work, Self and Society: After Industrialism.* London: Sage.

(2000). Sociology Sensing the Body: Revitalizing a Dissociative Discourse. In J. Hassard, R. Holliday and H. Willmott (eds.), *Body and Organisation.* London: Sage, pp. 52–70.

Charters, W. W. (1922). *How to Sell at Retail.* Cambridge, MA: Riverside Press.

Chia, R. and B. MacKay (2007). Post-Processual Challenges for the Emerging Strategy-as-Practice Perspective: Discovering Strategy in the Logic of Practice. *Human Relations,* 60 (1): 217–42.

Cicourel, A. (1968). *The Social Organization of Juvenile Justice.* New York: John Wiley.

Clark, B. (1972). The Organisational Saga in Higher Education. *Administrative Science Quarterly,* 17: 178–84.

Clark, C. (2004). Managing 'First Impressions' in Real-Life Retail Encounters: The Relationship Between Shoppers' Opening Turns and Sales Outcomes. *Cahiers du CEREN* (École Supérieure de Commerce de Dijon-Bourgogne), 7 (1): 2–12.

Clark, C. and T. Pinch (1988). Selling by Social Control. In N. Fielding (ed.), *Structures and Actions*. London: Sage, pp. 119–41.

(1992). The Anatomy of a Deception: Fraud and Finesse in the Mock Auction Sales Con. *Qualitative Sociology*, 15 (2): 151–75.

(1995a). *The Hard Sell: The Language and Lessons of Street Wise Marketing*. New York: Harper Collins.

(1995b). The Interactional Study of Exchange Relationships. *History of Political Economy*, special annual supplement to vol. 26, Transactors and Their Markets in the History of Economics (edited by Neil De Marchi and Mary S. Morgan), 370–400.

Clark, C., P. Drew and T. Pinch (1994). Managing Customer 'Objections' During Real-Life Sales Negotiations. *Discourse and Society*, 5 (4): 437–62.

(2003). Managing Prospect Affiliation and Rapport in Real-Life Sales Encounters. *Discourse Studies*, 5: 5–31.

Clark, T. and G. Salaman (1996). The Management Guru as Organisational Witchdoctor. *Organization*, 3 (1): 85–107.

(1998). Telling Tales: Management Gurus' Narratives and the Construction of Managerial Identity. *Journal of Management Studies*, 35 (2): 137–61.

Clayman, S. E. (1989). The Production of Punctuality: Social Interaction, Temporal Organization, and Social Structure. *American Journal of Sociology*, 95 (3): 659–91.

Clayman, S. and J. Heritage (2002). *The News Interview: Journalists and Public Figures on the Air*. Cambridge: Cambridge University Press.

Clayman, S. and A. Reisner (1998). Gatekeeping in Action: Editorial Conferences and Assessments of Newsworthiness. *American Sociological Review*, 63: 178–99.

Clegg S., C. Carter and M. Kornberger (2004). Get Up, I Feel Like Being a Strategy Machine. *European Management Review*, 1: 21–8.

Cohen, L. and G. Musson (2000). Entrepreneurial Identities: Reflections from Two Case Studies. *Organization*, 7 (1): 31–48.

Coleman, J. S. (1974). *Power and the Structure of Society*. New York: W. W. Norton.

Cooren, F. and G. T. Fairhurst (2004). Speech Timing and Spacing: The Phenomenon of Organizational Closure. *Organization*, 11 (6): 793–824.

Coulter, J. (1989). *Mind in Action*. Oxford, UK: Polity.

(2005). Language Without Mind. In te Molder and Potter 2005, pp. 79–93.

Cox, A. (2005). What Are Communities of Practice? A Comparative Review of Four Seminal Works. *Journal of Information Science*, 31 (6): 527–40.

Cuff, E. C. and W. W. Sharrock (1985). Meetings. In T. A. van Dijk (ed.), *Handbook of Discourse Analysis*, 4 vols. London: Academic Press, vol. III, 149–59.

Czarniawski, B. (2004). On Time, Space and Action Nets. *Organization*, 11 (6): 773–91.

Dale, K. (2000). *Anatomising Embodiment and Organisation Theory*. Basingstoke: Palgrave.

DiMaggio, P. and H. Louch (1998). Culture and the Economy. In N. Smelser and R. Swedberg (eds.), *Handbook of Economic Sociology*. Princeton: Princeton University Press, pp. 27–57.

DiMaggio, P. J. and W. W. Powell (1991). *The New Institutionalism in Organizational Research*. Chicago: University of Chicago Press.

Drew, P. (1992). Contested Evidence in Courtroom Cross-Examination: The Case of a Trial for Rape. In Drew and Heritage 1992b, pp. 418–69.

(2003). Precision and Exaggeration in Interaction. *American Sociological Review*, 68: 917–38.

(2006). When Documents 'Speak': Documents, Language, and Interaction. In P. Drew, G. Raymond and D. Weinberg (eds.), *Talk and Interaction in Social Research Methods*. London: Sage, pp. 98–122.

Drew, P. and J. Heritage (1992a). Analyzing Talk at Work: An Introduction. In Drew and Heritage 1992b, pp. 3–65.

(eds.) (1992b). *Talk at Work: Interaction in Institutional Settings*. Cambridge: Cambridge University Press.

du Gay, P. (1996). *Consumption and Identity at Work*. London: Sage.

(2000). *In Praise of Bureaucracy*. London: Sage.

du Gay, P. and G. Salaman (1992). The Cult(ure) of the Customer. *Journal of Management Studies*, 29 (5): 615–33.

Duguid, P. (2006). What Talking About Machines Tells Us. *Organization Studies*, 27 (12): 1794–1804.

Duneier, M. (1999). *Sidewalk*. New York: FSG.

Duneier, M. and H. Molotch (1999). Talking City Trouble: Interactional Vandalism, Social Inequality, and the 'Urban Interaction Problem'. *American Journal of Sociology*, 104 (5): 1263–95.

Durkheim, E. (1952). *Suicide: A Study in Sociology*. London: Routledge and Kegan Paul.

Edwards, D. (2005). Moaning, Whinging and Laughing: The Subjective Side of Complaints. *Discourse Studies*, 7: 5–29.

(2006). Facts, Norms and Dispositions: Practical Uses of the Modal *would* in Police Interrogations. *Discourse Studies*, 8 (4): 475–501.

(2007). Managing Subjectivity in Talk. In Hepburn and Wiggins 2007a, pp. 31–49.

Edwards, D. and N. Mercer (1987). *Common Knowledge: The Development of Understanding in the Classroom*. London: Routledge.

Edwards, D. and J. Potter (1992). *Discursive Psychology*. London: Sage.

(2001). Discursive Psychology. In A. W. McHoul and M. Rapley (eds.), *How to Analyse Talk in Institutional Settings: A Casebook of Methods.* London: Continuum International, pp. 12–24.

(2005). Discursive Psychology, Mental States and Descriptions. In te Molder and Potter 2005, pp. 241–59.

Eisenstein, E. E. (1983). *The Printing Revolution in Early Modern Europe.* Cambridge: Cambridge University Press.

Engestrom, Y. (1987). *Learning by Expanding: An Activity Theoretical Approach to Developmental Research.* Helsinki: Orienta-Consultit Oy.

Fleetwood, S. (2005). Ontology in Organisation and Management Studies: A Critical Realist Perspective. *Organization*, 12 (2): 197–222.

Fligstein, N. (1996). Markets as Politics: A Political-Cultural Approach to Market Institutions. *American Sociological Review*, 61 (4): 656–73.

Forray, J. M. and J. Woodilla (2002). Temporal Spans in Talk: Doing Consistency to Construct Fair Organisation. *Organization Studies*, 23 (6): 899–917.

Gabriel, Y. (1991). Turning Facts into Stories and Stories in Facts: A Hermeneutic Exploration of Organisational Folklore. *Human Relations*, 44 (8): 857–75.

(1995). The Unmanaged Organisation: Stories, Fantasies and Subjectivity. *Organization Studies*, 16 (3): 477–501.

(2000). *Storytelling in Organisation: Facts, Fictions and Fantasies.* Oxford: Oxford University Press.

Garfinkel, H. (ed.) (1967). *Studies in Ethnomethodology.* Englewood Cliffs, NJ: Prentice-Hall.

(1974). The Origins of the Term 'Ethnomethodology'. In Turner 1974a, pp. 15–18.

(ed.) (1986). *Ethnomethodological Studies of Work.* London: Routledge and Kegan Paul.

(1991). Respecification: Evidence for Locally Produced, Naturally Accountable Phenomena of Order, Logic, Reason, Meaning, Method, etc. in and as of the Essential Haecceity of Immortal Ordinary Society (I) – An Announcement of Studies. In Button (ed.) 1991, pp. 10–19.

(2006). *Seeing Sociologically: The Routine Grounds of Social Action.* Boulder, CO: Paradigm Publishers.

Garfinkel, H. and E. Bittner (1967). 'Good' Organisational Reasons for 'Bad' Clinic Records. In Garfinkel (ed.) 1967, pp. 186–207.

Garfinkel, H. and E. Livingston (2003). Phenomenal Field Properties of the Order of Service in Formatted Queues and Their Neglected Standing in the Current Situation of Enquiry. *Visual Studies*, 18 (1): 21–8.

Garfinkel, H. and H. Sacks (1970). On Formal Structures of Practical Actions. In J. C. McKinney and E. A. Tiryakian (eds.), *Theoretical Sociology: Perspectives and Developments.* New York: Appleton Century Crofts, pp. 337–66.

Geismar, H. (2001). 'What's in a Price?' An Ethnography of Tribal Art at Auction. *Journal of Material Culture,* 6 (1): 25–47.

Georges, R. A. (1969). Towards an Understanding of Storytelling Events. *Journal of American Folklore,* 82: 314–28.

(1980). A Folklorist's View of Storytelling. *Humanities in Society,* 3 (4): 317–26.

Gephart, R. P. (1978). Status Degradation and Organisational Succession: An Ethnomethodological Approach. *Administrative Science Quarterly,* 23: 553–81.

(1988). *Ethnostatistics: Qualitative Foundations for Quantitative Research.* London: Sage.

Gherardi, S. (2000). Practice-Based Theorising on Learning and Knowing in Organisations: An Introduction. *Organization,* 7 (2): 211–23.

(2001). From Organisational Learning to Practice-Based Knowing. *Human Relations,* 54 (1): 131–9.

(2006). *Organisational Knowledge: The Texture of Workplace Learning.* Oxford: Blackwell.

Gherardi, S. and D. Nicolini (2002a). Learning in a Constellation of Interconnected Practices: Canon or Dissonance? *Journal of Management Studies,* 39 (4): 419–36.

(2002b). Learning the Trade: A Culture of Safety in Practice. *Organization,* 9 (2): 191–223.

Giddens, A. (1979). *Central Problems in Social Theory: Action, Structure, and Contradiction in Social Analysis.* Berkeley: University of California Press.

(1987). *Social Theory and Modern Sociology.* Oxford: Polity.

Goffman, E. (1959). *The Presentation of Self in Everyday Life.* New York: Anchor Books.

(1961). On the Characteristics of Total Institutions. In D. R. Cressey (ed.), *The Prison: Studies in Institutional Organization and Change.* New York: Holt, Rinehart and Winston, pp. 15–67.

(1963). *Behavior in Public Places: Notes on the Social Organisation of Gatherings.* New York: Free Press.

(1983). The Interaction Order. *American Sociological Review,* 48: 1–17.

Goleman, D. (1996). *Emotional Intelligence: Why It Can Matter More than IQ.* London: Bloomsbury.

Goodwin, C. (1981). *Conversational Organisation: Interaction Between Speakers and Hearers.* New York: Academic Press.

(1984). Notes on Story Structure and the Organisation of Participation. In Atkinson and Heritage (eds.) 1984, pp. 225–46.

(1994). Professional Vision. *American Anthropologist*, 96 (3): 606–33.

(1995). Seeing in Depth. *Social Studies of Science*, 25: 237–74.

(2000). Action and Embodiment Within Situated Human Interaction. *Journal of Pragmatics*, 32: 1489–1522.

(2003). The Body in Action. In J. Coupland and R. Gwyn (eds.), *Discourse, the Body and Identity*. New York: Palgrave/Macmillan, pp. 19–42.

Goodwin, C. and M. H. Goodwin (1996). Seeing as Situated Activity: Formulating Planes. In Y. Engeström and D. Middleton (eds.), *Cognition and Communication at Work*. Cambridge: Cambridge University Press, pp. 61–95.

Goodwin, D., C. Pope, M. Mort and A. Smith (2005). Access, Boundaries and their Effects: Legitimate Participation in Anaesthesia. *Sociology of Health and Illness*, 27 (6): 855–71.

Granovetter, M. (1985). Economic Action and Social Structure: The Problem of Embeddedness. *American Journal of Sociology*, 91 (3): 481–510.

Grant, D., C. Hardy, C. Oswick and L. Putman (2004). *Organisational Discourse*. London: Sage.

Greatbatch, D. (1988). A Turn-Taking System for British News Interviews. *Language in Society*, 17 (3): 401–30.

Greatbatch, D. and T. Clark (2002). Laughing with the Gurus. *Business Strategy Review*, 13 (1): 10–18.

(2003). Displaying Group Cohesiveness: Humour and Laughter in the Public Lectures of Management Gurus. *Human Relations*, 56 (12): 1515–44.

(2005). *Management Speak: Why We Listen to What Management Gurus Tell Us*. London: Routledge.

Greatbatch, D. and R. Dingwall (1997). Argumentative Talk in Divorce Mediation Sessions. *American Sociological Review*, 62 (1): 151–70.

Greatbatch, D., G. Hanlon, J. Goode, A. O'Cathain, T. Strangleman and D. Luff (2005). Telephone Triage, Expert Systems and Clinical Expertise. *Sociology of Health and Illness*, 27 (6): 802–30.

Grimshaw, A. (1982). Sound–Image Data Records for Research on Social Interaction: Some Questions Answered. *Sociological Methods and Research*, 11 (2): 121–44.

Gronn, P. (1983). Talk as the Work: The Accomplishment of School Administration. *Administrative Science Quarterly*, 28: 1–21.

Handley, K., A. Sturdy, R. Fincham and T. Clark (2006). Within and Beyond Communities of Practice: Making Sense of Learning Through Participation, Identity and Practice. *Journal of Management Studies*, 43 (3): 641–53.

Harper, R., D. Randall and M. Rouncefield (2000). *Organisational Change and Retail Finance*. London: Routledge.

Harper, R. and A. J. Sellen (2002). *The Myth of the Paperless Office*. Cambridge, MA: MIT Press.

Hassard, J. (1993). Ethnomethodology and Organisational Research: An Introduction. In J. Hassard and D. Pym (eds.), *The Theory and Philosophy of Organisation*. London: Routledge, pp. 97–108.

Have, P. ten (1999). *Doing Conversation Analysis: A Practical Guide*. London: Sage.

Heath, C. (1986). *Body Movement and Speech in Medical Interaction*. Cambridge: Cambridge University Press.

Heath, C. and J. Hindmarsh (2000). Configuring Action in Objects: From Mutual Space to Media Space. *Mind, Culture and Activity*, 7 (1/2): 81–104.

(2002). Analysing Interaction: Video, Ethnography and Situated Conduct. In T. May (ed.), *Qualitative Research in Action*. London: Sage, pp. 99–121.

Heath, C., J. Hindmarsh and P. Luff (forthcoming). *Video in Qualitative Research*. London: Sage.

Heath, C., M. Jirotka, P. Luff and J. Hindmarsh (1995). Unpacking Collaboration: The Interactional Organisation of Trading in a City Dealing Room. *Computer-Supported Co-operative Work*, 3 (2): 147–65.

Heath, C. and P. Luff (2000). *Technology in Action*. Cambridge: Cambridge University Press.

(2007a). Gesture and Institutional Interaction: Figuring Bids in Auctions of Fine Art and Antiques. *Gesture*, 7 (2): 215–41.

(2007b). Ordering Competition: The Interactional Accomplishment of the Sale of Fine Art and Antiques at Auction. *British Journal of Sociology*, 58 (2): 63–85.

Heath, C., P. Luff and M. Sanchez Svensson (2002). Overseeing Organisations: Configuring Action and Its Environment. *British Journal of Sociology*, 53: 181–201.

Hepburn, A. (2003). *An Introduction to Critical Social Psychology*. London: Sage.

Hepburn, A. and S. Wiggins (eds.) (2007a). *Discursive Research in Practice: New Approaches to Psychology and Interaction*. Cambridge: Cambridge University Press.

(2007b). Discursive Research: Themes and Debates. In Hepburn and Wiggins 2007a, pp. 1–28.

Heritage, J. (1984). *Garfinkel and Ethnomethodology*. Cambridge: Polity.

(1997). Conversation Analysis and Institutional Talk: Analyzing Data. In D. Silverman (ed.), *Qualitative Research: Issues of Theory and Method*. London: Sage, pp. 161–82.

(2005). Cognition in Discourse. In te Molder and Potter (eds.) 2005, pp. 184–203.

Heritage, J. and D. Greatbatch (1986). Generating Applause: A Study of Rhetoric and Response at Party Political Conferences. *American Journal of Sociology*, 92: 110–57.

Heritage, J. and D. Maynard (2006). *Communication in Medical Care: Interaction Between Primary Care Physicians and Patients*. Cambridge: Cambridge University Press.

Heritage, J. and T. Stivers (1999). Online Commentary in Acute Medical Visits: A Method of Shaping Patient Expectations. *Social Science and Medicine*, 49: 1501–17.

Hess, R. L., S. Ganesan and N. M. Klein (2007). Interactional Service Failures in a Pseudorelationship: The Role of Organisational Attributions. *Journal of Retailing*, 83 (1): 79–95.

Hester, S. and D. Francis (2000). Ethnomethodology, Conversation Analysis and Institutional Talk. *Text*, 20 (3): 391–413.

Hindmarsh, J. and C. Heath (1998). Video and the Analysis of Objects in Action. *Communication and Cognition*, 31 (2/3): 111–30.

(2000). Sharing the Tools of the Trade: The Interactional Constitution of Workplace Objects. *Journal of Contemporary Ethnography*, 29 (5): 523–62.

(2007). Video-Based Studies of Work Practice. *Sociology Compass*, 1 (1): 156–73.

Hindmarsh, J. and A. Pilnick (2002). The Tacit Order of Teamwork: Collaboration and Embodied Conduct in Anaesthesia. *Sociological Quarterly*, 43 (2): 139–64.

(2007). Knowing Bodies at Work: Embodiment and Ephemeral Teamwork in Anaesthesia. *Organization Studies*, 28 (9): 1395–1416.

Hindmarsh, J., P. Reynolds and S. Dunne (2008). Demonstrating Dentistry. Unpublished paper, King's College London.

(forthcoming). Exhibiting Understanding: The Body in Apprenticeship. *Journal of Pragmatics*.

Hobbs, P. (2004). The Role of Progress Notes in the Professional Socialization of Medical Residents. *Journal of Pragmatics*, 36 (9): 1579–1607.

Housley, W. (1999). Role as an Interactional Device and Resource in Multidisciplinary Team Meetings. *Sociological Research Online* 4 (3), www.socresonline.org.uk/4/3/housley.html.

(2000). Category Work and Knowledgeability Within Multidisciplinary Team Meetings. *Text*, 20: 83–107.

Huczynski, A. (1993). *Management Gurus: What Makes Them and How to Become One*. London: Routledge.

Hughes, J. A., D. Randall and D. Shapiro (1992). Faltering from Ethnography to Design. In J. Turner and R. Kraut (eds.), *Proceedings of CSCW'92*

Conference on Computer-Supported Cooperative Work. New York: ACM Press, pp. 115–22.

Huisman, M. (2001). Decision-Making in Meetings as Talk-in-Interaction. *International Studies of Management and Organization*, 31(3): 69–90.

Huse, M. (2005). Accountability and Creating Accountability: A Framework for Exploring Behavioural Perspectives of Corporate Governance. *British Journal of Management*, 16: 65–79.

Iedema, R. (2007). On the Multi-modality, Materiality and Contingency of Organization Discourse. *Organization Studies*, 28 (6): 931–46.

Jackson, B. (2001). *Management Gurus and Management Fashions: A Dramatistic Inquiry*. London: Routledge.

Jarzabkowski, P. (2004). Strategy as Practice: Recursiveness, Adaptation and Practices in Use. *Organization Studies*, 25 (4): 529–60.

Jarzabkowski, P., J. Balogun and D. Seidl (2007). Strategizing: The Challenge of a Practice Perspective. *Human Relations*, 60 (1): 5–27.

Jefferson, G. (1978). Sequential Aspects of Storytelling in Conversation. In J. Schenkein (ed.), *Studies in the Organization of Conversational Interaction*. New York: Academic Press, pp. 219–48.

(1984a). On the Organisation of Laughter in Talk About Troubles. In Atkinson and Heritage 1984, pp. 346–69.

(1984b). Transcript Notation. In Atkinson and Heritage 1984, pp. ix–xvi.

(2004). Glossary of Transcript Symbols with an Introduction. In G. Lerner (ed.), *Conversation Analysis: Studies from the First Generation*. Amsterdam and Philadelphia: John Benjamins, pp. 152–205.

Jefferson, G., H. Sacks and E. A. Schegloff (1987). Notes on Laughter in Pursuit of Intimacy. In G. Button and J. R. E. Lee (eds.), *Talk and Social Organisation*. Clevedon, UK: Multilingual Matters, pp. 152–205.

Johnson, G., L. Melin and R. Whittington (2003). Guest Editors' Introduction. Micro Strategy and Strategizing: Towards an Activity-Based View. *Journal of Management Studies*, 40 (1): 3–22.

Johnson, G., K. Scholes and R. Whittington (2005). *Exploring Corporate Strategy*. London: Prentice-Hall.

Kendon, A. (1990). *Conducting Interaction: Patterns of Behaviour in Focused Encounters*. Cambridge: Cambridge University Press.

Kennon, T. (2006). *How to Avoid 'Just Looking': And Other Ways to Increase Your Retail Sales*. New York: Author House.

Keynes, J. M. (1936). *The General Theory of Employment, Interest and Money*. New York: Harcourt, Brace.

Kirshenblatt-Gimblett, B. (1975). A Parable in Context: A Social Interactional Analysis of Storytelling Performance. In D. Be-Amos and K. S. Goldstein (eds.), *Folklore: Performance and Communication*. The Hague and Paris: Mouton, pp. 105–30.

Klemperer, P. (2004). *Auctions: Theory and Practice.* Princeton: Princeton University Press.

Knights, D. and G. Morgan (1991). Corporate Strategy, Organisations and Subjectivity: A Critique. *Organization Studies,* 12 (2): 251–73.

Knorr Cetina, K. and U. Bruegger (2002). Global Microstructures: The Virtual Societies of Financial Markets. *American Journal of Sociology,* 107 (4): 905–50.

Krishna, V. (2002). *Auction Theory.* London: Academic Press.

Lave, J. and E. Wenger (1991). *Situated Learning: Legitimate Peripheral Participation.* New York: Cambridge University Press.

Lavin, D. and D. Maynard (2001). Standardization vs. Rapport: Respondent Laughter and Interviewer Reaction During Telephone Surveys. *American Sociological Review,* 66: 453–79.

Lawson, T. (1995). Economics and Expectations. In S. Drew and J. Hillard (eds.), *Keynes, Knowledge and Uncertainty.* Aldershot, UK: Edward Elgar, pp. 77–106.

Lerner, G. H. and C. Kitzinger (2007). Introduction: Person Reference in Conversation Analytic Research. *Discourse Studies,* 9: 427–32.

Levy, M. and B. A. Weitz (1998). *Retailing Management,* 3rd edn. Boston: Irwin, McGraw-Hill.

Lilley, S. (2001). The Language of Strategy. In R. Westwood and S. Linstead (eds.), *The Language of Organisation.* London: Sage, pp. 66–88.

Llewellyn, N. (2004). In Search of Modernization: The Negotiation of Social Identity in Organizational Reform. *Organization Studies,* 25 (6): 947–68.

(2005). Audience Participation in Political Discourse: A Study of Political Meetings. *Sociology,* 39 (4): 697–716.

(2008). Organization in Actual Episodes of Work: Harvey Sacks and Organization Studies. *Organization Studies,* 29 (5): 763–91.

Llewellyn, N. and R. Burrow (2007). Negotiating Identities of Consumption: Insights from Conversation Analysis. In A. Pullen, N. Beech and D. Sims (eds.), *Exploring Identity: Concepts and Methods.* Basingstoke: Palgrave, pp. 302–15.

(2008). Streetwise Sales and the Social Order of City Streets. *British Journal of Sociology,* 59 (3): 561–83.

Luff, P., C. Heath and D. Greatbatch (1992). Tasks in Interaction: Paper and Screen Based Activity in Collaborative Work. In J. Turner and R. Kraut (eds.), *Proceedings of CSCW' 92 Conference on Computer-Supported Cooperative Work.* New York: ACM Press, pp. 163–70.

Luff, P., J. Hindmarsh and C. Heath (eds.) (2000). *Workplace Studies: Recovering Work Practice and Informing System Design.* Cambridge: Cambridge University Press.

Lynch, M. (1993). *Scientific Practice and Ordinary Action: Ethnomethodology and Social Studies of Science*. New York: Cambridge University Press.

MacBeth, D. (2000). On an Actual Apparatus for Conceptual Change. *Science Education*, 84 (2): 228–64.

Maitlis, S. (2005). The Social Processes of Organisational Sense Making. *Academy of Management Journal*, 48: 21–49.

Mangham, I. L. and A. Pye (1991). *The Doing of Managing*. Oxford: Basil Blackwell.

Martin, J., M. S. Feldman, M. J. Hatch and S. B. Sitkin (1983). The Uniqueness Paradox in Organisational Stories. *Administrative Science Quarterly*, 28: 438–53.

Martin, J. and M. E. Powers (1983). Truth or Corporate Propaganda: The Value of a Good War Story. In L. R. Pondy, P. J. Frost, G. Morgan and T. C. Dandridge (eds.), *Organizational Symbolism*. Greenwich, CT: JAI Press, pp. 93–107.

Maynard, D. W. (1988). Language, Interaction, and Social Problems. *Social Problems*, 35: 101–24.

(1991). Interaction and Asymmetry in Clinical Discourse. *American Journal of Sociology*, 97: 448–95.

Maynard, D. and N. C. Schaeffer (2002). Standardization and Its Discontents: Standardization, Interaction, and the Survey Interview. In D. W. Maynard, H. Houtkoop-Steenstra, N. C. Schaeffer and J. van der Zouwen (eds.), *Standardization and Tacit Knowledge: Interaction and Practice in the Survey Interview*. New York: Wiley, pp. 3–46.

Mazeland, H. (2004). Responding to the Double Implication of Telemarketers' Opinion Queries. *Discourse Studies*, 6 (1): 95–115.

McConkie, M. L. and W. R. Boss (1986). Organisational Stories: One Means of Moving the Informal Organisation During Change Efforts. *Public Administration Quarterly*, 10: 189–205.

McDonald, T. and M. D. Hakel (1985). Effects of Applicant Race, Sex, Suitability, and Answers on Interviewer's Questioning Strategy and Ratings. *Personnel Psychology*, 38 (2): 321–34.

McGoldrick, P. J. (1990). *Retail Marketing*. London: McGraw-Hill.

McHoul, A. W. (1978). The Organisation of Turns at Formal Talk in the Classroom. *Language in Society*, 7: 183–213.

Meehan, A. (1986). For the Record: Organizational and Interactional Practices for Producing Police Records on Juveniles. Ph.D dissertation, Department of Sociology, Boston University.

Mehan, H. (1979). *Learning Lessons*. Cambridge, MA: Harvard University Press.

Menzes, F. M. and P. K. Monteiro (2005). *An Introduction to Auction Theory*. Oxford: Oxford University Press.

Meriläinen, S., J. Tienari, R. Thomas and A. Davies (2004). Management Consultant Talk: A Cross-Cultural Comparison of Normalizing Discourse and Resistance. *Organization*, 11 (4): 539–64.

Meyer, J. and B. Rowan (1977). Institutionalized Organisations: Formal Structures as Myth and Ceremony. *American Journal of Sociology*, 83: 340–63.

Miles, M. B. (1979). Qualitative Data as an Attractive Nuisance: The Problem of Analysis. *Administrative Science Quarterly*, 24 (4): 590–601.

Miller, D. (2002). Turning Callon the Right Way Up. *Economy and Society*, 31 (2): 218–33.

Mintzberg, H., B. Ahlstrand and J. Lampel (2002). *Strategy Safari*. London: Prentice-Hall.

Mirivel, J. and K. Tracy (2005). Premeeting Talk: An Organisationally Crucial Form of Talk. *Research on Language and Social Interaction*, 38 (1): 1–34.

Moeran, B. (2007). A Dedicated Storytelling Organisation: Advertising Talk in Japan. *Human Organization*, 66 (2): 160–70.

Moore, R. J. (2008). When Names Fail: Referential Practice in Face-to-Face Service Encounters. *Language in Society*, 37 (3): 385–413.

Moore, R. J. and D. Maynard (2002). Achieving Understanding in the Standardized Survey Interview: Repair Sequences. In D. W. Maynard, H. Houtkoop-Steenstra, N. C. Schaeffer, and J. van der Zouwen (eds.), *Standardization and Tacit Knowledge: Interaction and Practice in the Survey Interview*. New York: Wiley, pp. 281–312.

Mulkay, M., C. Clark and T. Pinch (1993). Laughter and the Profit Motive: The Use of Humor in a Photographic Shop. *Humor*, 6 (2): 163–93.

Mulkay, M. and G. Howe (1994). Laughter for Sale. *Sociological Review*, 42 (3): 481–500.

Mumby, D. (1987). The Political Function of Narrative in Organisations. *Communication Monographs*, 54: 113–27.

Nicolini, D. (2007). Stretching Out and Expanding Work Practices in Time and Space: The Case of Telemedicine. *Human Relations*, 60 (6): 889–920.

Nicolini, D., S. Gherardi and D. Yanow (eds.) (2003). *Knowing in Organisations: A Practice-Based Approach*. Armonk, NY: M. E. Sharpe.

Orr, J. (1996). *Talking About Machines: An Ethnography of a Modern Job*. Ithaca: Cornell University Press.

Osborne, D. and T. Gaebler (1992). *Reinventing Government: How the Entrepreneurial Spirit Is Transforming the Public Sector*. Reading, MA: Addison-Wesley.

Pilnick, A., J. Hindmarsh and V. Gill (eds.) (2009). *Communication in Healthcare Settings: Policy, Participation and New Technologies*. London: Blackwell.

Pinch, T. and C. Clark (1986). The Hard Sell: 'Patter-Merchanting' and the Strategic (Re)Production and Local Management of Economic Reasoning in the Sales Routines of Market Pitchers. *Sociology*, 20 (2): 169–91.

Pollio, H.R., R. Mers and W. Lucchesi (1972). Humor, Laughter, and Smiling: Some Preliminary Observations on Funny Behaviors. In J.H. Goldstein and P.E. McGhee (eds.), *The Psychology of Humor*. New York and London: Academic Press, pp. 211–39.

Potter, J. (1996). *Representing Reality: Discourse, Rhetoric and Social Construction*. London: Sage.

Potter, J. and A. Hepburn (2003). I'm a Bit Concerned: Early Actions and Psychological Constructions in a Child Protection Helpline. *Research on Language and Social Interaction*, 36: 197–240.

(2007). Chairing Democracy: Psychology, Time and Negotiating the Institution. In Tracy, McDaniel and Gronbeck (eds.) 2007, pp. 176–204.

Potter, J. and C. Puchta (2007). Mind, Mousse and Moderation. In Hepburn and Wiggins 2007a, pp. 104–203.

Potter, J. and H. te Molder (2005). Talking Cognition: Mapping and Making the Terrain. In te Molder and Potter (eds.) 2005, pp. 1–54.

Potter, J. and M. Wetherell (1987). *Discourse and Social Psychology*. London: Sage.

Potter, J., M. Wetherell and A. Chitty (1991). Quantification Rhetoric: Cancer on Television. *Discourse and Society*, 2: 333–65.

Puchta, C. and J. Potter (2004). *Focus Group Practice*. London: Sage.

Pye, A. and A. Pettigrew (2005). Studying Board context, Process and Dynamics: Some Challenges for the Future. *British Journal of Management*, 16: 27–38.

Rawls, A. (2008). Harold Garfinkel, Ethnomethodology and Workplace Studies. *Organization Studies*, 29 (5): 701–32.

Raymond, G. (2006). Questions at Work: Yes/No Type Interrogatives in Institutional Contexts. In P. Drew, G. Raymond and D. Weinberg (eds.), *Talk and Interaction in Social Research Methods*. London: Sage, pp. 115–34.

Reitlinger, G. (1982). *The Economics of Taste*, vol. II, *The Rise and Fall of Picture Prices 1760–1960*. New York: Hacker Art Books.

Rendle-Short, J. (2006). *The Academic Presentation: Situated Talk in Action*. Aldershot, UK: Ashgate.

Ritzer, G. (1998). *The McDonaldization Thesis: Explorations and Extensions*. Thousand Oaks, CA: Sage.

Ritzer, G. and T. Stillman (2001). From Person to System Oriented Service. In A. Sturdy, I. Grugulis and H. Willmott (eds.), *Customer Service: Empowerment and Entrapment*. London: Palgrave, pp. 102–16.

Roberts, J. (2006). Limits to Communities of Practice. *Journal of Management Studies*, 43 (3): 623–39.

Robinson, J. D. (1998). Getting Down to Business: Talk, Gaze and Body Orientation During Openings of Doctor–Patient Consultations. *Human Communications Research*, 25: 98–124.

Rogers, L. (1988). *Retail Selling: A Practical Guide for Sales Staff*. London: Kogan Page.

Rosenthal, P. and R. Peccei (2007). The Work You Want, The Help You Need: Constructing the Customer in Jobcentre Plus. *Organization*, 14 (2): 201–23.

Roy, Donald, F. (1960). Banana Time: Job Satisfaction and Informal Interaction. *Human Organization*, 18: 156–68.

Sacks, H. (1972). Notes on the Police Assessment of Moral Character. In D. N. Sudnow (ed.), *Studies in Social Interaction*. New York: Free Press, pp. 45–65.

(1974). On the Analyzability of Stories by Children. In J. J. Gumperz and D. Hymes (eds.), *Directions in Sociolinguistics: The Ethnography of Communication*. New York: Rinehart & Winston, pp. 325–45.

(1984). Notes on Methodology. In Atkinson and Heritage (eds.) 1984, pp. 21–7.

(1992). *Lectures on Conversation*, 2 vols. Edited by G. Jefferson with an introduction by E. A. Schegloff. Oxford: Basil Blackwell.

Sacks, H., E. A. Schegloff and G. Jefferson (1974). A Simplest Systematics for the Organisation of Turn-Taking for Conversation. *Language*, 50 (4): 696–735.

Samra-Fredericks, D. (1996). The Interpersonal Management of Competing Relationalities: A Critical Ethnography of Board–Level Competence for 'Doing' Strategy as *Spoken* in the 'Face' of Change. Unpublished Ph.D., Brunel University.

(2003a). A Proposal for Developing a Critical Pedagogy in Management from Researching Organisational Members' Everyday Practice. *Management Learning*, 34 (3): 291–312.

(2003b). Strategizing as Lived Experience and Strategists' Everyday Efforts to Shape Strategic Direction. *Journal of Management Studies*, 40 (1): 141–74.

(2004a). Talk-in-Interaction/Conversation Analysis. In C. Cassell and G. Symon (eds.), *Essential Guide to Qualitative Methods in Organizational Research*. London: Sage, pp. 214–27.

(2004b). Understanding the Production of 'Strategy' and 'Organisation' Through Talk Amongst Managerial Elites. *Culture and Organisation*, 10 (2): 125–41.

(2005a). Strategic Practice, 'Discourse' and the *Everyday* Interactional Constitution of 'Power Effects'. *Organization*, 12: 803–41.

(2005b). Understanding Our World as It Happens. Paper presented to the 1st Organisation Studies workshop, Greece.

(2007). Me and My Shadow and Our Dance of Reflexivity. Paper presented at European Group for Organisation Studies Conference, Austria, July.

Samra-Fredericks, D. and F. Bargiela-Chiappini (2008). Introduction to the Symposium on the Foundations of Organising: The Contribution from Garfinkel, Goffman and Sacks. *Organization Studies*, 29 (5): 653–75.

Schatzki, T. (2005). The Site of Organizations. *Organization Studies*, 26 (3): 465–84.

Schatzki, T. R., K. Knorr Cetina and E. von Savigny (2001). *The Practice Turn in Contemporary Theory*. London: Routledge.

Schegloff, E. A. (1979). The Relevance of Repair to Syntax-for-Conversation. In T. Givon (ed.), *Syntax and Semantics XII: Discourse and Syntax*. New York: Academic Press, pp. 261–86.

   (1991). Reflections on Talk and Social Structure. In Boden and Zimmerman 1991b, pp. 44–70.

   (1993). Reflections on Quantification in the Study of Conversation. *Research on Language and Social Interaction*, 26 (1): 99–128.

   (1997). Whose text? Whose context? *Discourse and Society*, 8: 165–87.

   (1998a). Body Torque. *Social Research*, 65 (3): 535–96.

   (1998b). Reply to Wetherell. *Discourse and Society*, 9: 413–16.

   (1999). Discourse, Pragmatics, Conversation Analysis. *Discourse and Society*, 11 (4): 405–35.

   (2006). A Tutorial on Membership Categorization. *Journal of Pragmatics*, 39: 462–82.

   (2007). *Sequence Organisation in Interaction, vol. I, A Primer in Conversation Analysis*. Cambridge: Cambridge University Press.

Schegloff, E. A. and H. Sacks (1973). Opening Up Closings. *Semiotica*, 8: 289–327.

Scott, W. R. (1981). *Organisations: Rational, Natural, and Open Systems*. Upper Saddle River, NJ: Prentice-Hall.

Sharrock, W. and G. Button (1991). The Social Actor: Social Action in Real Time. In Button (ed.) 1991, pp. 137–75.

Sheets-Johnstone, M. (2000). Kinetic Tactile-Kinesthetic Bodies: Ontogenetical Foundations of Apprenticeship Learning. *Human Studies*, 23: 343–70.

Shor, R. E. (1978). The Production and Judgement of Smile Magnitude. *Journal of General Psychology*, 98: 79–96.

Silverman, D. (1997a). *The Discourses of Counseling: HIV Counseling as Social Interaction*. London: Sage.

   (1997b). Studying Organisational Interaction: Ethnomethodology's Contribution to the New Institutionalism. *Administrative Theory and Praxis*, 19 (2): 178–95.

(2001). The Construction of 'Delicate' Objects in Counselling. In M. Wetherell, S. Taylor and S. J. Yates (eds.), *Discourse Theory and Practice: A Reader*. London: Sage, pp. 119–37.

Silverman, D. and J. Jones (1973). Getting In: The Managed Accomplishment of 'Correct' Selection Outcomes. In J. Child (ed.), *Man and Organisation: The Search for Explanation and Social Relevance*. London: George Allen and Unwin, pp. 63–106.

Sinclair, J. and M. Coulthard (1975). *Towards an Analysis of Discourse*. Oxford: Oxford University Press.

Smart, G. (1999). Storytelling in a Central Bank: The Role of Narrative in the Creation and Use of Specialized Economic Knowledge. *Journal of Business and Technical Communication*, 13 (3): 249–73.

Smith, C. W. (1990). *Auctions: The Social Construction of Value*. Berkeley: University of California Press.

(1991). Comment on Siegelman's Review of Auctions. *American Journal of Sociology*, 96 (6): 1539–41.

Smith, D. E. (1990). *Texts, Facts, and Femininity: Exploring the Relations of Ruling*. New York: Routledge.

(1996). Telling the Truth after Postmodernism. *Symbolic Interaction*, 19 (3): 171–202.

Smith, D. E. and J. Whalen (1997). Texts in Action. Unpublished paper, Institute for Research on Learning, Menlo Park, CA.

Snyder, M. and W. B. Swann (1976). When Actions Reflect Attitudes: The Politics Of Impression Management. *Journal of Personality and Social Psychology*, 34 (5): 1034–42.

Solomon, M. R., C. Surprenant, J. A. Czepiel and E. G. Gutman (1985). A Role Theory Perspective on Dyadic Interactions: The Service Encounter. *Journal of Marketing*, 49 (1): 99–111.

Speer, S. A. and I. Hutchby (2003). From Ethics to Analytics. Aspects of Participants: Orientations to the Presence and Relevance of Recording Devices. *Sociology*, 37: 315–37.

Stinchcombe, A. L. (1990). Work and the Sociology of Everyday Life. In K. Erikson and S. P. Vallas (eds.), *The Nature of Work*. New Haven, CT: Yale University Press, pp. 99–116.

Strati, A. (2003). Knowing in Practice: Aesthetic Understanding and Tacit Knowledge. In Nicolini, Gherardi and Yanow (eds.) 2003, pp. 53–85.

Strauss, A. (1985). Work and the Division of Labor. *Sociological Quarterly*, 26 (1): 1–19.

Sturdy, A. (1998). Customer Care in a Customer Society: Smiling and Sometimes Meaning It? *Organization*, 5 (1): 27–53.

Suchman, L. (1987). *Plans and Situated Actions: The Problem of Human–Machine Interaction*. Cambridge: Cambridge University Press.

(1997). Centers of Coordination: A Case and Some Themes. In L. B. Resnick, R. Säljö, C. Pontecorvo and B. Burge (eds.), *Discourse, Tools, and Reasoning: Essays on Situated Cognition*. Berlin: Springer-Verlag, pp. 41–62.

(2000). Making a Case: Knowledge and Routine Work in Document Production. In Luff, Hindmarsh and Heath (eds.) 2000, pp. 29–45.

(2005). Affiliative Objects. *Organization*, 12 (3): 379–99.

Suchman, L. and B. Jordan (1990). Interactional Troubles in Face-to-Face Survey Interviews. *Journal of the American Statistical Association*, 85: 232–41.

Suchman, L. and J. Whalen (1994). Standardizing Local Events and Localizing Standard Forms. Paper presented at the Annual Meetings of the Society for Social Studies of Science. New Orleans, LA.

Swedberg, R. (1997). New Economic Sociology: What Has Been Accomplished, What Is Ahead? *Acta Sociologica*, 40: 161–82.

Tartter, V. C. (1989). Happy Talk: Perceptual and Acoustic Effects of Smiling on Speech. *Perception and Psychophysics*, 27: 24–7.

Taylor, S. S., D. Fisher and R. L. Dufresne (2002). The Aesthetics of Management Storytelling: A Key to Organisational Learning. *Management Learning*, 33 (3): 313–30.

te Molder, H. and J. Potter (eds.) (2005). *Conversation and Cognition*. Cambridge: Cambridge University Press.

Townley, B. (1993). Foucault, Power/Knowledge and Its Relevance for Human Resource Management. *Academy of Management Review*, 18 (3): 518–45.

Tracy, K, J. P. McDaniel and B. E. Gronbeck (eds.) (2007). *The Prettier Doll: Rhetoric, Discourse and Ordinary Democracy*. Tuscaloosa: University of Alabama Press.

Trowler, P. (2001). Captured by the Discourse? The Socially Constitutive Power of New Higher Education Discourse in the UK. *Organization*, 8 (2): 183–201.

Tullar, W. L. (1989). Relational Control in the Employment Interview. *Journal of Applied Psychology*, 74 (6): 971–77.

Turner, R. (ed.) (1974a). *Ethnomethodology: Selected Readings*. Harmondsworth: Penguin Books.

(1974b). Words, Utterances and Activities. In Turner 1974a, pp. 197–215.

Underhill, P. (1999). *Why We Buy: The Science of Shopping*. New York: Simon & Schuster.

Uzzi, B. (1997). Social Structure and Competition in Interfirm Networks: The Paradox of Embeddedness. *Administrative Science Quarterly*, 42: 35–67.

van Maanen, J. and S. Barley (1984). Occupational Communities: Culture and Control in Organisations. *Research in Organisational Behavior*, 6: 287–365.

Vinkhuyzen, E. and M. H. Szymanski (2004). Would You Like to Do It Yourself? Service Requests and Their Non-Granting Responses. In K. Richards and O. Seedhouse (eds.), *Applying Conversation Analysis*. London: Palgrave Macmillan, pp. 91–106.

Walker, E. (1995). Making a Bid for Change: Formulations in Union/ Management Negotiations. In A. Firth (ed.), *The discourse of negotiation*. Oxford: Pergamon, pp. 101–40.

Watson, D. R. (1990). Some Features of the Elicitation of Confessions in Murder Interrogations. In G. Psathas (ed.), *Interactional Competence*. Washington, DC: University Press of America, pp. 263–96.

(1997). Ethnomethodology and Textual Analysis. In D. Silverman (ed.), *Qualitative Research: Theory, Method and Practice*. London: Sage, pp. 80–98.

Watson, T. (1995). *Sociology of Work and Industry*. London: Routledge.

Weber, M. (1948). *From Max Weber: Essays in Sociology*. Edited by H. H. Gerth and C. Wright Mills. London: Routledge and Kegan Paul.

(1978). *Economy and Society*, 2 vols. Los Angeles: University of California Press.

Weick, K. (1979). *The Social Psychology of Organising*. Reading, MA: Addison Wesley.

(1993). The Collapse of Sense Making in Organisations: The Mann Gulch Disaster. *Administrative Science Quarterly*, 38: 628–52.

(1995). *Sensemaking in Organisations*. London: Sage.

Wenger, E. (1998). *Communities of Practice: Learning, Meaning and Identity*. New York: Cambridge University Press.

Wetherell, M. (1998). Positioning and Interpretative Repertoires: Conversation Analysis and Post-Structuralism in Dialogue. *Discourse and Society*, 9: 387–412.

Wetherell, M. and J. Potter (1992). *Mapping the Language of Racism: Discourse and the Legitimation of Exploitation*. London: Harvester.

Whalen, J. (1995). A Technology of Order Production: Computer-Aided Dispatch in Public Safety Communications. In P. ten Have and G. Psathas (eds.), *Situated Order: Studies in the Social Organisation of Talk and Embodied Activities*. Washington, DC: University Press of America, pp. 187–230.

(1997). Making Standardization Visible. Unpublished paper, Palo Alto Research Center, Palo Alto, CA.

Whalen, J., M. Whalen and K. Henderson (2002). Improvisational Choreography in Teleservice Work. *British Journal of Sociology*, 53: 239–59.

Whalen, J., Zimmerman, D. and M. Whalen (1988). When Words Fail: A Single Case Analysis. *Social Problems*, 35 (4): 335–62.

Whalen, M. R. and D. H. Zimmerman (1987). Sequential and Institutional Context in Calls for Help. *Social Psychology Quarterly*, 50: 172–85.

White, H. (1981). Where Do Markets Come from? *American Journal of Sociology*, 87: 517–57.

Whittington, R. (2006). Completing the Practice Turn in Strategy Research. *Organization Studies*, 27 (5): 613–34.

Wieder, D. L. (1974a). *Language and Social Reality*. The Hague: Mouton.

(1974b). Telling the Code. In Turner 1974a, pp. 144–72.

Wilkins, A. (1983). Organisational Stories as Symbols Which Control the Organisation. In L. Pondy, P. Frost, G. Morgan and T. Dandridge (eds.), *Organizational Symbolism*. Greenwich, CT: JAI Press, pp. 81–92.

(1984). The Creation of Company Cultures: The Role of Stories and Human Resource Systems. *Human Resource Management*, 23: 41–60.

Willis, P. (1978). *Learning to Labour*. Aldershot, UK: Ashgate.

Willmott, H. (2005).Theorizing Contemporary Control: Some Post-Structuralist Responses to Some Critical Realist Questions. *Organisation*, 12 (5): 747–80.

Wittgenstein, L. (1953). *Philosophical Investigations*. Oxford: Blackwell.

Woodilla, J. (1999). Workplace Conversations: The Text of Organising. In D. Grant, T. Keenoy and C. Oswick (eds.), *Discourse and Organisation*. London: Sage, pp. 31–50.

Woolgar, S. (2004). Marketing Ideas. *Economy and Society*, 33 (4): 448–62.

Wray-Bliss, E. (2001). Representing Customer Service: Telephones and Texts. In A. Sturdy, I. Grugulis and H. Willmott (eds.), *Customer Service: Empowerment and Entrapment*. London: Palgrave, pp. 38–59.

Zimmerman, D. (1971a). The Practicalities of Rule Use. In J. Douglas (ed.), *Understanding Everyday Life*. London: Routledge, pp. 221–38.

(1971b). Record Keeping and the In-Take Process in a Public Welfare Bureaucracy. In S. Wheeler (ed.), *On Record: Files and Dossiers in American Life*. New York: Russell Sage, pp. 319–54.

Index

accounting practices, role in
    ethnomethodological studies 4
adjacency pairs (paired actions) 27–8
    question–answer pair 35–7
auctions
    approaches to the study of economic
        action 120–2, 137–9
    auctioneer's system of ordering bids
        122–6
    authenticity of bids 127–31
    commission bids 128–31
    economic action as social interaction
        121–2
    establishing and preserving runs
        125–6, 131–6
    establishing only two bidders at any
        one time 125–6
    incremental structure for bids 123–5
    institutional forms of market
        activities 136–9
    interactional organisation 136–9
    pace and rhythm of bidding 126
    revealing the source and integrity of
        bids 127–31
    social and organisational issues 119–20
audio and/or video records, *see* recorded
    materials

Barbiegate, *see* school board meeting
body movements, significance in
        interactions 39–41
bureaucratic conduct,
        ethnomethodological study 19–21

call centres, asymmetries in interactions
    37–9
Chair of a meeting
    dilemmas associated with the role
        58, 61–2
    role 33–4

classroom interactions
    role of feedback 34–5
    turn-taking 34–5
communities of practice
    analysis of a dental community of
        practice 220–1
    approaches to study
        218–19
    centripetal trajectories 218
    concept 218–19
    critical contributions of peripheral
        participants 236–40
    ethnomethodological
        approach 219
    learning by observation and
        modelling 221–5
    overlapping communities of practice
        237–8
    participation and peripherality
        236–40
    peripheral trajectories 237–40
    professional vision in apprenticeship
        training 221–5
    real-time organisation of action and
        interaction 220–1
comparative method of conversation
        analysis 32–3
context, relevance to sequential
        interactions 28–30
conversation analysis (CA)
    approach to storytelling in
        organisations 97–100
    comparative method 32–3
    organisational discourse
        approach 9–10
    perspective on organisational
        events 49–50
    see also ethnomethodology
        and conversation analysis
        (EM/CA)

dental community of practice
analysis 220–1
apprenticeship of UK dental
students 220
approaches to the study of
communities of practice 218–19
centripetal trajectories 218
concept of communities of practice
218–19
critical contributions of peripheral
participants 236–40
ethnomethodological approach 219
interaction between demonstrators
and dental students 221–5
learning by observation and
modelling 221–5
managing uncertainties in front of the
patient 229–32
overlapping communities of practice
237–8
participation and peripherality 236–40
patient orientation to the training
situation 225–9, 232–6
patient's critical role in community
practices 236–40
patient's peripheral role in the
community of practice 225–9
peripheral trajectories 237–40
presence of the patient during
assessment and diagnosis 229–32
professional vision in apprenticeship
training 221–5
real-time organisation of action and
interaction 220–1
training and supervision of UK dental
students 220
discursive psychology, perspective on
organisational events 49–50, 52–3
document processing, *see* standard forms
Durkheim, Émile 14

economic actions, *see* auctions
embodied properties of work and
organisation 39–41
ethnography 6
ethnomethodological approach
avoidance of imposition of analytic
categorisation 16
focus on mundane or routine
activities 15

guiding assumptions 13–16
practices and procedures that achieve
order 13–15
relevance of each party's conduct
embodied in the other 16
study policies 13–16
ethnomethodological studies
organisation in the details of ordinary
activities 11–13
relevant themes within organisation
studies 16–23
role of accounting practices 4
subject matter 4
ethnomethodological themes
16–23
ordering of identity at work 21–3
rules 19–21
skill, knowledge and images of work
17–19
standardised forms and
procedures 21
subjects of work 21–3
working with bureaucracy 19–21
ethnomethodology
analysis of recorded materials 5–6
criticisms from management and
organisation studies 8
distinctive features 23
intersections with organisational
studies 7–11
potential contribution to organisation
studies 6–7
references from new institutionalism
8–9
references from organisational
sensemaking 9
references in organisation and
management studies 7–10
ethnomethodology and conversation
analysis (EM/CA)
distinctive approaches to the study of
work 4–5
and the 'practice turn' in organisation
studies 10–11
relationship to management and
organisation studies 4–5

feedback, turn-taking in the classroom
34–5
form-filling, *see* standard forms

Garfinkel, Harold 5–6
  guiding assumptions of
    ethnomethodology 13–16
  production of social order 25
  references in organisation studies 7–10
Goleman, Daniel 96–7
  see also storytelling in organisations

identity, ordering of at work 21–3
institutional settings, asymmetries in
  interactions 33, 37–9
Institutional Talk Programme 32–3
instructional triad, turn-taking 34–5
interaction
  interplay with practice 92–5
  reflexivity with the setting 75–7
interactional asymmetries, institutional
  settings 33, 37–9
interactional dimensions of storytelling
  116–18
interview orthodoxy
  participant orientation to 75–7, 87–9
  as a resource for practice 87–9
interviews, *see* recruitment interview
  study

Jeffersonian transcription 42–4, 50, 56
job interviews, *see* recruitment interview
  study

knowledge and skills at work 17–19

laughter and authority 60–1
lexical choice, institutional interactions 33

management studies
  references to ethnomethodology 7–10
  relationship to EM/CA 4–5
market activities, *see* auctions
meetings, *see* school board meeting
methodologies
  comparative analysis of interactions
    32–3
  distinctive approaches of
    ethnomethodology 44–5
  sequential analysis of interactional
    details 25–32
  transcription of recorded data 41–4
  use of recorded data 24–32
  use of video data 39–41

new institutionalism, references to
  ethnomethodology 8–9

organisation in the details of ordinary
  activities 11–13
organisation studies
  criticisms of ethnomethodology 8
  descriptive approach to work
    activities 3–4
  intersections with ethnomethodology
    7–11
  nature of records of work activity 3
  potential contribution from
    ethnomethodology 6–7
  references to ethnomethodology 7–10
  relationship to EM/CA 4–5
  relevant themes for
    ethnomethodological studies 16–23
organisational details, use of transcripts
  to recover 41–4
organisational discourse
  focus of empirical studies 9–10
  references to EM/CA 9–10
organisational interaction
  comparative method of analysis 32–3
  institutional character of talk 32–9
  interactional/institutional
    asymmetries 33, 37–9
  lexical choice 33
  sequential organisation 33, 35–7
  structural organisation 32
  turn design 33
  turn-taking organisation 32, 33–5
organisational sensemaking, references
  to ethnomethodology 9

paired action, *see* adjacency pairs
plans, relation to actions 51–2
practice, interplay with interaction 92–5
'practice turn' in organisation studies
  intersections with EM/CA 10–11
  links with ethnomethodology 74–5
professional vision
  achievement of 201–3, 209–11
  in apprenticeship training 221–5
psychological orientations of meeting
  participants 66–72

question–answer adjacency pair 35–7
questions, strategic use at work 35–7

recorded materials
  advantages and limitations 24–5
  collection of recorded data 26
  transcription 41–4
  use in EM/CA studies 24–5
  use in studies of work activities 3
recorded materials analysis 26
  ethnomethodological approach 5–6
  range of research applications 6
  sequential analysis of interactional
    details 25–32
recovering organisational details, use of
    transcripts 41–4
recruitment interview study
  answers as objects of assessment 78–84
  assessment of candidates'
    achievements 79–81
  assessment of quality of answers 81–4
  ethnomethodological analysis of the
    data 92–5
  interplay between practice and
    interaction 92–5
  interview orthodoxy as a resource for
    practice 87–9
  links to the 'practice turn' within
    organisation studies 74–5
  mild interrogation by the interviewer
    84–7
  participant orientation to interview
    orthodoxy 75–7, 87–9
  power of the interviewer 90–2
  previous study approaches 77
  reflexivity between setting and
    interaction 75–7
  scoring of candidates' answers 78–84
  study methodology 77–8
reflexivity between setting and
    interaction 75–7
research, applications of analysis of
    recorded materials 6
retail shopping analysis
  actively-avoiding-contact SUs 144
  actively-seeking-contact SUs 144,
    157–61
  bodily conduct components of
    integrated communication 164–8
  bodily conduct in verbal contact
    avoidance 161–3
  bodily conduct in verbal contact
    seeking 157–61

browsing MPSUs 154–7
browsing SUs 144, 153–4
establishing and avoiding verbal
  encounters 144–8
eye contact before verbal encounters
  144–8
insights for sales staff training 168–9
low- and high-involvement bodily
  conduct 148–52
misunderstanding of retail encounters
  141–3
MPSUs (groups of shoppers) 143,
  154–7
open-to-contact MPSUs 154–7
open-to-contact SUs 144, 148–52
potential economic consequences of
  findings 168–9
pre-verbal encounter conduct 144–8
research approaches 140–1
shopper and salesperson involvement
  148–52
shoppers being served by a currently
  absent salesperson 163–4
situational basis of shoppers' conduct
  165–8
SUs (single shoppers) 143
  see also specific types
traditional assumptions about retail
  encounters 141–3
types of SUs 144
verbal contact-avoidance bodily
  conduct 161–3
verbal contact-seeking bodily conduct
  157–61
retrospective sensemaking 9
rules
  control and co-operation dilemma
    61–2
  ethnomethodological study 19–21
  local construction of 62–3
  negotiation of time allowed
    64–72
  operation in organisations 50–2
  relation to practices 50–2
  resistance to 64–72

Sacks, Harvey 5–6
  distinctive features of EM/CA 23
  focus on mundane or routine
    activities 15

'order at all points' dictum 15
relevance of each party's conduct
embodied in the other 16
sequential organisation in CA 25–6
strategic use of questions at work
35–7
salesperson encounters, *see* retail
shopping analysis
school board meeting (Barbiegate)
analytic approach 54, 72–3
Chair's actions to bring DT to a close
70–2
Chair's disclaimer and imposition of
rules 61–2
Chair's display of hearing the timer
68–70
Chair's introduction 56–8
control and co-operation dilemma for
the Chair 61–2
conversation analysis perspective
49–50
dilemmas associated with chairing
58, 61–2
dilemmas associated with rules 61–2
discursive psychological perspective
49–50, 52–3
initial interaction between DT and
Chair 64–6
interactions that end DT's
presentation 66–72
laughter and authority 60–1
materials available for analysis 53–4
nature of the controversy 53
negotiation of the rules concerning
time allowed 64–72
opening of DT's presentation 64–6
physical layout of the meeting room
54–6
psychological orientations as the
presentation is ended 66–72
resistance to time constraint rules
64–72
rules and the Chair's disclaimer 61–2
rules as constructed by the Chair 62–4
terms used to describe participants
54–6
theoretical perspectives 50–3
use of the description 'Chair' 54–6
selling, *see* auctions; retail shopping
analysis

sensemaking approach, references to
ethnomethodology 9
sequential organisation of interactions
25–32
adjacency pairs (paired actions) 27–8
analysis of recorded data 26
collection of recorded data 26
embedded nature of talk and action
26–8
evidence for claims 30–2
institutional interactions 33, 35–7
recognition and orientation by social
actors 27–8
relevance of context 28–30
strategic use at work 35–7
setting
as product of and means to create
interaction 75–7
reflexivity with interaction 75–7
shopping, *see* retail shopping analysis
situated production of stories
conversation analytic approach 100
effects of different paralinguistic and
visual conduct 111–18
functions of stories in organisations 96
influence of situation on meaning
96–7, 99–100
interactional dimensions of
storytelling 116–18
limitations of stories-as-text approach
96–100, 115–16
management guru Daniel
Goleman 96–7
storytelling as a communicative act
97–100
variety of approaches to research
97–100
skills and knowledge at work 17–19
social sciences, approach to analysis of
recorded materials 6
standard forms
changing role of front counter
employees 193–5
chronic insufficiency of standard
forms 185–6
co-ordinating role in activity systems
172–5, 195–7
creative methods used to make the
form work 185–6
de-coding of the instructions 186–93

standard forms (cont.)
enabling action at a distance 172–5,
195–7
ethnomethodological studies 173
form filling as a collaborative
achievement 181–5
historical roles of written
documents 172
mundane details of the situated use of
documents 195–7
non-standard methods of description
185–93
objectives of standardisation 174–5
re-introduction of non-standard
features 185–93
role in face-to-face service
encounters 172
taking a customer order 176–81
use of annotation to make the form
work 185–6
web submission by customers 194–5
standardised forms and procedures 21
storytelling in organisations
conversation analytic approach 100
effects of different paralinguistic and
visual conduct 111–18
functions served by 96
influence of situation on meaning
96–7, 99–100
interactional dimensions 116–18
limitations of stories-as-text approach
96–100, 115–16
management guru Daniel Goleman
96–7
storytelling as a communicative act
97–100
variety of approaches to research
97–100
strategic plan creation
achievement of professional vision
201–3, 209–11

approaches to research on strategy
199–201
challenges of strategic management
199–201
conceptions of the strategic plan 200
contributions of EM/CA studies to
organisation studies 213–16
ethnomethodological approach 198–9
interactional assembly of the plan
203–7
stratagem to mitigate the 'power
effects' of the document 211–13
strategic planning cycle 200
strategy work and practice 199–201
use of classificatory language and
coding schemes 202–3, 207–9
structural organisation, institutional
interactions 32

time constraints, negotiation of the
rules 64–72
transcription
Jeffersonian 50, 56
of organisational details 41–4
turn design, institutional interactions 33
turn-taking organisation, institutional
interactions 32, 33–5

video data, embodied properties of
work 39–41
see also recorded materials

work
delineation of subjects of work 21–3
images of 17–19
knowledge and skills 17–19
ordering of identity at work 21–3
work activity studies
analytic approach 3–4
descriptive approach 3–4
work orders, *see* standard forms

For EU product safety concerns, contact us at Calle de José Abascal, 56–1°,
28003 Madrid, Spain or eugpsr@cambridge.org.